NORTHWOODS WHITEWATER

A Paddler's Guide to Whitewater
of Minnesota, Wisconsin, Ontario and Michigan

by

Jim Rada

Dedicated to

Karen Sweetness Jensen

Published by SangFroid Press

Text copyright ©2003 Jim Rada

Photographs copyright ©2006 Doug Nelson and others as attributed.

All maps and illustrations copyright ©2006 Steve Stratman.

ISBN 0-917939-03-4

Published in the United States of America by

SangFroid Press

SangFroid Press
34 Water Street
Excelsior, Minnesota 55331
952-474-6220
www.sangfroidpress.com

RE-EVOLUTION

Book designed by Steve Stratman
Re-evolution Studio
612-824-5252

All rights reserved under International and Pan-American copyright Conventions. No part of this book may be reproduced, stored in a retrieval system or transmitted in any form or by any means, digital, electronic, electrostatic, magnetic, tape, mechanical, photocopying, recording or otherwise without written consent of the publisher.

Printed in Canada on recycled paper.

Cover photo: Lover's Leap falls, Cascade River. Boater is Paul Everson. ©2006 Doug Nelson
Back cover photo: Poplar River. Boater is John Kiffmeyer, ©2006 Doug Nelson. Inset photo: Jim Rada, ©2006 Doug Nelson

"...You should not expect a guidebook to show the way. Even the best of guidebooks is only a Zen-like "finger pointing." You must do the paddling, scouting, eddy hopping, sweeper dodging, portaging and enjoying. I will give you advice and a sense of what the rivers are like."

– Jim Rada

John Alt, Discretion Drop, Cascade River, Minnesota. ©2006 Doug Nelson

NORTHWOODS WHITEWATER

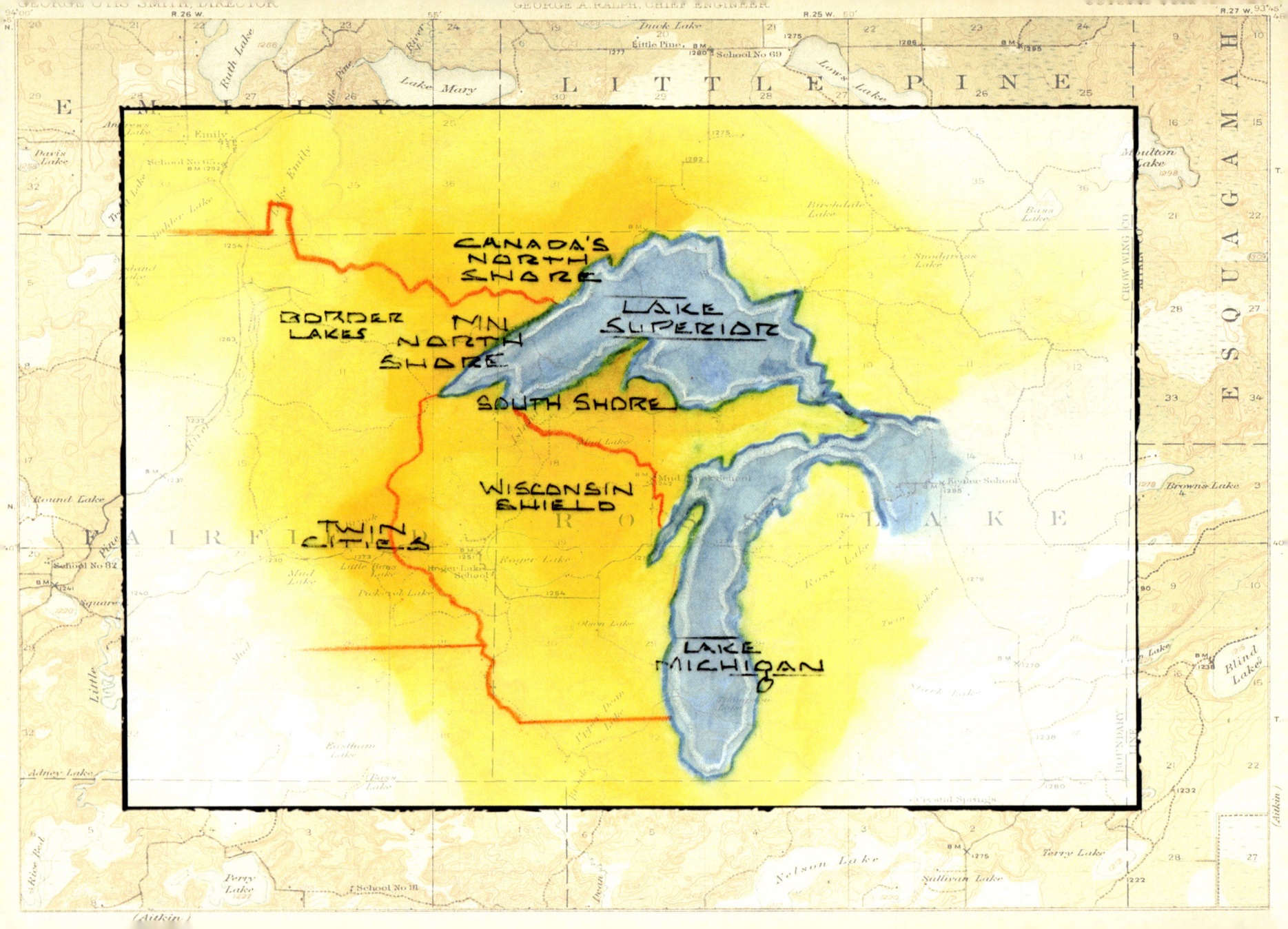

CANADA'S NORTH SHORE
BORDER LAKES
MN NORTH SHORE
LAKE SUPERIOR
SOUTH SHORE
WISCONSIN SHIELD
TWIN CITIES
LAKE MICHIGAN

TABLE OF CONTENTS

The Northwoods Whitewater Flipbook begins on page 13.

Fan through the pages with your right thumb and watch kayakers hurl themselves off the big drops.

Foreword 6

Whitewater In The North 8

Minnesota's North Shore 10

St. Louis River 12
Amity Creek 16
Lester River 17
French River 18
Sucker River (Also Called Big Sucker Creek) 19
Knife River 20
Encampment River 21
Crow Creek 22
Gooseberry River 23
Split Rock River 24
Beaver River 26
Baptism River 28
Manitou River 36
Cross River 39
Temperance River 43
Poplar River 44
Cascade River 47
Devil's Track River 50
Kadunce River 56
Brule River 57
Pigeon River 61
Other Creek Runs On The North Shore 63
North Shore Photo Gallery 64–71
Lower Cascade River 70

Canada's North Shore 72

Kaministiquia River 74
Shebandowan River 75
Mackenzie River 77
Current River 78
Thunder Bay Rivers 79
Jackpine River 80

South Shore Of Lake Superior 82

Nemadji River 84
Black River (Near Superior, WI) 84
Amnicon River 85
Bois Brule River (Near Superior, WI) 86
Brunsweiler River 87
Mellen Area Streams 88
Montreal River 90
West Fork Of The Montreal 91
Upper Montreal (East Fork Of Montreal) . . 93
Black River (Upper Peninsula) 94
Presque Isle River 98
Copper Creek 104
Rock River 105
Sturgeon River 106
Falls River 108
Silver River 109
Slate River 112
West Branch Of The Huron 113
Huron River (East Branch Of The Huron) . 114
Yellow Dog River 116
Baltimore 118
Other Creek Runs On The South Shore . . . 119
South Shore Photo Gallery 120–123

Border Lakes Canoe Country 124

Stony River 126
Vermilion River (Near Crane Lake) 127

Wisconsin's Canadian Shield Country 130

Wolf River 132
Peshtigo River 135
Menominee River 136
Wisconsin River (Grandfather Falls Section) . 137

Twin Cities Rivers 138

Vermillion River (In Hastings, MN) 140
Black River (Near Black River Falls, WI) . . 141
Eau Claire River (Big Falls) 142
Sauk Rapids 143
Sand Creek 144
Apple River 144
Kinnickinnic River 145
St. Croix River At Taylor's Falls 146
Snake River 147
Kettle River 148

Other Pleasures 155

River Skiing 156
Summer Options 157
Devil's Track Canyon 159

Water Flows 160

Paddlers' Resources 165

Thanks 166

About Jim Rada 167

FOREWORD

Ah, yes, Northwoods Whitewater.

By Paul Everson

Jim Rada's book is a labor of love, compiled over 23 years. Originally published in loose-leaf binder form, its humorous stories and crisp descriptions of the best rivers in our region have been a staple of the upper Midwest boating scene.

Jim's love of rivers brings North Woods boating alive. This book contains excellent technical descriptions of rivers, falls and rapids, as well as colorful tall tales. All have carried boaters through the long Minnesota winter and inspired them to seek out new rivers.

After Jim's untimely death in 2003 I have felt an undefinable tweaking from above . . . or maybe from downstream . . . to contribute to the completion of this work. Maybe it is a way of saying thanks to Jim for the profound influence that he's had on my life. Working with his wife, Karen Jensen, and other friends, we have left his manuscript in its original form, adding only notes and a few missing descriptions.

Jim's enthusiasm for being alive is still inspiring. It certainly rubbed off on anyone who spent any amount of time with him. I first got to know Jim Rada and his future wife Karen Jensen while raft guiding at Superior Whitewater on the St. Louis River in 1989. It was easy to see they had a relaxed, and mutually devoted relationship. Of course I soon learned that Jim usually managed to make everything, even work, a bit more interesting. When in a particularly bored or devilish mood, Head Raft Guide Jim might become "Grock," the wild haired squirt boating caveman-guide, grunting and pointing, but refusing to speak complete sentences to his bemused customers.

Adventuring with Jim was an experience. He exerted a strong but charming presence in any group. He usually sported an ancient battered hockey helm, pilled and faded pile, and ancient plastic boats bandaged crudely but effectively with duct tape and inner tube pieces. Jim was as proud of the wear and tear on his gear as a knight of his battle scars! Meeting him, you quickly realized his elfish (trollish?) nature in the way his eyes twinkled like a baby's with awe and amused wonder at the intricate beauty of creeking.

He loved the competitive action of river running and old school play boating: "Throw your paddle, dude!" It was pretty intense to bike, ski, and kayak with Jim. But never in the time that I knew him did he let competitiveness or pursuit of glory taint his decision-making process. Jim always wanted to live to boat another day. What he truly valued in boating and life was not adrenaline fueled glory but experiencing living and paddling as beautifully as he could.

In an obituary published in AMERICAN WHITEWATER JOURNAL Sept./Oct. 2003; our friend Hal Crimmel described him well:

> "His independent streak defined his kayaking. He was a purist who favored action over talk, a man who didn't let the latest paddling fads get in the way of communing with the wild rivers he loved. Running a river with Jim was special, because he was a person who distilled paddling to its essence, and sought only to experience it in its purest form. The sun glinting off the late spring snow pack, the rumble of the rapids, the boreal forest at the edge of the moving water—all were as profoundly important to Jim as the people he spent time with."

Scarcely a day goes by when I don't find myself remembering my first creeking trip to the North Shore with Jim. The pack of boaters initiating me that weekend in 1991 also included pioneering patriarch Pete Cary, John Alt and Robert "Texas Bob" Ruffner. Having been clued in to the melt, and fired up with enthusiasm and motivation that was somewhat uncharacteristic for me at that time in my life, I had power-driven solo to meet them for my North Shore initiation. Putting on at a pretty decent flow, I realized with some trepidation that I understood very little of what was about to happen as I slipped into the swollen flowage gliding beneath the overhanging trees. The intense

Paul Everson ©2006 Doug Nelson

browns, greens and grays in the creek's canyon created an overwhelming visual backdrop to the task at hand– keeping my wits together and paying attention to the rapids.

Distracted by the discomfort of numb toes inside my wool socks and tennies, and brand new drysuit with its fresh, constricting gaskets, I struggled to stay focused. Nervously and somewhat clumsily, I followed my guides, sliding through Class III and IV boulder beds into eddies, guided attentively by Jim and John. During precarious portages we trudged through thigh deep snow past fascinatingly horrific falls.

The next day I was thoroughly baptized in Gauge Hole, obliging Alt to pursue my boat and gear out into the lake. As terrified as I was, caught in that frothing fount, I don't think I had ever felt that alive and purified. As I floundered around, I got glimpses of Pete and Jim cheering from the eddy. A few cycles and I emerged downstream, smiling and appreciating that my new drysuit with tight gaskets was working perfectly.

Jim's death of a heart attack in May 2003 was an unexpected shock. Jim died in his boat. We watched as he fought valiantly in a hole at the bottom of Triple Drop on the Presque Isle, with ropes and safety boaters in place. As he floated upside down towards Class V Nokomis Falls, we felt powerless, realizing nothing could be done. We frantically searched downstream and returned the next day recovering his body. But somehow even the ordeal of that weekend seemed elementally beautiful. There was still an oddly compelling urge to surf the exit waves at the end of the run and admire the brilliant sunset. The warm, sunny Presque Isle was Jim's favorite river.

A Cautionary Note

Please always use caution, especially when preparing to attempt new rivers described in this book. Many have serious hazards not adequately described here. As anyone who runs rivers knows, the risk factors are substantial. Over the years, I have had several close calls on the rivers and creeks described in this book, witnessed numerous bad situations, and know of dozens more in our region. I have also lost two friends to kayaking.

North and South Shore rivers are dangerous, and Jim rightly was concerned someone might die. With rare exception, higher flows and cold temperatures exponentially increase the danger of difficult runs. Danger also increases as the learning curve steepens and probably whenever video is present, tempting boaters to take risks for the sake of digital glory. I like to think about the inherent risk of a particular river or drop in terms of a fun-to-danger ratio. If you are going to do it, it had better be pretty high!

Since Jim's writing some items such as gauge readings, including the Presque Isle and Devil's Track, have changed. Be sure to use a topo map to confirm put-ins and takeouts. Get the intel from someone knowledgeable.

As many of his close friends can attest, Jim was a prankster. In fact, he sometimes talked about including one bogus river in his book, just so folks might be more inclined to take proactive measures to ensure the pleasure of their river day. To reiterate his advice, "You must do the paddling, scouting, eddy hopping, sweeper dodging, portaging and enjoying."

Jim Rada

©2006 Doug Nelson

WHITE WATER IN THE NORTH

Over twenty years ago I saw pictures of people paddling through rapids in kayaks. Then and there the idea of visiting mysterious canyons, plunging over foaming drops and splashing through rolling waves was planted in the fertile soil of my soul. The past twenty years have led me on a continuing adventure by kayak, one that has enriched my life with exciting moments, wonderful friends and places of unimagined beauty. Perhaps you are a kayakist or would like to become one? Perhaps your spirit is drawn to rushing waters? Perhaps you, too, would enjoy the cooling spray of a falls on a hot summer day? If so this book is for you.

Of course to be a kayakist, you have to be able to find the rivers! Almost everyone has heard of the Grand Canyon of the Colorado and kayakists from around the world flock to Idaho, California and even West Virginia. But mention "Minnesota" or "Wisconsin" or "Michigan" and the image that comes to mind is of birch bark canoes on sky blue lakes amidst the whispering pines. So it might seem even to those who have spent their whole lives in these states. I know differently!

Jim Rada ©2006 Karen Jensen

In this book I will encourage you to push back the pine boughs and take a peek at the rivers of the Northwoods. Hidden in the forest you will find whitewater that will challenge any paddler, beauty that will seduce all who love the Northwoods and opportunity for adventure on a Sunday afternoon in your own backyard. If you search for whitewater challenge, beauty and adventure in the Northwoods with this guidebook you will find all these things and more, I promise! Ready? Then let me tell you more about when and where you can find this whitewater excitement.

This book will concern itself primarily with the whitewater that lies within a 550 mile crescent that rims the western half of Lake Superior from around Nipigon, Ontario to Marquette, Michigan. I'll also include whitewater runs from the canoe country of northern Minnesota, the Canadian Shield country of northern Wisconsin and some whitewater in the Twin Cities area around Minneapolis-St.Paul. These additions will give variety and extend the season for the enthusiastic paddler.

As I write this, I am aware that whitewater exists within this realm that I haven't paddled. Some of these rivers are quite distant, others are rarely runnable, others have easier whitewater that has made them less attractive for kayaking during the spring snowmelt. I'd like to be able to paddle every run mentioned in this book before writing about them, but as twenty years of concerted effort hasn't let me paddle them all, I'll note those runs that I haven't personally experienced and also refer you to other guidebooks that might fill in some holes. I'm a kayakist, but I hope that my descriptions will be useful to canoeists and other river lovers, too.

When does the action occur? Most of these rivers rely on snowmelt and spring rain–running high when the winter's accumulated water runs off over frozen soil and under leafless trees. As the vegetation comes out, the rivers still can be brought up, but for shorter periods, by heavy summer or fall rains.

Some rivers, such as the Kettle, Wolf, Vermilion, Menominee and St. Louis run at paddlable levels much of the summer. Even these major rivers can become low and "rocky." However, smaller rivers, such as the Baptism, usually experience at least a couple of summer/fall renaissances each year. These rains spice up the summer whitewater diet that consists mainly of those few runs on large or dam-controlled rivers. Fall rains in September and October are more successful in bringing up levels as the trees soak up little water and there's less evapotranspiration. With the end of October comes the end of Northwoods' paddling for most.

It's important then to be ready for the spring snowmelt season to see many of these streams. So let's get a bit more specific about the natural clock that these rivers run by. Snowmelt in southern Wisconsin and the Twin Cities area usually begins about mid March. Short runs on Sand Creek, the Vermillion in Hastings, the Apple near Somerset, and the Kinnickinnic near River Falls usually start the season off for Twin Cities paddlers. I imagine the Black River near Black River Falls, WI might start things off in southern Wisconsin.

These runs are fading as April nears, but in late March the snowmelt has moved north to unleash the Snake and Kettle in Minnesota, the Wolf and Peshtigo in Wisconsin. During some years the Montreal and Presque Isle in Michigan's Upper Peninsula (known as the U.P.) break up and let March leave roaring like a lion.

As April develops the frenzy of whitewater roars to fever pitch! Early to mid-April sees the southern runs of the North Shore near Duluth such as the Lester, Amity and Sucker quickly rise and fall. Meanwhile the nearby St. Louis begins to swell towards a peak in late April usually in the 15-20,000 cubic feet per second (CFS) range. Mid-April often sees the Kettle high, in excess of five feet on the Highway 23 gauge and the Wolf and Peshtigo pushing over 20 inches on their respective gauges. The second or third weekend in April finds the U.P. throbbing with high quality whitewater as the Montreal, Presque Isle, Black, Silver and other South Shore rivers crest. If I had to pick a week for excitement it would run from April 17-24 with so many runs and such high water as to confuse paddlers who don't know what to grab first.

The last week of April sees the South Shore beginning to drop (unless of course a rainstorm hits!) but now the rivers of Minnesota's North Shore kick in: Baptism, Brule, Temperance and others flush out the ice and draw the warmly dressed and adventurous. Some runs are great at the peak of flow: Baptism, Manitou, Temperance, Brule, Poplar, Pigeon—others can be treacherous—notably the Cascade and Devil's Track. Run the big "classics" and the Split Rock during late April and early May; then do some "hair raising" on the smaller and steeper runs. Keep in mind the advice to chase the snow north as levels drop.

With the North Shore beginning to fade in mid May head for the "bush" near Thunder Bay, Ontario. The Canadian Shore holds jewels with names as mystical as any: Shebandowan, Kaministiquia (Kam!!). Beyond, near the edge of our world in this book, roars the mighty Jackpine. For those who don't want to run all the way to Canada, runs fringing the BWCA (Boundary Waters Canoe Area) become prime targets in mid to late May: the Vermilion near Crane Lake, the Stony and the Namakan being possibilities for Memorial Day fun. With the end of May the snowmelt effect is completely gone.

June begins with rivers falling but swamps and ground saturated and ready to respond to rain. Almost invariably early June (June is Minnesota's wettest month) brings a rainstorm somewhere and mid-June brings another. Where is somewhere? Grab the weather reports and phone!! Kettle? Peshtigo? Baptism? St. Louis? Now it becomes a little harder as June blossoms out and boaters turn to larger rivers: Vermilion, St. Louis, Menominee and St. Croix provide boating that tapers through June and on into July.

As Northwoods rivers head towards their summer low levels, some Northwoods paddlers head towards a summer vacation–Idaho anyone? or Colorado? Yes, friend, some people do plan summer vacations to coincide with the end of reliable Northwoods water and peak of Rocky Mountain pleasure. When you return to the Northwoods, you'll find the water getting pretty thin during late July and August—watch for thunderstorms which will pump up rivers in a given area for a few days to a week—or go canoeing in the BWCA or surfing or sea kayaking on Lake Superior!

Fall usually sees a couple of resurgences as air and water cool down. Labor Day and mid-October often seem to bring rains that allow the boater another shot at Northwoods whitewater. It can be fun running down the Baptism as the salmon run up the Baptism from Lake Superior!! Even at lower flows a color tour down the Kettle or St. Louis or with luck the West Fork of the Montreal seems not only a treat but a mellow way of saying adieu to the rivers til ski season or next spring. And then come the gales of November. . .

Snow and skis let you visit the slumbering giants during winter. There is a special calm to be found in seeing the drops smoothed in snow, the roar of whitewater turned to boreal stillness or muted gurgling. Perhaps you'll want to check out some new runs for the coming spring, or see old friends in a new way.

This scenario would be for a "typical" year, which of course rarely happens. Yet the dates and sequence of events are useful for planning your paddling year, which for most Northwoods paddlers extends from mid March til early October. With a summer trip elsewhere, it's possible to have a diverse and satisfying six months of paddling. The winter can lead to different pursuits: work?!, relationships, river skiing . . . or you can pack your paddles for the Andes!

MINNESOTA'S NORTH SHORE

The shoreline of Lake Superior contained in Minnesota embraces rocky lakeside cliffs, numerous state parks, rugged hills dropping sharply toward the Lake and over a dozen rivers sliding down this escarpment. The rivers tend to be small, some just creeks, and bedrock ledges and slides make up most of the rapids of interest. Gradients are high, with most rivers having sections of 100+ feet per mile descent. Just about every river has at least one unrunnable falls on it, and a few, such as the Gooseberry, expend much of their vertical drop as falls.

These North Shore streams roughly parallel each other, so as you drive the 150 miles from Duluth to the Canadian border, you encounter a whitewater run about every ten miles. This makes for a lot of boating choices with very little driving!

The rivers are also quite pristine and the water tinted brown by tannic acid from tree roots and bogs. Our "root beer" water flows best in April and May, with boating seasons sometimes lasting only a few weeks. We always hope for warm weather rain revivals, and sometimes we get lucky.

Boreal woods of spruce, fir, birch, cedar, pine and aspen shade the rapids and canyons. Several of the runs end on Lake Superior, giving a strange and beautiful sense of completion on reaching the Lake. The North Shore is a very special place, whether the water is high or not, and the numerous parks and hiking trails allow you to glimpse its intimacies by foot—but by boat is best!

The North Shore on Lake Superior, Minnesota. ©2006 Doug Nelson

MINNESOTA'S NORTH SHORE

ST. LOUIS RIVER

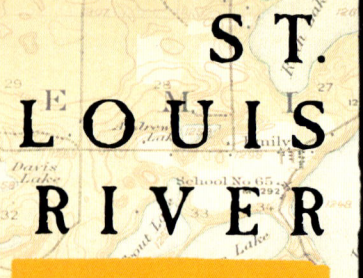

SECTION: I (UPPER)

LENGTH: 3 MILES

CLASS: II–III

SUMMER: YES

QUICK DESCRIPTION:
EASY, SIX RAPIDS, PLAY/SQUIRT

PUT-IN:
CARLTON COUNTY 61 AT SCANLON

TAKE-OUT:
THOMSON DAM, MINNESOTA 210

The St. Louis is one of the largest of Lake Superior's tributaries. This large drainage area provides whitewater to paddle from breakup in mid-April 'til freezeup in November. During this period the flow will range from a low of about 500 CFS to peak flow of 15,000 CFS or more.

These figures should tell you that summer flows can provide technical whitewater with boulder dodging and sharp drops, while snowmelt and heavy rains can bring big water complete with glorious waves, holes and ender spots. I will describe two sections of the St. Louis, though upper stretches also hold class II whitewater in a near wilderness setting.

SECTION I

CARLTON COUNTY 61 AT SCANLON TO THOMSON RESERVOIR AT MINNESOTA HIGHWAY 210.

This section of the St. Louis, first pioneered by Greg Breining and friends in the early 1980's has become an extremely popular run with whitewater paddlers of every stripe. Open canoeists and less experienced kayakists find the mixture of enjoyable class II and III drops, recovery pools, scenic rock outcroppings and easy access from Interstate I-35 to be just the recipe for a day of fun. Add in deep holes for squirt boaters, a few excellent surfing waves and summer flows that permit the luxury of "lifejacket only" paddling and you have a "winner."

The run contains six named rapids and an abundance of flatwater. The mixture of intermittent rapids and rustic scenery provides a very enjoyable daytrip. Commercial rafting can be arranged through Superior Whitewater out of Carlton, Minnesota. This conscientious whitewater company operates in such a way as to rarely inconvenience the private paddler. UMD's Kayak and Canoe Institute also uses this section as a classroom for teaching whitewater skills. The Kayak and Canoe Institute has an "outpost" for instructional purposes right next to the boater parking lot at the Highway 210 bridge over the St. Louis. The outpost is a hub of boater activity during the summer months and has a bulletin board listing such things as the river flow for the day, upcoming events, etc.

Shortly after passing under the I-35 bridge, the paddler encounters a broad class I boulder field. This riffle signals the approach to a constriction producing the first named rapid, "The Wave." The Wave is a very benign playspot of class II nature. At flows typical of summer (1000-1500 CFS) the rapid features a broad surfing wave with an excellent approach eddy on river left. At some levels The Wave is a smooth surfing slick, sometimes a foamy sidesurfer, sometimes a pop-up spot and at higher flows (above 5000 CFS) altogether absent. The Wave, with the boat length hole just below, can provide a lot of surfing, pop up, hole riding, squirting and mystery move fun. At summer flows it`s the best playspot on the run. Some local paddlers will come just to play The Wave and then portage and paddle back to the put-in.

Following The Wave comes two-thirds of a mile of leisurely flowing flatwater. Rounding a bend to the left, you'll see a cable spanning the river. This marks the entrance to a 100 yard long easy boulderbed rapid: Two Hole. Two Hole is ordinarily an easy class II boulder field that has a couple of large boulders over which the water barely flows. As the flow rises above 1500 CFS these two spots develop into holes that become quite nice with a few thousand CFS.

The holes are narrow and easily avoided, but can be good side surfing at moderate to high water (3000-7000 CFS). At flows above 10,000 CFS, Two Hole is largely washed out, but can hold a couple of surfable rolling waves.

Below Two Hole large pines and small cliffs appear on river left: Boatsmear rapid. Boatsmear is a broad class II rapid which can feature a nice surfing wave midway through and a cliffside pop-up spot on the left when flows are in the 3000-5000 range. Squirt boaters will enjoy the deep swirling waters that pass the cliffs and those inclined to a picnic lunch will appreciate the small sand beach tucked between low black outcrops on the right. Boatsmear ends in a congenial spot with pines, blueberries, poison ivy and cliffs which have been jumped in boats.

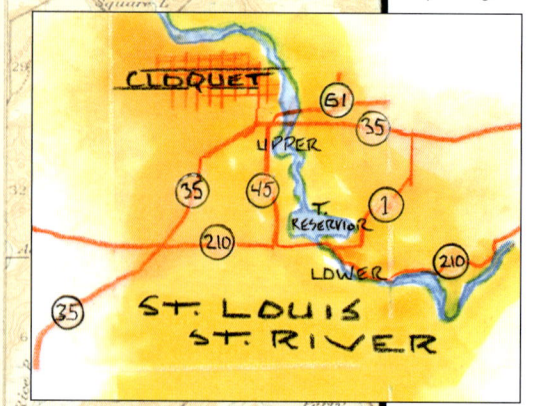

A hundred yards below Boatsmear a horizon line gives warning of Hidden Hole, a somewhat steeper boulder and ledge rapid about 100 yards long. There can be some nice waves in this class II rapid, which grow as the flow goes up. I'd call it a III when the flow is a few thousand CFS and the big boulder in the center at the end forms a hole hidden amongst the waves.

A quarter-mile downstream from Hidden Hole, a set of powerlines crosses above the river, sending a tingle of electricity through approaching paddlers, for Electric Ledge is upon us. Electric Ledge is formed by a sharp drop of 5-6 feet across the whole river. The right side is more or less a vertical falls and the left side a twisting series of stairsteps. In the middle is the chute. The middle route provides a thrilling and sudden descent into backrollers at the bottom.

Class III even at low flows, the central chute becomes a glorious big water rush at flows over 10,000 CFS. At high flows a less violent route opens on the left, curving along the shore. At very high flows the central chute verges on class IV and is really a thrill.

Following Electric Ledge a short recovery pool (which disappears at high flow) allows regrouping before the last rapid–Little Kahuna. Kahuna is class II+ at low flows and big water III at high flows. High or low it usually provides some of the biggest waves on the river, which are located right of center at the bottom. At peak you'll find some five footers and some difficult but exhilarating surfing.

A word of caution: Little Kahuna forms the main channel lying left of a series of long, skinny, pine-studded islands. To the right of this series of islands is a smaller channel that opens with an ugly eight foot drop over a set of razor rocks that many people call Boat Buster Falls. I call it "Slice and Dice," and I have never run it–it doesn't look fun. I have heard of a successful run (water level unknown) and a vertical pin. Be sure to either scout or avoid this drop. It's easy to ignore it entirely since it's on a channel that's far right below Electric Ledge.

However, there is a nice little rapid further down the right channel, "Upstream-Downstream." At flows above 5000 CFS this can contain a nice pop up/ender spot. Upstream-Downstream can be reached by paddling to the left and upstream after running Little Kahuna.

Below Kahuna the action ends and a half-mile later the St. Louis hits the Thomson Reservoir. The reservoir looks a bit like a BWCA lake with rocky islands studding it. As you round the end of an island you should be able to see the dam about a half-mile away. Paddle towards the dam, but give it a wide berth, taking out at the outcrops/dock to the left. Carry down the trail about two hundred feet to the boaters' parking area just north of Minnesota 210.

SECTION II

THOMSON DAM TO POWERPLANT ROAD (THROUGH JAY COOKE STATE PARK)

The Jay Cooke State Park run holds beautiful scenery, one of the finest slalom courses in the country and "hair" whitewater drops as well as a few playspots and a mile-long stretch of class II whitewater.

Unless Section I is running at over 1500 CFS, Section II will only have a 350 CFS flow to keep fish alive as 1500 CFS of flow is diverted at Thompson Reservoir down a diversion canal to Forebay Lake and thence down a set of tubes to a hydropower facility operated by Minnesota Power and Light (MP&L). The flow in Section I is the flow at Knife Falls Dam and can be obtained from MP&L or Superior Whitewater of Carlton. The flow in Section II is generally 1500 CFS less than the flow in Section I; however one or two world class slaloms are held each summer in June or July, usually with 1200-1500 CFS of warm water released Fri.-Sun. for the race. These releases can provide a guaranteed warm weather cruise if you're an expert paddler or a willing-to-portage advanced paddler. There's no need to wait for releases, though, as spring (and even summer rain) provides many days when the canal can't drink all of the St. Louis. I should note that the

ST. LOUIS RIVER

SECTION: II (LOWER)
LENGTH: 5 MILES
CLASS: II–V
SUMMER: SOME
QUICK DESCRIPTION: POWER, BIG LEDGES, VI WHEN HIGH
PUT-IN: THOMSON DAM, MINNESOTA 210
TAKE-OUT: POWERPLANT 1.5 MI. E. OF OLDENBURG POINT

ST. LOUIS LEVELS PHONE INFO
- Minnesota Power: 1-800-582-8529
- "KNIFE FALLS:" this is the CFS for the Upper.
- "THOMSON DAM DISCHARGE:" this is the CFS for Lower St. Louis.

welcome to
the northwoods
whitewater
flipbook frames:

START
FLIPPING!

diverted water serves racers, who often leave a swiftwater slalom course hung for training over the canal just above Forebay Lake.

Section II through Jay Cooke State Park is an incredible spectacle during the peak of spring runoff. It may be viewed or scouted from the Minnesota Highway 210 bridge just east of Carlton, from the "Swinging Bridge" (a pedestrian footbridge near the Jay Cooke State Park office) or from Oldenburg Point picnic area, also in Jay Cooke State Park.

Hiking trails along the river are found in the Swinging Bridge area. Upstream of the Swinging Bridge are several runnable ledges and the rapid a quarter mile below the Swinging Bridge is one of the most difficult on the run. This heavy rapid below the Swinging Bridge sported an honest 20 foot crashing wave one spring as 15-20,000 CFS roared through a section of 150 foot per mile gradient. I was safely on shore and still consider a high water run nearly insane, certainly an expedition as a maze of holes, waves and channels confronts the paddler. I would recommend flows of race level (about 1200-1500 CFS) and would recommend scouting and a possible takeout at the Swinging Bridge as a way to introduce yourself to this lovely but demanding section.

A boater boofs the seven foot falls before Swinging Bridge, Lower St. Louis River. ©2006 Doug Nelson

Putting in on river right one hundred yards below the dam, the paddler enters the race course section of the run. The first major drop occurs almost immediately as the river plunges down a sloping ledge that drops roughly seven feet into a powerful hydraulic. I call this drop "Superhole" after its appearance at high water. Though punchable at race levels it can still stop and trash a boater who's sloppy or off line. Superhole is visible looking upstream from the Minnesota 210 bridge and gives a feel for the nature of the big ledges on the run through Section II. The race course contains great play waves and an ender spot in the vicinity of the 210 bridge and then continues with a wavy canyon which ends as you pass under an old railroad bridge which is now a bike trail. The bike trail marks the end of the race course and permits boaters to practice or play the quarter-mile race course section and then take out. Otter Creek, a run in itself, enters the St. Louis on the right just below the bike trail.

Then the river turns sharply left and in the next two-thirds of a mile passes a nice surfing wave (at high flows) and about three or four very regular ledge drops each two to four feet in height. One of these has a hydraulic capable of backendering boats. After this section of small drops comes a two hundred foot pool as the river backs up behind a natural ledge dam. Best scouted on the left, the river mostly zig-zags through a slot while dropping about eight feet. This impressive class V rapid goes by the name of Octopus and is hard to run nicely, but is easily snuck by chutes spilling right of the main drop.

After the main pitch of Octopus the St. Louis immediately falls away steeply over a series of ledges. There's a good route on the left and an apparent route on the right; both require fast and precise maneuvering. The next mile below these class IV+ ledges is a collection of boulderbed and small ledges in a very wide river channel, class II.

The nature of the river changes about 200 yards above the Swinging Bridge where a route through a series of ledges runs along river left. A narrow sloping drop of about nine feet, a fifty foot pool, then a twist to the right to fall over a fun seven foot falls and a final tussle with a very regular four foot ledge bring you to the Swinging Bridge, if you follow the channel next to the left shore. The middle and right channels in this area await exploration.

The Swinging Bridge offers a convenient takeout: to this point the paddler has enjoyed some fine play spots and a number of good class IV-IV+ drops.

14

Continuing beyond the Swinging Bridge brings a very challenging rapid. The river shoots off a five foot falls and then turns sharply left into a miniature gorge between parallel vertical fins of rock. This setting prompts me to suggest the name "Fin Falls" for this class V rapid. This little gorge heads downhill in a hurry, funneling into a large hydraulic at the base of one of the fins. This hydraulic stops and/or flips most boaters, but doesn't hold on too long—at least so far. It's a mighty drop—scout it!

Following close upon Fin Falls come a couple of sharp ledges, one of which can totally submerge the paddler in foam at its base, sucking everything down deep. Below these drops you feel fantastic; a real surge of adrenalin has passed. The river relents for maybe half a mile, with a broad channel and small ledges.

It would be good to scout the section just upstream from Oldenburg Point from a hiking trail on river right as the St. Louis churns towards its last major rapids: The Wall. The Wall is a frenzied section dropping sixty feet in less than a quarter-mile. I'd recommend a route that heads to the right shore and jumps a six foot falls and then returns to the center. The Wall is descended going center to right down a series of drops that magically match (if you don't vertically pin), a short pool and then another machinegun series of drops leading right to left. A couple more small ledges and WAHOO!!!—you're through. Looking upstream is tremendous—black rock, white foam, root beer brown cascades—you wonder how you got down that amazing Wall.

For those who prefer a more "vertical" descent of the Wall, Paul Everson has pioneered a run in the center that includes a falls of about sixteen feet. I have yet to check this route out.

After the Wall, you can carry up to Oldenburg Point on river left or continue downstream to a "road" takeout. One and a half miles of riffles and flatwater bring you around Oldenburg Point to the powerplant where the St. Louis regains the water stolen from it at the Thomson Reservoir. Take out on the left and carry up the dirt access road to the gate near Highway 210, and relish a feeling of euphoria.

Alan Faust, below the Swinging Bridge drop. ©2006 Paulina Cuevas

This section of river was first run in the mid-70's by a group containing early explorers Fred Young, Al Button and Pete Cary. They were the first of several groups to reach the Swinging Bridge. The section below the Swinging Bridge had to wait til 1988 to be run in its entirety by a group including myself and the infamous Anoka Boys during a summer race release. I expect the river to be run more often in the future as more boaters discover the summer pleasure and excitement that this section holds.

The Thomson Dam has recently been relicensed until 2025 and thanks in part to American Whitewater, whitewater boating is now a formal element of project operation as there are 10 scheduled releases each summer. Check the flow hotline at 1-800-582-8529.

steve stratman
illgen falls
baptism river

©2006 ephram holyoak

AMITY CREEK

LENGTH: 2 MILES

CLASS: IV–V

SUMMER: RARE

QUICK DESCRIPTION: STEEP CREEK, SLIDES, ONE FALLS

PUT-IN: SKYLINE PARKWAY, NEAR SEVEN BRIDGES ROAD

TAKE-OUT: SUPERIOR STREET BRIDGE NEAR JUNCTION WITH LESTER RIVER

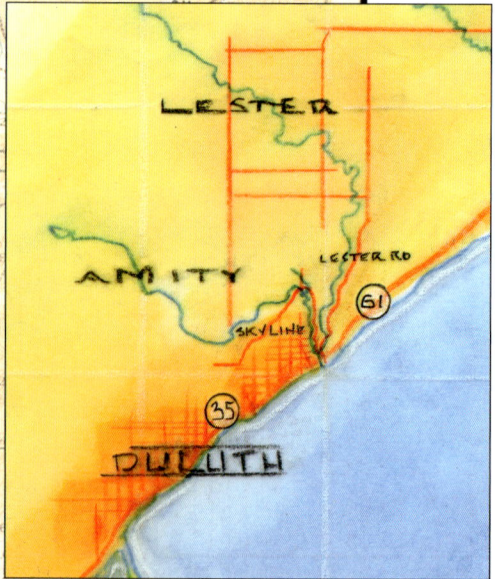

Amity Creek is an amazing example of what can be paddled in a plastic boat. Dan Theis and Randy Carlson of Duluth were the first to run this river in 1989 and since that time many parties have skittered down this Duluth river which drops over three hundred feet in about 1.5-2 miles as it charges toward Lake Superior. It's even scenic! Though within the city of Duluth, it flows through a wooded valley that contains some beautiful pines as you near its juncture with the Lester and the riverbed is largely interesting bedrock.

Amity Creek is runnable only during snowmelt peak and after heavy rains. It has a short season but displays quite a variety of drops as it falls from the east end of Skyline Parkway toward the Lake. Fortunately, it is crossed time and again (seven times!) by the Seven Bridges Road which facilitates scouting, spectating and support. Once Amity enters Lester-Amity Park it's paralleled by foot trails. One drop of about twenty feet, a steeply sloping falls, remained unrun until 1995 by John Linn. "Gazebo Falls" occurs just below a footbridge that spans Amity shortly after entering Lester-Amity Park. There is a gazebo next to the river here, hence the name.

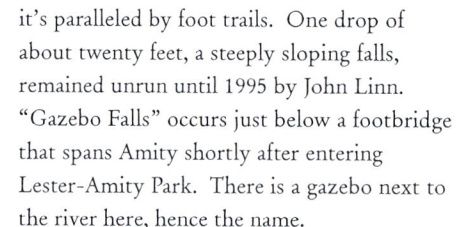

If you can handle the slides at the beginning of the trip, all should be well. Otherwise it might be an Amityville horror! Take out just before the Lester River confluence or add one more challenge by running the last falls on the Lester. Generally a class IV-IV+ steep creek descent.

Dan Theis in Smiley Face rapid. ©2006 Mike Cotten

An unstrapped helm atop Paul Everson on Gazebo Falls. ©2006 Kay Holmgren

The Lester is the largest of Duluth's whitewater creeks and contains an excellent short run. It is most easily caught during snowmelt, but it seems to come up with rain a few times each year. It can drop quickly so it's nice to have a Duluth connection. The gradient increases sharply right at the put-in, where an inconspicuous pulloff from the Lester River Road leads to the river only 100 feet away. This will give you a run of about 1.5-2 miles to the Superior Street bridge.

The action starts immediately with a double drop at the put-in followed in a hundred yards by a class IV twisting drop between low

LESTER RIVER

Descending Almost Always the Lester folds into a narrow tongue of water and crashes 20-25 feet down into a pool. A pretty spot, Almost Always is close to the Lester River Road about a half mile above the Lester-Amity Creek confluence.

Below Almost Always the Lester enters a very picturesque section of Lester-Amity Park, where the big pines tower over the river and small ledges make good fun for the paddler. Just after passing under a pedestrian bridge the Lester arcs over a four to five foot Baby Falls, an easy smiler.

Many take out at the Superior Street bridge. If you don't mind bothering the ever present stream fishermen, run the twisting drop into Railroad Hole. This is an excellent class IV+ drop which has more ummph due to the addition of Amity Creek's water just as the rapid starts. On one occasion I ran this drop into a swarm of fishermen to be greeted by both cheers and curses.

I first paddled the Lester in 1986 on a solo exploratory and consider this short accessible run to be a real find: fun and exciting steep creek boating. It reminds me of the Silver in Michigan's Upper Peninsula.

LENGTH: 2 MILES

CLASS: IV–V

SUMMER: RARE

QUICK DESCRIPTION: STEEP, FUN LEDGES, SCENIC PINES

PUT-IN: LESTER RIVER RD, 1.5 MILES ABOVE SUPERIOR STREET

TAKE-OUT: SUPERIOR STREET BRIDGE, PARK UPSTREAM

Paul Douglas in Limbo Falls on the Lester.   ©2006 Mike Cotten

rock walls. This twisting drop, Limbo Falls, is a good gauge of the river's level and your skill as it mirrors the steep technical nature of many of the Lester's drops.

Continuing downstream at least a half dozen class IV drops worthy of scouting will appear. Naked Man is a long sluiceway that suddenly drops eight feet vertically, another a stairstep drop of probably twenty feet as the river bends gradually to the left. The scenery is pretty with little evidence of the Lester River Road nearby on the left. A noteworthy drop where the water races down a nine foot sloping plunge to constrict near the reddish left wall was christened "Holy Shit" by the Anokas when one paddler after another pronounced these words after breaking through the wave at the bottom and snagging an eddy.

Good idea to snag an eddy, too, as following Holy Shit around a bend to the right comes "Almost Always." Almost Always is almost always portaged on the right. Almost Always has actually been run a couple of times; the first runs I know of belong to Paul Everson and Chris Brobin on a beautiful August day in 1995 when the sun was shining and the water perfect.

steve stratman
illgen falls
baptism river

©2006 ephram holyoak

17

FRENCH RIVER

LENGTH: 1.6 MILES

CLASS: III–IV

SUMMER: RARE

QUICK DESCRIPTION: TINY POOL-DROP STEEP CREEK

PUT-IN: ST. LOUIS COUNTY 33 CULVERT

TAKE-OUT: RYAN ROAD BRIDGE JUST UPSTREAM FROM EXPRESSWAY

I feel very lucky to have been involved in paddling during the Northwoods "Age of Exploration" when many whitewater streams were descended for the first time. One by one the more obvious runs were done and it became harder to find "virgin" rivers. Sometimes I'd begin to think there were no more worthwhile exploratories left, but I still believe there are a few runs hiding out in the woods.

My optimism about finding new runs was bolstered by a first descent of a two mile section of the French River in the spring of 1993. This section of the French had drawn my attention with its very uniform loss of elevation from the put-in at St. Louis County 33 to the takeout a quarter mile above the Highway 61 expressway. Two hundred feet of descent seemed to be spread quite evenly over the 1.6 mile run. Shortly below the takeout, the Ryan Road bridge, the French goes down a steep cascade that's visible from the expressway. This drop no doubt gave boaters the wrong impression of the French!

My eagerly anticipated first look at the riverbed came in February 1992. My girlfriend, Karen Jensen, and I took a hike upriver from the takeout on the frozen French. I was delighted and excited! The walk revealed many drops set in a pretty woods setting. While the drops were smoothed by snow and marked by ski tracks (it looks like a good ski run) it was obvious that the drops had enough size to be interesting. Some were in the 15-20 foot range but many more were smaller. All in all it looked very interesting.

Then came the spring paddling season. After our hike my main concern was if it would carry enough water to be boatable. As the runoff began I was able to sneak off for a peek at the put-in: encouraging, but not high enough to run at the time. A week later a heavy rain pushed up the runs in the Duluth area. Now was the time!

Many of the current generation of boaters haven't had the opportunity to do an exploratory so it was easy to persuade Ross Peterson, Marcus Witt, Chris Nybo and John McLaughlin to join old hands Ed Schneider, Scott Bridgham and myself on an exploratory run.

The run was termed a "first class boondoggle," quite a compliment! Many drops were encountered similar to the one at the put-in as well as some bigger ones. Everything proved runnable and most of the drops were boat-scoutable. The river was surprisingly free of sweepers and debris, considering that it's just an oversized creek. At first the river ran through stands of medium-sized deciduous trees but later there were lots of conifers and the river seemed quite "remote" despite its proximity to Duluth. The drops were enjoyable class III and IV, overall a pleasing run with a lot of interesting pool-drop action packed into a short run. Plastic boats were in order and John McLaughlin's short Topolino seemed right at home here.

The French is pretty small, which means it's best caught when all the surrounding rivers are running quite high. I'd guess that it's runnable whenever Amity Creek is runnable, but would be best on those days (which do occur!) when Amity and the Lester are high enough to be "gnarly." The Lester, Amity and French are all short and could be done in one steep-creekin' day! I'd say that the French is the easiest and most straightforward of the three, but certainly doesn't lack for action.

Are there other worthwhile runs waiting in the Northwoods for the kayakist? I think so but I'm going to be tight lipped about them. You other explorers need to unroll your maps! Maybe you'd like the French below the takeout I've listed here???

SUCKER RIVER

ALSO CALLED BIG SUCKER CREEK

LENGTH: 3 MILES

CLASS: IV–IV+

SUMMER: RARE

QUICK DESCRIPTION:
STEEP CREEK, QUITE SMALL

PUT-IN:
BERQUIST ROAD BRIDGE

TAKE-OUT:
OLD HIGHWAY 61 SCENIC ROUTE

The first time I heard of anyone paddling the Sucker was when Fred Young (Fearless Fred) took a visiting Charlie Walbridge down to run it. Fred reported that, "You'd like it, lots of steep drops." Indeed, there are a lot of steep drops, but it was several years before I decided to check it out.

After putting in where Berquist Road crosses the Sucker, you definitely have the feeling of being on a big creek. The first mile or mile and a half contains nothing more serious than one medium size (four foot) sloping ledge. In fact on my first run, a canoeist who lived near the river saw us putting in, ran home, got his canoe and led the trip for the first bit. He did the upper part frequently and said the Sucker responded nicely to rain.

The bottom falls out after passing under a powerline and it's open boat water no more. Tall pines emerge, the slides and ledges come fast and furious just below a house on river left. Small trails can be found on both the left and the right as the river drops about 150 feet in two-thirds of a mile. Almost everything is runnable, the exception for me being a very narrow vertical falls that looks blasted and as if it could contain severe pinning/broaching possibilities. I understand that Paul Everson found a way to avoid the worst of this spot, but it still scares me. This drop is about a third of the way through the steep stuff. Another unforeseen hazard that may exist is ice shelves in early spring. The river is small and well shaded, so it sometimes still has ice jutting from the shore blocking the eddies even when the Sucker is running good.

The end of the steep section is signaled by a drop of about 20 vertical feet where the preferred route is a staircase on the right down several steps with strong hydraulics—quite exciting! Another half mile of easier but still interesting whitewater brings you to your first possible takeout—a dirt road called the Old North Shore Road. However, I'd recommend continuing past this to enjoy a half-mile of nice water to the North Shore Scenic Route. This also includes culvert paddling under U.S. Highway 61—interesting! In winter I think the Sucker would be a pretty ski, though I haven't skied it yet.

Sucker River as snow and ice melt. ©2006 Mike Cotten

steve stratman
illgen falls
baptism river

©2006 ephram holyoak

KNIFE RIVER

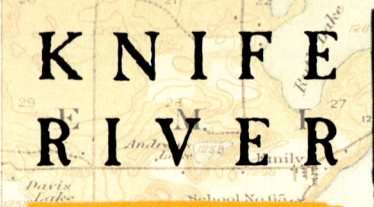

LENGTH: 3.5 MILES

CLASS: II–III

SUMMER: RARE

QUICK DESCRIPTION:
NICE II-II+, TWO TOUGHER LEDGES

PUT-IN:
LAKE COUNTY 102 BRIDGE

TAKE-OUT:
REST AREA AFTER EXPRESSWAY OR LAKE SUPERIOR

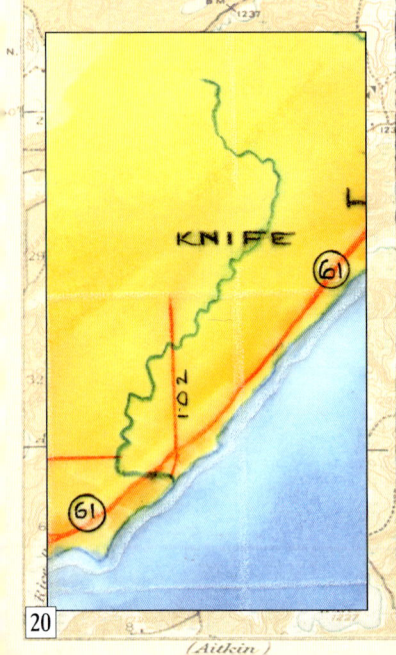

After having heard about the Knife from an open boater, after having looked at it on topo maps and after having hiked in to look at a dry riverbed, I finally got to run the Knife in April 1991. It was actually a nice short intermediate run and I was amazed at how many times I drove past it before giving it a chance.

One possible takeout for a three mile run is the wayside rest on river left just downstream of the Duluth-Two Harbors Expressway. The large, multi-step ledge you see at the wayside rest area is atypical of the river. It's far and away the biggest drop on the run and is easily avoided by taking out on the left above it. On river right is a USGS river gauge, and readings from this have been used to make the hydrograph found elsewhere in this book.

Another takeout option is right at Lake Superior in the town of Knife River. Chris Nybo has recommended this option, telling me that there's some interesting water in the last half mile to the Lake. The view of Knife Island is another bonus for those who run the last piece down to the Lake.

The put-in for the run is the Lake County 102 bridge, reached by driving two thirds of a mile east of the Knife on the Expressway and then turning north on 102. You'll come to the river in a couple of miles. The first mile and a half of this 3.5 mile run is just swiftwater and class I boulderbed. You'll pass red clay banks that taint the water, a group of log structures and then encounter a couple of small ledges.

The calm is broken when you reach a sharp ledge 6 or 7 feet high. It can easily be portaged on the right, but it also has a "ramp" on the right making it an easy slide. An island in the middle separates the ramp from a curving, three ledge stairstep that is a bit tricky, but fun. I've heard this stairstep referred to as the "Fish Ladder." The ramp is simple; the Fish Ladder is a III-IV proposition.

From this ledge to the takeout you'll have about a mile and a half of class II-II+ whitewater. The first two-thirds mile of this is the best–lots of small, smooth redrock ledges in a pretty valley with low rock walls decked with cedars and some nice pines. It was medium going on low when I ran it, and there were some small playspots. Apparently at high water there are some nice play features.

The banks fade away and the riverbed changes to boulders, as the river continues to plug along at class II intensity. Under the Expressway bridge and you're at the rest area, so take out left or scout the big ledge either left or right. I found a constricted chute on the extreme left to be a fun class IV run at the water level I encountered. All that's left after the big ledge is the last half-mile of interesting stuff to the Lake for those who want a bit more.

I'd think this run would please a lot of boaters—a short after-work run for Duluth paddlers, a good run for intermediate kayakists and experienced open boaters to enjoy. This run gives a little taste of North Shore scenery below the upper ledge and is large enough to not have a lot of sweeper danger. Its nature is such that it would be a good high water run when some rivers might be dangerously high. As a bonus the easy access at put-in and takeout makes this a good "quickie" run. You do a mile and a half of flatwater for an equal amount of interesting class II with a couple of drops to add zest or an easy portage. Not bad for a river I've passed by for fifteen years!

The Encampment River

Warning!! The Encampment River flows through private lands belonging to the "Encampment Forest Association," a group that has posted the land against trespassing. You will have to figure out for yourself how to approach this obstacle to access this beautiful and intimate river. We put in on lands outside the Association's holdings and took out at the mouth of Crow Creek. Our takeout necessitated a 1.5-2 mile flatwater paddle on Lake Superior to avoid trespassing on Association lands. Our encounter with the Association was mixed: the guests staying in the cabins were very curious and friendly, the caretaker couple we talked to viewed us and future kayakists as a trespassing nuisance and

ENCAMPMENT RIVER

LENGTH: 3 MILES

CLASS: III–V

SUMMER: RARE

QUICK DESCRIPTION: STEEP CREEKIN', HUGE PRIVATE FOREST

PUT-IN: SHORT SPUR ROAD OFF LAKE COUNTY 3, THREE MILES FROM LAKE

TAKE-OUT: AT THE MOUTH OF CROW CREEK AFTER LAKE PADDLE TO AVOID TRESPASSING

---

only reluctantly granted us permission to finish our run. We were attempting to be as discreet and unobtrusive as possible but you'll have to handle this yourself.

The private ownership of the land and the tiny size of the Encampment kept paddlers away until 1996, when spring high water provided ideal conditions for this interesting run. The Encampment Forest Association has protected the river corridor from development, which means the Encampment area hasn't been logged and displays a forest of huge pines. This forest is one of the few reminders of the past magnificence of the North Shore's old growth forests. The Association also has some rustic foot trails along the river that facilitate scouting and portaging without detracting from the setting.

Robert Ruffner, Paul Everson, Chris Brobin and I did a first descent in April 1996 after I'd scouted the river on an October hike. We put in on one of the branches of the Encampment that was crossed by a dead end dirt road that branched off Lake County 3. The first mile of our three mile run involved weaving through brush and swiftwater as the Encampment gained strength from other branches. The whitewater begins about where the Superior Hiking Trail crosses the Encampment.

It was interesting to compare my notes from the dry water hike to the reality of the Encampment with water. I found that everything was generally about one class harder than I'd guessed it would be! For instance, the low ledges that start to appear near the hiking bridge were more class III than II and the bouldery drop that came a third of a mile below the bridge was closer to IV than to III.

This meant that the serious water, which begins less than a quarter-mile from the boulder drop was intense indeed. When you see a log footbridge spanning the river–get out! Scouting from the right will reveal a tantalizing piece of whitewater. Just upstream from the bridge the river drops sharply about nine feet over a ledge that looks like it could "upset your plans." The runout from the nine footer is a slide into a fifty foot pool followed by an arcing falls that spills 25 feet into a bowl-like amphitheater. On my dry water hike, the thought of running this pitcher falls stuck with me as one great reason to run the Encampment. Unfortunately, the strength of the lead-in drop combined with the presence of an angled log at the base of the falls made a run seem reckless.

We carried over the footbridge and used the forest trail to portage downstream. If one could put in just below the falls, you'd have the "opportunity" to bounce down a 15 foot boulder drop. It didn't look pretty, but a 12 foot mini-falls another hundred feet downstream did look clean and pretty. Even better, it wasn't too hard to carry down to the pool just above the little falls, and we enjoyed a fun run on this class IV+ drop.

Below the little falls, the river turned into a slalom course with small ledges and boulders. This led to a bridge and just below the bridge was a rocky 20 foot drop onto more rock, which is quickly portaged on the left. At this point you are only a hundred yards from Highway 61 and in the midst of some cabins owned by the Association, so we made tracks downstream and under Highway 61.

Just after passing under 61 you come to the most enjoyable rapids on the run: a series of slides over the bedrock that lasts a hundred yards and drops thirty feet. It was a rush to zoom down those slides blasting through hydraulics and hitting waves. It provided entertainment for us and the cabin guests clustered along the river.

We regrouped in the pool below this class IV and scouted the next drop, another IV which included a 5 foot ledge followed by some tight maneuvering. Though not as much "fun" as the previous slide, it was technically challenging and enjoyable, and also the last rapid on the run.

Friendly folks called to us from a footbridge and then the currents of the Encampment merged with Lake Superior. We'd done it! We smiled as we paddled off toward Encampment Island and our Crow Creek takeout. We'd enjoyed the forbidden fruit.

MAP ON NEXT PAGE.

CROW CREEK

LENGTH: .35 MILES

CLASS: III–V

SUMMER: RARE

QUICK DESCRIPTION:
TINY CREEK, SLOT GORGE, SUPER SLIDE

PUT-IN:
0.35 MILES ABOVE SUPERIOR HIKING TRAIL BRIDGE (BEHIND TRAILER HOME)

TAKE-OUT:
SUPERIOR HIKING TRAIL BRIDGE OVER CROW CREEK

This little run hid out for years until Robert Ruffner sniffed it out. As one drives over Crow Creek on Highway 61 you notice a deep valley and wonder, "Hmmm, wonder what's upstream?" Somebody from Duluth claimed to have walked it and found it uninteresting. I had actually crossed it on the Superior Hiking Trail while sneaking in to look at the forbidden Encampment. Pretty, but too small to be a run I thought. Robert, however, went for a winter ski with Paul Everson and discovered one of the most picturesque canyons on the Shore.

When the big water spring of 1996 began to roar, some of us knew what to do—head for those tiny creeks! Robert, Paul, Chris Brobin and I had descended the neighboring Encampment on Saturday and next scouted the Crow Creek slot canyon thoroughly from the river left cliffs. One log, portagable, and one screaming drop that was unportagable, caught our eyes. The drop looked clean but it was hard to gauge the size and speed from a hundred feet above. We decided to give it a go on Sunday, and joined by Charles Griffiths, away we went on a first descent!

After receiving permission from the very friendly landowner, we put in behind the trailer home about .35 miles north of the Superior Hiking Trail parking lot on the dirt road that runs just east of Crow Creek. I believe the road is Lake County 106. We encountered easy rapids for a hundred and fifty yards and then a fun seven foot sliding falls. This was followed by some cool water . . . big boulders forming a class III slalom in the pint-sized creek. The slalom ended with a sharp right turn and drop, followed by a sharp turn back to the left. Here we got out to portage the log and then took turns sliding one by one down from a snow shelf towards the crux of the run.

A hundred yards below the hairpin sheer, reddish cliffs rose straight out of the water on both sides of the creek, with the creek plunging out of sight through this gate. The plunge began with an easy seven foot ledge, best run on the right, and then continued by twisting right, forcing the paddler to bank off the left wall. The last part of the slide drops about fifteen feet.

I don't use this word too much, but this drop filled me with an AWESOME exhilaration—you fly towards the cleft, drop, bank and scream down into the pool below. The view looking upstream from the pool is marvelous: you can only see upstream fifty feet to where the creek seems to squirt out of solid red rock.

Robert, Paul and I had all run and waited an eternity in the pool for Charles and Chris. Suddenly, Charles blasted around the corner and down the slide yelling, "Have you blokes seen the bloody paddle?!?" No, we said, we'd been unaware of any problems upstream. Chris's paddle had slid into the river and disappeared as he prepared to seal launch on the snow where the log was. Caught upstream without a paddle!! Robert and I raced downstream, climbed out of the canyon and rushed upstream with a paddle for Chris. He was just about to rope his boat out. We told him what a blast the run was and now he was equipped to fly—and he did!

On reaching the Superior Hiking Trail bridge, the takeout, we were all in a party mood. What a thrill that third of a mile had been! Robert was beaming; he'd discovered a little jewel. It might not run often and you do need to check carefully for logs before descending, but Crow Creek is an unqualified rush, one you can experience in five minutes.

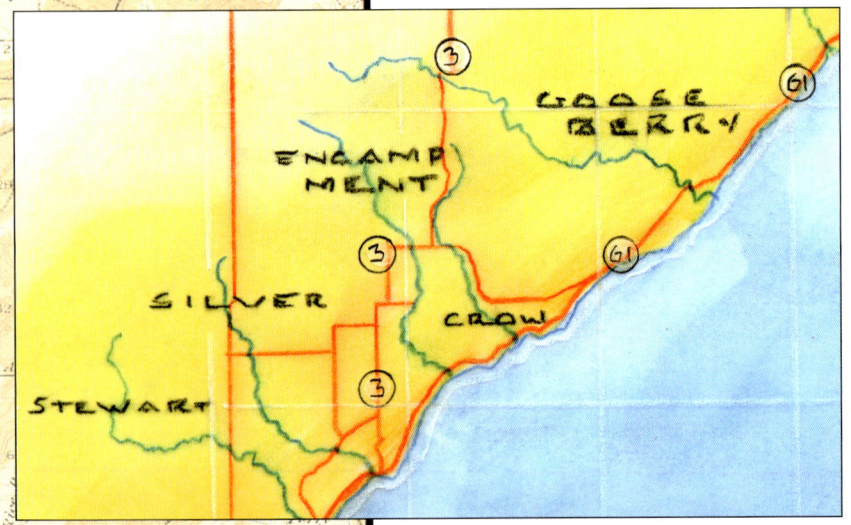

GOOSEBERRY RIVER

The Gooseberry is probably one of the best known of the North Shore streams as far as tourists are concerned. There are many beautiful waterfalls, including one that's visible looking upstream from the Highway 61 bridge. From the bridge to the Lake the river crashes over one falls after another.

For kayakists the Gooseberry offers two options: run all the way from Lake County 3 to Highway 61 encountering lots of easy water, or carry up from Highway 61 to run the last nice section. After accessing it several miles inland off of Lake County Highway 3, Tom Schellberg and I ran to the falls just above Highway 61. The upper river was often gravel bedded with occasional stretches of boulderbed and lots of winding curves. I remember one nice section of steep boulderbed (class III) on this upper section.

When within a mile of Highway 61 a major tributary, Skunk Creek, adds considerable flow. The river changes character three-quarters of a mile above Highway 61 to a bedrock river, with a few enjoyable red rock slides and ledges. This change occurs as you approach Fifth Falls, recognized by a footbridge spanning the Gooseberry just after a nice, snaking section of class III. Fifth Falls, actually a sequence of drops, may be portaged on either the left or right using Gooseberry Falls State Park trails. There's a nice ledge a couple hundred feet below Fifth Falls, and if you carry on the right you can put in above this drop, with a little difficulty.

The next two-thirds of a mile to the takeout on river right above Upper Falls is the nicest part of the run. In addition to the drop just below Fifth Falls, the paddler will find three more broad ledges of shallow pitch. Each of these III-III+ drops is easily scouted and the rapids between drops are just fun class II. This last piece is short but nice, and would justify carrying your boat up one of the Gooseberry Falls State Park trails from Highway 61 to Fifth Falls. A "hike up" technique could be used to run the fine lower stretches of the Split Rock, Cross and Brule as well. Each would repay a carry of a mile or less with excellent rapids.

The nature of the rapids above and below Fifth Falls make the Gooseberry one of the least difficult North Shore runs. The pretty scenery below Fifth Falls combined with the easy ledges should whet an intermediate paddler's appetite for the harder runs.

MAP ON PREVIOUS PAGE.

Snow falls on Gooseberry Falls, Gooseberry River ©2006 Dewey James

LENGTH: 6 MILES

CLASS: II–III

SUMMER: RARE

QUICK DESCRIPTION: MOSTLY EASY I-II, SOME III AT END

PUT-IN: LAKE COUNTY 3 BRIDGE

TAKE-OUT: UPSTREAM FROM U.S. 61, GOOSEBERRY FALLS STATE PARK

steve stratman
illgen falls
baptism river

ephram holyoak

SPLIT ROCK RIVER

LENGTH: 5.5 MILES

CLASS: IV–V

SUMMER: RARE

QUICK DESCRIPTION:
FLAT EARLY, THEN STEEP CREEK

PUT-IN:
LAKE COUNTY 3 BRIDGE OVER WEST FORK

TAKE-OUT:
LAKE SUPERIOR, U.S. 61

Mike "Turbo" Goglin hugs the hero route on Winfrey's Whimper, Split Rock River. ©2006 Paul Everson

The Split Rock is a river that sports many steep slides and redrock ledges, is very picturesque and is rarely paddled. The explanation for the lack of paddling activity is threefold:

#1. You must paddle two to three miles down either the East or West Fork of the Split Rock to get to where the gradient steepens and the water is sufficient. We once came in on the West Fork which is basically a big creek with numerous down trees to portage. I've since opted for the two mile carry up from the takeout to do this run.

#2. You need high flows to keep the Split Rock from being too scrapey—and at high flows many enjoyable and accessible Shore rivers are nearby.

#3. The whitewater of the Split Rock is extremely steep, unappealing to some because of piton hazard. I know of one piton incident resulting in a broken ankle on this run and was personally involved in a vertical pin myself. I got out of my boat easily, but at least half an hour and the pull of a six man crew orchestrated by Pete Cary and Fred Young was necessary to extract my boat.

Some say it's a better ski river than a boating run. However, I'd encourage the expert steep creek paddler to give it a whirl. Why? Because of its enchanting scenery and the exhilarating drops. The river has eroded the layered red rock into tiny steps that make great slides and staircases amid cliffs and small pinnacles of the same red rock. Add a few cedars and it's a beautiful sight.

The real action begins just above where a footbridge of the Superior Hiking Trail crosses the river, less than a mile below the confluence of the East and West Fork. From that point on you don't need a guidebook, you need two good eyes, good eddy catching ability, judgement and your wits. "Scout at will" is the motto. Despite their large vertical size, most of the drops are extremely smooth because of the erosion of the layered rock and come about as close to natural water slides as you could hope for.

I would say that there are about six to eight distinct major drops in the mile and a half before the Split Rock calms down. Between these drops lie short stretches of class II. One day I was entranced by running drop after drop, some descending twenty feet and more in a flash–then the vertical pin reminded me of some facts of life.

The recently constructed (late '80s) segment of the Superior Hiking Trail loops up the right side of the river from a wayside parking lot on the north side of Highway 61 and crosses the Split Rock as the rapids begin. The hiking trail then follows the Split Rock on the left side for perhaps a half mile. The Superior Hiking Trail is a great resource for portaging, scouting rapids or looking at the run during low water periods.

In fact, given the brushy nature of the upper forks, I feel that portaging your boat up from the parking lot on 61 is the way to go. A one and a half to two mile carry allows a preliminary scout of the 1.5 miles of slides, saves a lengthy shuttle and some bushwacking. I've gone down the West Branch and hiked from the bottom and I definitely prefer hiking. At least one group did the run by starting on the East Branch, and they reported smooth sailing. You make the choice, but I like the carry.

The drops on the river are beyond individual description other than to say that they are class IV and V in nature. It would be best to scout on your own. The two rapids that have caused the most trouble and are the most likely portages are Winfrey's Whimper and Under the Log. Winfrey's Whimper is about the fifth major drop below the Superior Hiking Trail bridge. If you carried up on the trail on river right you walked right next to it. It bounces down sharply in the first pitch and terminates by running into a rock shelf under the water. This is where Winfrey long ago broke his ankles by pitoning.

Under the Log is the last drop of the run. Here the river charges down a steep slide that drops about fifteen feet and then careens abruptly to the left. The name commemorates a huge tree that for many years blocked the right side of the rapid. Paul Everson made the first descent with the log still there, and rather than missing the log, he found himself pushed up to it and swept "under the log." He emerged unscathed, but lasting mental scars remain on the cortexes of the boaters watching the run. It was one scary moment I'm told. As of 1996, the log is gone from Under the Log, and the rapid has been run with a little less "action" than Paul had on his first run.

Immediately following Under the Log is a small drop that is surprisingly powerful, and in fact quite capable of producing enders when the river is running high. Enjoy some play here if the water is right and savor the fine run during the winding half-mile of flatwater that brings you to the Lake.

Split Rock River. If you're carrying to the put-in, this is halfway. ©2006 Paul Everson

BEAVER RIVER

SECTION: WEST FORK

LENGTH: 3 MILES

CLASS: II

SUMMER: RARE

QUICK DESCRIPTION:
ONE III-IV DROP EARLY

PUT-IN: LAKE COUNTY 3 THREE MILES FROM LAKE COUNTY 4 BRIDGE

TAKE-OUT: LAKE COUNTY 4 BRIDGE, OR JUST BEFORE GLEN AVON FALLS

SECTION: EAST FORK

LENGTH: 2 MILES

CLASS: III+

SUMMER: RARE

QUICK DESCRIPTION:
LEDGES, BOULDERS, RUNNABLE FALLS

PUT-IN: LAKE COUNTY 5 BRIDGE

TAKE-OUT: LAKE COUNTY 4 BRIDGE OVER THE WEST FORK, YOU MUST PADDLE UP THE WEST FORK 1/4 MILE.

Glen Avon Falls, West Fork of the Beaver

WEST FORK OF THE BEAVER

The West Fork of the Beaver affords a short intermediate run putting in at the Lake County Highway 3 bridge about 5 miles from Beaver Bay. I would recommend taking out above Glen Avon Falls, about two miles downstream. While it's possible to run Glen Avon, sliding down the rocky shelves, or to portage it on the left, there is little whitewater from Glen Avon until the confluence with the East Fork of the Beaver.

The run contains mostly class I and II boulder rapids, but there is one notable exception. A sharp ledge approximately one mile below the put-in is certainly class III and develops a strong hydraulic capable of stopping boats along the river right shore.

EAST FORK OF THE BEAVER

Though smaller than the West Fork, the East Fork has considerably more interesting whitewater. You can extend the run by putting in where Lake County 4 crosses the East Beaver, but most of the good whitewater can be run by putting in at the Lake County 5 bridge. Just below County 5 you enter a wild area with rocky hills flanking the river. It seems remote and in fact a group of us had a mother bear and two cubs swim across the river ahead of us once.

The placid paddling is soon over and excellent steep boulderbed appears. Set in this section of boulderbed are a couple of substantial ledges (III+/IV-), one pinching the current tightly to the right and shortly thereafter another abrupt drop. It's best not to get too carried away by the fine whitewater in this section because approximately a mile below the Highway 5 bridge a series of three waterfalls breaks the river's downhill progress.

These falls lie in the vicinity of an above-ground pipeline associated with the taconite refining facility in Silver Bay. This pipeline, which is readily visible from County 4, carries a slurry of taconite tailings inland for on-land disposal. The company has suggested from time to time that the excess water from the tailings disposal be dumped in the Beaver, augmenting flow with water possibly enriched with asbestos.

The three falls also remind me of an interesting experience with a visiting expert C-1 paddler. We scouted the eddy on river right above the first falls before our run, and I heard him say, "Oh, I can generally sniff out waterfalls pretty well anyway." We then ran from County 4 down and when we pulled into the portage eddy he was surprised when someone told him, "We usually portage here." His old "sniffer" had failed!

The moral of this story is that North Shore falls often come up in the midst of innocuous whitewater. Since many of these streams are small, winding and densely forested there's little warning so you must know where to take out. I have had reservations about including some north shore runs just because of this aspect. If at all possible scout poten-

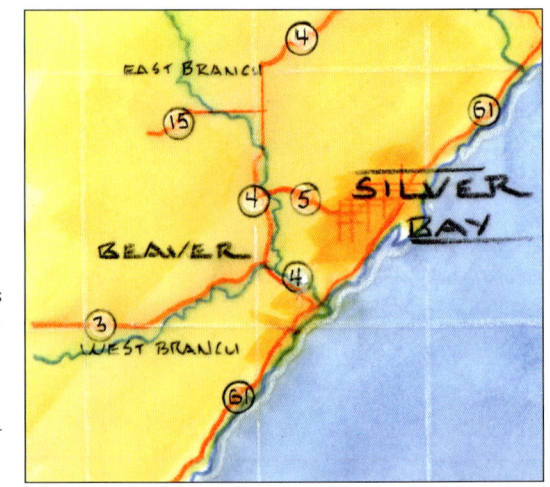

Doug Demerest runs second falls on the East Fork, Beaver River.

tial portage areas by ski or hiking or a quick look before paddling. It's extra nice, though not always possible, to go with someone familiar with the river.

Many of the rivers in this book can be run by a watchful, experienced paddler with guidebook information but a few such as the Devil's Track and Cascade can be treacherous at the wrong water level or for kayakists who "bomb" downriver. Catch eddies and take a look if you're not sure what's ahead. A guidebook can't do it all for you! Treat these rivers with respect, almost like exploratories on your first run, and all should be well. Be especially careful on the smaller runs where a down tree can block the whole river.

Back on the East Beaver, the first falls is a steep runnable slide but is followed in a hundred feet by the second falls, a 20-25 foot drop of great hydraulic power. All three falls were run in the summer of 1992 by Chris Nybo and a visiting Wisconsin paddler. I don't know what the water level was, but it was probably low during summer. I do know that Nybo was "trashed" here during a spring time run and I've watched one other shaky run. There have been successful runs but be careful in your approach to falls #2.

Most parties have portaged the first two and run the last, a joyous 15 foot leap. There are several runnable chutes or tongues on the third falls. The safest is the sloping tongue left of center. There are also "streamers" on the right that allow a vertical leap. Be careful on the rightside streamers if the water is low, though, because the pool isn't as deep then. I know because I broke my little toe here once, partially because of the low water and partially because I let the boat enter the pool too vertical. On all other occasions, falls #3 has been great fun for everyone.

Following the falls comes a section I find extremely pleasant. The tiny East Fork enters a half mile playground of continuous class II-III water with small ledges and fun boulderbed interspersed with kayak-sized eddies. The rapids wane as the river goes through the Beaver Bay Country Club golf course and then the East Fork joins the West Fork. Paddle upstream on the west fork a quarter mile to take out where County 4 crosses the West Beaver, about one and a half miles from Beaver Bay.

MAIN BEAVER

BELOW THE CONFLUENCE OF EAST AND WEST FORK

The Beaver below the confluence is placid until it comes within a mile of Lake Superior. Then it develops steep ledges, which look runnable, interspersed with stretches of boulderbed for about a half-mile. I know of only one attempt on this section, which apparently was a portage-fest. Looking from the safety of the Superior Hiking Trail during low water, some of these large ledges appeared as though boatable at higher flows.

This half-mile segment starts after running under the snowmobile/hiking trail bridge. The last third of a mile of river is visible from the Highway 61 bridge and displays a tumultuous Beaver with one glorious falls and many ledges stacked one on top of another–looks like "scareball" video material to me!!!

BAPTISM RIVER

SECTION: I

LENGTH: 4 MILES

CLASS: II–III

SUMMER: RARE

QUICK DESCRIPTION:
BOULDERS, PORTAGE, PLAY LEDGES

PUT-IN:
STATE FOREST CAMP-GROUND IN FINLAND

TAKE-OUT:
ECKBECK CAMPGROUND AT MINNESOTA 1 BRIDGE

This is one of the Northwoods classics! Repeat, a classic! Just as the Chattooga or the Tuolumne or the Gauley or the Arkansas, the Baptism has a special personality. Any boater who paddles from Finland to Lake Superior will experience a memorable journey: great whitewater, splendid waterfalls and cascades, intimate and sublime beauty with a finale of the other world aura of Lake Superior. If this makes you want to see this river you should! I remember a boater who after his "baptismal" run on the Baptism said, "Can we do this every weekend?"

Fortunately the Baptism is "up" more days out of the year than most Lake Superior rivers. There are two reasons for this: it has a relatively large drainage area and it has a high percentage of runoff for water coming into this drainage area. I once saw a study of rivers in Minnesota potentially suitable for hydropower development. Of the rivers studied, the Baptism collected more out of each inch of rainfall than any other river in the group.

This characteristic actually shows up for river runners: a summer rain may bring only a moderate rise in low summer levels of other Shore rivers, but the Baptism will be boatable! I attribute this peculiarity to the steep and rocky terrain in the Baptism's drainage—quick runoff and "flashy" level changes. Another point that helps boaters is that the Eckbeck-Illgen section of the Baptism is quite constricted, and that means good boating can be had with low flows. Being one of the larger North Shore runs also minimizes the danger of down trees and means there's an official USGS river gauge located just upstream of the Highway 61 bridge on the right shore. It should be mentioned that there is a newer USGS gauge on the river right shore a couple hundred yards above the Highway 61 bridge. The older gauge, "in the shadow" of the bridge, is the one I and other boaters refer to. Two feet on the bridge gauge is probably the absolute boat scraping low level, 2.5 feet makes for enough water to enjoy the lower two sections, 3.0 feet puts some juice into the drops and gets rid of "boniness" on the upper section and flows above 3 feet don't happen that often and should definitely be enjoyed, particularly the Eckbeck-Illgen stretch which is just great!!

Although the classic run from Finland to the Lake is easily done in a day, I'll break the river into three sections that are often pad-

A shallow landing prevents descents of High Falls; even Al Sabean puts in the pool below. ©2006 Mike Cotten

BAPTISM RIVER

SECTION: II

LENGTH: 1.3 MILES

CLASS: II–IV

SUMMER: SOME

QUICK DESCRIPTION: NARROW, LEDGES, PRETTY

PUT-IN: ECKBECK CAMPGROUND AT MINNESOTA 1 BRIDGE

TAKE-OUT: ILLGEN FALLS, NEAR MINNESOTA 1, ONE MILE FROM ECKBECK

---

dled independently because of differences in difficulty, flow characteristics or time available: I. Finland to Eckbeck, II. Eckbeck to Illgen Falls and III. Illgen Falls to the Lake.

SECTION I

FINLAND TO ECKBECK CAMPGROUND

This section, while containing one portage, is suitable for intermediate paddlers. After putting in at the state forest campground at Finland, the river passes through easy, wide open boulderbed rapids for a couple of miles. There are also two or three minor ledges which produce small but enjoyable surfing waves. If the river level is about 2.9 feet or higher on the Highway 61 gauge, there won't be many rocks. The river gets quite scrapey by 2.5 feet.

The lone portage is Avalanche Falls, a sloping cascade which drops about twenty five feet. It's evident from above as a horizon line breaks the class I riffles preceding it. As far as I know, Avalanche Falls has never been run. There are a couple good small takeout eddies on river right above the falls and a reasonable portage over rock outcrops on the right side. If the river is high, it might be a little challenging re-entering the river at the base of the falls.

Shortly below Avalanche Falls comes a short class II-III ledge drop. Not much further one enters Paul Bunyan's Steps—a 200 yard long section containing several class III ledges that embrace a number of fine holes for sidesurfing. The play spots here are the best on the Finland to Eckbeck run, so take advantage. Below the Paul Bunyan's Steps the river returns to a boulderbed nature that's similar to the miles above Avalanche Falls until Eckbeck Campground, which is on river left just above the Minnesota Highway 1 bridge over the Baptism. Eckbeck is a pretty little state forest campground and a convenient and relaxing place to camp in the Baptism area.

SECTION II

ECKBECK TO ILLGEN FALLS

The next mile and a half downstream from Eckbeck Campground is one of the nicest miles of river to be found in the Northwoods, or by my judgement anywhere in the country (I know, I'm prejudiced!!). It's very intimate, the river narrowing considerably from its width at Eckbeck campground and this permits boating even if the river near Eckbeck looks a bit "thin" on water. Certainly a good run at 2.5 feet, it can be run lower.

Confinement Canyon of the Baptism. ©2006 Dewey James

Passing beneath the Highway 1 bridge, a small surfing wave appears on the right, then come 150 yards of easy class II boulderbed as the river bends right. A sudden narrowing of the river, a house on the right and low rock cliffs let you know that you've reached Confinement Canyon. This is an exhilarating class III+ flume of whitewater that runs nonstop for a hundred yards down a narrow slalom course of waves, ledges and holes. There are some kayak-sized eddies, too! See how many you can catch!

The tail end of Confinement Canyon is very picturesque with a little creek (or ice fall depending on temperature!!) spilling in from the right beneath tall pines and cedar. The river narrows ominously and bends left. The paddler is greeted by a four or five foot drop, with a left and right channel. I recommend the left channel as the right has caused bow pinning and pitoning.

Below Confinement Canyon the Baptism runs along as a mellow, pretty class II for about half a mile. You will notice an ever so slight increase in intensity as you paddle along, especially as you notice the boulders becoming bigger and the gradient steeper. The water will take on class III nature as you weave through "bed-sized" boulders.

Don't fall asleep now! The bed-sized boulders form a 150 yard lead-in to "Kramer's Choice," an honest class IV that should be scouted from the left if you've never seen it. An eight foot diameter boulder sits squarely in the middle of the river below a complex fifty yards of drops and waves. Boats have been broached on Kramer, the big rock. Boats have been bridged across the main channel to the left of Kramer. It's turbulent and exhilarating, and Kramer does offer a good pillow to help you. When I first started boating, I didn't choose a side, I just paddled, let Kramer choose, and tried to keep the boat straight! I think it's easier to go left.

Downstream from Kramer's Choice the Baptism enters a shady mini-canyon with low rock walls, beautiful old conifers and rocky ledges. One hundred fifty yards of calm and small ledges ends with a horizon line as the river drops, then turns sharply to the left. This is Gustafson's Falls, a III+/IV drop of about six or seven feet. A runnable tongue on the right is the usual route threading a tight line between Forever Eddy on the right, the rock wall straight ahead and a hole to the left. Quick and turbulent, it makes you move.

Another hundred yards below Gustafson's Falls the river twists sharply to the right over a short abrupt dropoff of about four feet, House Rock Drop, a III. House Rock Drop is named for a cabin high above the river on the left. The reversal here is surprisingly powerful, causing back pop-ups and swims at some levels. The hole is just wide enough to side surf a boat—and to lock you in with a rock wall on the left. I once put my nose in to try for an ender, got grabbed sideways and yelled at friends to help me, to pull out my bow from shore. Needless to say, Greg Breining was more than happy to help me after I swam out.

The next quarter-mile reverts to class II-III boulderbed water, fun!! and then a class III multi-ledge stairstep followed by a pool. You're now about a quarter-mile from Illgen, so after the pool run another hundred yards of boulders, slide over a set of ledges on a sharp left turn (Elbow Bend Ledges) and then head left, taking out fifty yards below Elbow Bend Ledges on the left.

You've arrived at Illgen! If you carry out to Highway 1 here, you'll notice a house on river left. It's my understanding that this house has been acquired by Tettegouche State Park (and hopefully will be removed!). However, it would be best to be on good behavior and ask permission before portaging or accessing the river here. The portage trail around Illgen is on river left, atop the cliffs that overlook Illgen's plunge pool. It's also probably possible to portage Illgen on the right, but it would be brushy and not as desirable. Many parties take out here after a short run, so do be on your best behavior when in the vicinity of this access point.

Illgen Falls!

Illgen Falls is a beautiful, mesmerizing sight. The Baptism pours its soul over a bedrock outcrop dropping thirty feet in the process. A huge plunge pool and boil fill a kettle-like amphitheater at the base of the falls. The usual route at Illgen is around it, walking with boat on back along a steep narrow trail that reaches some "seal launch" rocks about 200 feet downstream of Illgen.

Illgen has been swum by a boater who abandoned ship at the small ledge that's perhaps fifty feet above Illgen. It must have been a terrifying few moments to see your boat go over the brink and then to realize that you are about to follow. Fortunately, the paddler went deep into the plunge pool and escaped unscathed, to be the star of the show at the bar that night. This incident scares me, though, because it is one of a handful of incidents on the North Shore in which a boater was swept over something he had no intention of running. When that happens, death is a real possibility. Please, please approach these rivers with respect and skill!

Illgen has been run on a several occasions, usually when the Baptism is at a flow that would make the Eckbeck-Illgen run a bit scrapey. At high flows the hydraulic at the base of the falls is extremely powerful and surges towards the surrounding cliff walls very strongly. At very low flows the plunge pool isn't as well aerated and paddlers risk a sharp impact if they "pancake" on landing.

Fred Young (Fearless Fred) was the first over the falls in the late 70's. After a summer of romantic heartbreak, Fred was ready to go it alone in his C-1. The atmosphere was electric as he paddled towards the edge and over. The hull of his boat bounced lightly off of a water-covered projection just right of river center and he hit the pool at an angle "porpoising" up smartly.

BAPTISM RIVER

Then it was my turn. I distinctly remember the gut wrenching sensation of seeing tree tops beyond the lip as I neared the brink, then going over smoothly with the water. The landing was unexpected bliss, just softly piercing down and down into the depths of aerated water at the bottom—unbelievably soft. After total submersion I popped up to be pressed gently against the left cliffs, where I rolled and then paddled on. What a feeling!!

We measured the falls with a throw rope and found it to be thirty feet seven inches high. Fred returned another day with some Idaho paddlers for more successful runs. Ross Peterson, Marcus Witt, Chris Nybo, John Alt and John McLaughlin are among the growing cadre of North Shore experts who've taken the plunge.

I returned during the low water spring of 1988 with the Anokas (Mike Cotten, Dean Johnson, Mark Gibson, Al Sabean, Paul Douglas and Steve Henderson). This time all runs though different went well until the last. Paul charged over the lip but the bow of his boat hit the same projecting rock that Fred had touched years before. Instead of just bouncing off his boat twisted so as to land almost flat. The impact severely compressed his back and he floated up to us still in his boat writhing in pain. We extracted him from the boat, and while no permanent injury was done, our exuberance was dampened.

Illgen can be run safely–but at low flow you must either avoid the rock projection or gather enough speed to clear it after cresting the lip. At higher flows you must decide how you will deal with the hydraulic. To date all runs have been successful with the only injury being Paul Douglas's temporary back injury. No doubt about it, Illgen is a mighty drop.

SECTION III:
ILLGEN FALLS TO THE LAKE

This section, while not sustaining quite the high level of boating found on the Eckbeck-Illgen run, contains two of the most difficult rapids on the river, two spectacular falls, enchanting scenery and a wonderful feeling of completion on reaching Lake Superior.

SECTION: III

LENGTH: 2.5 MILES

CLASS: II–V

SUMMER: RARE

QUICK DESCRIPTION:
SCENIC, FALLS, PORTAGES, TWO STEP

PUT-IN:
ILLGEN FALLS, PRIVATE LAND

TAKE-OUT:
LAKE SUPERIOR, TETTE-GOUCHE STATE PARK AND WAYSIDE

The first descent of Illgen Falls by Fearless Fred Young. ©2006 Tom Aluni

steve strathman
illgen falls
baptism river

©2006 ephram holyoak

Doug Demerest lines up for Illgen Falls.

©2006 Steve Stratman

Immediately below Illgen the river stumbles over and around a series of small ledges and boulders that come in rapid fire succession, fun class III water that occasionally holds a snag. Then, in the next half-mile, several minor ledges provide an opportunity for some play. The last of these ledges has a hand painted sign next to it naming the four foot drop "Patty Cake Falls."

The river changes to class II boulderbed and flows between low banks for about a third or half a mile below Patty Cake Falls. It's time to get out immediately when you see a footbridge over the river. This bridge is for the Superior Hiking trail and provides an access to the Tettegouche State Park campground if you'd like to hike in (or out!) at High Falls. Take out on river left where the shore turns into a rock shelf, right near the bridge supports. Heed this warning for just around the corner is High Falls, about a sixty foot drop.

A nice trail on the left brings you a view of High Falls roaring over a slab of bedrock. It appears to hit the bedrock sheet again near the pool and has never been run. On one occasion a hiker was swept over the falls. The hiker survived but suffered some temporary partial paralysis. Continuing along the trail on river left you will reach a branch in the trail where you can descend to the base of the falls. Make sure to feel the "hurricane wind" coming off the base of the falls and check out the foam pile on river right. A spectacular place.

When you head downstream, you'll see a couple large boulders, then a medium ledge. Time to wake up since "Two Step" is just ahead. Two Step resides about a third of a mile below High Falls and should definitely be scouted from the left. Some will choose to portage and above 3 feet on the gauge, the hole at the base of the second step will scare away most. The first drop is a joy–the paddler shoots over a rooster tail ramp to "boof" into a deep and foamy pool eight feet below. There's an eddy below the first step to recover in. Pete Cary needed it when he ran too far right on a pioneering run and bottomed out, cracking some ribs. A small ledge between the Steps has distracted a boater or two as they approached the second step of Two Step, fifty feet from the first step.

The second step provides nine or ten feet of exhilaration as the river sweeps over an intricate crescent-shaped ledge. Going far right over the "shoulder" of water banking off the right wall is the most straightforward route, "The Missouri Route," named for some down south visitors. It'll immerse you and clean out your nostrils! Another approach is to ferry right to left and aim to get to the left side of the crescent, a delicate move. The center can hold boat and paddler–it has been demonstrated. John Amren also demonstrated that you can survive running the lower drop upside down in a C-1 but it's not recommended.

Expert paddlers have been injured, and there have been some swimmers and boats have been lost, such as Steve Drobnick's low volume race craft–never seen again. Two Step is serious stuff, IV+ or V, depending on water level.

You're past the major drop of the lower run now, but approaching a dangerous spot: The Cascades. At The Cascades the river slams through a narrow cut (6-8 feet) into a washing machine pothole, spews out and slides down a rocky incline that drops twenty feet or more in a hundred feet. It has never looked like a run to me, but it's a beautiful spot. There's a rather rugged portage on the left that ends up sliding down a muddy ravine to put in at the base of The Cascades.

Lenny Sheps runs the first "step" of Two Step rapid.
©2006 Steve Stratman

diameter hole drilled in it by the current. Sometimes this hole is under water. This "drilled" rock gave the rapid its name.

You are now about a half mile from the Lake. The river eases until just above the Highway 61 bridge when a staccato series of ledges sends you scrambling. One hole near the river gauge has entertained guests from Missouri, Wisconsin and elsewhere. Waiting at the gauge for unsuspecting newcomers to hit the "Gauge Hole" is one of the chief amusements for North Shore regulars. A couple more drops and bends and you reach the gravel bar at the river's mouth—a beautiful and serene place to end a river trip.

I usually enjoy a short paddle at the mouth of the Baptism after each river run, admiring Shovel Point to the east and the view of Palisade Head to the west. Sometimes big breakers are coming in—once we spent forty hair raising minutes recovering swimmers and boats unwittingly trashed in big surf.

The danger here is in the approach to The Cascades, for the river slowly increases in difficulty from easy class II to become harder. The whitewater won't overwhelm you, but you may not notice that the left shore has turned into a slick slope of moss covered rock slipping smoothly into the river. It has a couple of narrow one boat eddies early on, but provides no shelter when the rapids take off, a funnel enticing you to go just a little too far. I encourage first-time adventurers to get out a little early and check it out from shore.

Once on shore, be careful; the rocks are slippery, as Jim Pedginski found out. He was portaging just ahead of me when he slipped, fell on one knee breaking his kneecap. The impact jolted his boat out of his grasp and it slid into the river and over The Cascades. We recovered the boat from the boulders below.

Below The Cascades is a fun boulder drop, then class II boulderbed for a half-mile which includes an island. A hundred yards after the island, the river twists sharp right. This is the lead-in to "Hole-in-the-Rock," a IV. Nice waves, as the river drops evenly through a narrows then turns exciting at the end as the river plunges down a six foot drop amongst a tangle of boulders. Paddle hard! One of the boulders on the left has a half foot

steve stratman
illgen falls
baptism river

©2006 ephram holyoak

A boater known as Fish takes the Missouri Route of Two Step. ©2006 David Fawcett

It was a lazy Saturday morning in June.

by Tom Aluni

Five kayakers were gathered at Pete Cary's home to discuss the best rivers to run. There wasn't a lot to pick from. It was late in the year for North Shore streams. We didn't have a lot of enthusiasm. After all, who could enjoy thumping down rocks along an overexposed river bed?

Suddenly one of us had an idea! "Let's call Fred Young and tell him Jim Rada decided to run Illgen Falls." In those days, Fred Young was the Midwest's most admired whitewater boater. That is how he became known as "Fearless Fred." But, time and tide were taking their toll, and Jim Rada had been rapidly replacing Fred as "Most Daring Boater." We could always feel a little tension between them.

That morning, Pete called Fred at his home near Chicago. After a little small talk, Pete set the hook. "Oh, by the way, Jim Rada decided to run Illgen Falls today!" Chuckles and smirks filled the room. Then Pete's expression turned from glee to surprise. All we heard was "Okay, 10:30am. Duluth Airport." Then he hung up the phone.

Fred was devastated. He told Pete to hold up the action until he got there. Illgen wasn't going to be run without him. At least he would become the second boater to run it. No one was going to take that away from him too. He told Pete he would fly to Duluth and asked to be picked up there so he could be present as the big event unfolded.

For Midwestern Boaters of the late 1970s, Illgen Falls was the shining prize of the boating community. As far as we knew no vertical waterfall over 30 feet had yet been run. Snugly tucked away on Minnesota's North Shore lay Illgen Falls, a 30 foot vertical drop into a deep calm pool. It appeared to be perfectly runnable. The only barrier was that waterfall jumping was still in its infancy making the distance of the drop quite intimidating.

It was now mid-afternoon. Everyone was in place along the Baptism River. Greg Breining, Henry Kinukan, and I were positioned among the cliffs just down from Illgen Falls. Our cameras were poised and ready. Jim Rada and Fred Young stood on a rock shelf above the falls. Pete Carey was running safety in the pool below the drop. Jim and Fred were dressed in their boating gear with their boats sitting along the rocky shore of the Baptism. We could see Jim intensely studying the lead-in to the

Fortunately, the lower Baptism is protected by Tettegouche State Park. Tettegouche State Park offers camping and many miles of wonderful hiking trails, some of which give boaters a chance to scout parts of the river from High Falls down. The Tettegouche information station and rest area off of Highway 61 is a great place to load up on state park maps (free!), maps for the Superior Hiking Trail (free!), books about the North Shore and other interesting literature.

So there you have it, the three sections of the Baptism: falls, playspots, class II, III, and IV plus a class V, cliffs, cascades, an ending on the biggest lake in the world. All this leads me to a conclusion: The Baptism would be a classic in any kayaking guidebook.

drop. We waited five minutes, then ten, then fifteen. Nothing! We were getting a little flustered. Why isn't Jim getting in his boat? Jim disappeared from our sight. Finally, he was ready! Maybe not! He suddenly popped up behind us. He had cold feet. Disappointed, we began to pack up our equipment and leave our perches.

Suddenly, someone motioned to us from the ledge above Illgen. It was Fred. We didn't need to have anyone tell us what was going through Fred's mind. Jim forfeited his opportunity for the day. The writing was clearly on the wall. It wasn't going to be much longer, now, before Jim or someone else actually finished the job. It was now or never! He held his arm over the falling water, looked in our direction, and gave the thumbs up! Fred was going to run Illgen!

Within minutes he was in his boat and at the rim. He plunged over the lip; fell straight downward hitting a protruding rock midway down Illgen's face. His boat bounced hard forward and pancaked firmly on the surface of the pool. He, amazingly, landed upright clearing all the turbulence of the falling water. Suddenly, he tipped over and bailed out of his boat without even attempting a roll. As Pete pulled him to shore, he asked him why he gave up and bailed. He told Pete, he was so relieved to have it over, it just happened automatically.

Then Jim got into his boat, took the consolation prize for being the second boater to run Illgen and the rest is boating history.

Jim Rada ponders Illgen moments before Fred Young's first descent. ©2006 Tom Aluni

Jim Rada runs Illgen. ©2006 Mike Cotten

steve buchman
illgen falls
baptism river

©2006 ephram holyoak

35

MANITOU RIVER

LENGTH: 5.5 MILES

CLASS: II–IV

SUMMER: RARE

QUICK DESCRIPTION: BOULDERS, LEDGES, PLAY, PORTAGES

PUT-IN: LAKE COUNTY 7 BRIDGE

TAKE-OUT: 0.3 MILE UP FROM HIGHWAY 61, PARK AT 61 ON RIGHT

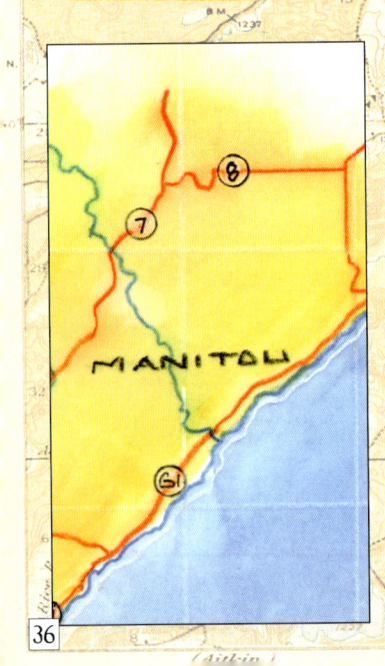

The Manitou has become one of the most popular of North Shore streams, probably because it has a bigger drainage than many other North Shore rivers and because it sports a lot of II-IV whitewater in a setting of rock outcrops and big trees. Much of the river can be explored by foot, ski or snowshoe using the backcountry trails and campsites of Crosby-Manitou State Park.

The put-in is reached by taking Lake County Highway 7 east out of Finland for about eight miles til you cross the Manitou. The takeout is on either river left or river right upstream of the powerline crossing a third-mile upstream from the Highway 61 bridge. Your shuttle car may be parked on a dirt road, river right, that breaks off Highway 61 about a quarter-mile west of the Manitou. This dirt road is the old Highway 61 route. To reach this parking spot from the powerline takeout above Rain-falling-up Falls, make use of the narrow woodsy hiking path that runs along the river right side. Be sure not to proceed downriver past the powerlines as the Manitou plunges into a heavy rapid, over Rain-falling-up Falls and into a deep dark gorge.

A gauge can be found on the river left downstream side of the culverts under Highway 61. Normally I don't look at the gauge. I usually evaluate the flow by looking at the riverbed just below the culverts. If it looks rocky the run will be, too. On the other hand, when the river is high you're in for a real treat! The Manitou's moderate gradient makes great use of high water and the run becomes a "gas" for experienced paddlers. This makes the Manitou very popular when conditions are high enough to make some North Shore runs treacherous.

The Manitou is not a run for intermediates without guidance, however. This run is no pushover because you must be able to catch small eddies in class III rapids reliably. The difficulties include mandatory portages to be made, the possibility of down trees around any corner, short bursts of continuous intense class III+ water and serious rapids to be scouted. Those "moderate" gradients I mentioned are relative to the North Shore as 90 feet per mile would be considered "steep" many other places. If you are unsure about your ability, wait til the levels are near the low end and not so pushy. Then explore the Manitou—your boat may not like this but it'll be safer!

The first mile and a half of the run is a meander as the stream passes through boreal lowlands. Then you'll notice some rocky knobs rising. This marks a beautiful series of falls that require a portage on the right. There's a Crosby-Manitou State Park hiking trail here that makes the hundred yard portage a breeze.

The first mile and a half of flatwater holds a bizarre story from the highwater spring of 1996. It was the first weekend of paddling on

An unrun falls opens up the action in Crosby-Manitou State Park. ©2006 Dewey James

the North Shore that year, with the creeks and small rivers near Duluth busted loose and roaring. On Sunday morning after some good creek runs on Saturday, the boaters at Pete Cary's house split into two groups. One group went to the Split Rock and Crow Creek and had a fabulous day with warm spring weather and the other group (who will remain unnamed except for "Sweetness" Jensen) went to the Manitou for an ordeal.

They came to the Manitou and found that there were still sections of the first few miles that were ice covered, so they paddled the pools and slid over the ice till they got to the first falls. Here they found huge ice sheets going over the falls and breaking up into ice chunks that filled the eddies below. A pow-wow was held: continuing downstream would have been crazed, with eddies filled with ice and known portages ahead. Hiking out would be extremely difficult, with waist deep snow in the woods after a record snow year. The only option was to go back up river the mile and a half to the put-in.

This might sound easy but with no current to help out our adventurers crossing the ice sheet in their boats was not a possibility, so they had to walk on the ice sheet dragging their boats. Then the ice sheet started to break up, so they had to run with their boat ahead of them, prepared to jump on it if the ice gave way beneath. Still, some people broke through the ice and had to be pulled up out of the river. The river was actually breaking loose as the team worked its way upstream. The return to the put-in was extremely draining both physically and psychologically, with a total of seven and a half hours spent going one and a half miles downstream to the falls and then back to the top. I was in the group that "had a nice day" and when I met the others back at Pete's house they were all so drained-looking I thought someone had drowned. Fortunately, all were ok. I guess the lesson is that the little rivers on the south end of the Shore throw their ice off easier and quicker than the big runs that have swampy headwaters. Everyone has an ordeal sooner or later on the North Shore!

Back to the Manitou run—below the opening falls the whitewater gets rolling with class II boulderbed slowly increasing in intensity to class III. After a half to two-thirds of a mile of this, the river bends sharp left. Take out here and scout the IV+ drop below, "Pinball." It's studded with big boulders and has lots of "juice" at high water. Maybe too much juice! Since boaters sometimes careen

Just downstream of Machine Gun Ledges. ©2006 Dewey James

steve stratman
illgen falls
baptism river

©2006 ephran holyoak

37

and bounce off these boulders, Pinball is appropriately named. Pete Cary once ran Pinball when a log was bridged over the big boulders and he had to roll under it! Yikes!!! This rapid is deceptively steep and fast, requiring quick moves.

A short pool exists below Pinball, then a small ledge, then be sure to get out immediately if you haven't gotten out already, as a steep drop onto rock is just ahead. Trust your own judgement here and not that of others—once I asked a boater on shore what the next eddy looked like—he said it was ok, but it proved to be a scramble with a fallen tree blocking most of the river. I then formulated a rule for boating, "If it's worth looking at, it's worth looking at yourself!"

The carry begins here or above Pinball, but either way it used to be a bad one, struggling through deadfalls and up and over a hill on river left to reach a long, ledge-riddled section below the rocky portage. This "traditional" route over steep terrain through brushy woods where you couldn't see was, as Mark Gibson would say, "as much fun as a sharp stick in the eye." Those who didn't want to paddle the furious class IV "Machine Gun Ledges" were faced with another hundred yards of this joy!

Today things are a bit easier. In 1992 the Superior Hiking Trail was completed in this area and a footbridge now crosses the Manitou just below the Machine Gun Ledges. The trail heads upstream on both river left and right and provides some welcome new routes to "portageurs." On the left side it's possible to hit the trail by walking away from the river and then you can carry to the bridge avoiding some of the "brushthrashing" of the old days. On the right it's even easier, just a steep carry uphill before or after Pinball and you encounter the trail for an easy walk to the bridge. Once at the bridge you can put in or if you'd like to run the Machine Gun Ledges, carry upstream from the bridge a hundred yards on the right to some small eddies.

Maybe you think the portage is still nasty but now the real fun begins: nothing but paddling and rapids for the next three miles to the takeout! A quarter mile of fun boulderbed roars up to the lip of a seven foot "surprise" drop which has a nice pool at its base. Then two-thirds of a mile of low ledges and boulderbed sometimes coming at a frenzied pace—fun! Parts of this section approach class IV at high water with holes grabbing at you one after another.

When you see a sharp left as low rock walls rise on your right, look for a little playhole. If you're already nervous, get out on the river right side just above the playhole to scout. Two hundred feet downstream and around the next right hand bend is the Red Rock Slide. It can be scouted from above on the right and if run on the extreme right is a fun sliding drop of about eight feet. Run it left and you can encounter a heavy hole. I call Red Rock Slide a IV-. Red Rock Slide has low cliffs on either side just above the drop, so if you wish to scout you must get out at the sharp left hand turn above the playhole. The 150 yards below Red Rock Slide contain several nice waves and side-surfing holes as the river slips over smooth sheets of red bedrock.

Now it's "Mellow Time!" The last two miles are very pleasant class II boulderbed sprinkled with several ledges of moderate size, class III. Some of the ledges have holes for sidesurfing amidst surroundings of pine and cedar. I'm always struck by the park-like beauty of the river here as it roars through the ancient forest.

When you see a black sand bluff on the right you're well over half done with the final two mile section. Look for a ninety degree left turn where you encounter a good series of ledges and holes—now you're a third-mile from the takeout. Below this series of ledges boulderbed gradually narrows and steepens to class III. Go as far as you choose, but watch for the powerlines and eddies; don't get "carried away!" There is a wild rapid just below the takeout eddies where the water banks off the left side wall. It looks class IV-V but I wouldn't advise running it since it ends a mere hundred feet from the big falls.

You can carry out either left or right. I prefer the right where a narrow trail heads to the old Highway 61 crossing, the gravel parking area mentioned earlier. Either way, left or right, stop and admire the splendid falls that sends the Manitou hurtling into a black cliff and drops of mist hurtling skyward as the wind from the falls counters gravity. I think of this drop as Rain-falling-up Falls. Peer into the narrow black gorge—mysterious and powerful. There will be more opportunities to glance down into this dark chasm as you carry your boat along the narrow path to the parking area. The black gorge may be paddlable—skiers have said that with the exception of one drop right below mighty Rain-falling-up Falls there are no more major drops to Highway 61. It would be worth checking out. Paddling that black gorge would be an incredible way to end the trip.

The observant will note that the Manitou continues past Highway 61!! It plunges over several large drops and falls in its final quarter mile, entering Lake Superior via a beautiful thirty footer. Hiking down to look at those falls is a nice way to enjoy the tired satisfaction that comes after a Manitou run with memories of Pinball, playspots, portages, pristine woods and Rain-falling-up Falls. The hike is especially nice because you're in your warm dry fuzzies!

CROSS RIVER

The Cross is a river that gets done relatively infrequently—most paddlers I've known who've done it don't return to it often, yet all consider it a worthy and interesting run. It seems different than many of the other North Shore streams in that after putting in at the FR 166 crossing, many miles of this 7 mile run are spent slicing through the backwoods on swift class I water. However, the last 2.5 miles holds the kind of whitewater for which the North Shore is renowned.

Although the first 4.5 mile section is easy water through alders and boreal forest, there are two drops which should be looked for: "Z" and "Elbow Falls." It's difficult to estimate distances on this river, but Z is about 2 miles into the run. Z is a zigzag rapid where the Cross spills over steep ledges in rapid succession, a good class III+. You can boat scout from river right just above the horizon line. It works well to run the first ledge, next go left and then scurry right to avoid the extreme left at the end. A play hole or two is tucked into Z.

Then it's back to pretty paddling through the woods another mile to mile and a half to Elbow Falls, a IV+/V- cascade which slides downhill a vertical 15-20 feet. The river picks up to class II not far above Elbow Falls and a hundred yards above it a very small channel forks left off of the main Cross. After this fork expect to see a horizon line with small eddies on the left. Here the left shore offers the best vantage of a big drop which funnels into a narrow and turbulent outwash. The big drop has been run on extreme left into a slot and off a curving tongue just right of center. See for yourself. Fred Young banged his elbow during a big C-1 brace here, thus "Elbow Falls."

The river reverts to class I and occasional II for the next mile below Elbow Falls. Sometimes a sweeper will be encountered from here on down and the paddler should be more alert for down trees and whitewater as the Cross narrows and winds into a deeper valley. The whitewater will pick up as the Cross constricts and big boulders create tight class III water. Eddyhop City! Be sure to eddyhop now and be careful as you are approaching "Slither Slide."

Following a quarter mile of eddy snagging class III you'll see a

Falls thunder in the Black Canyon of the Cross River. ©2006 Dewey James

LENGTH: 7 MILES

CLASS: II–V

SUMMER: RARE

QUICK DESCRIPTION:
COMBINES EASY AND HARD, PORTAGES!

PUT-IN:
SUPERIOR NATIONAL FOREST ROAD 166

TAKE-OUT:
0.25 MILE ABOVE HIGHWAY 61, TRAIL FROM 61 ON RIGHT

©2006 dan monskey
joerg steinbach
second drop
devils track

John Alt runs Elbow Falls. ©2006 Henry Kinnucan

Slither Slide. ©2006 Henry Kinnucan

four foot ledge across the river. Either run this and eddy out right immediately or eddy out above the ledge and scout right. You'll notice a low, crumbly rock wall on the right here—warning of class V Slither Slide.

Slither Slide is part of the reason the Cross doesn't get a lot of return visits. It's an intriguing drop where a snappy lead in ends in a bobsled slide losing 15-20 vertical feet. The bobsled run terminates in a very powerful recirculating hole and lies between low, crumbling cliffs of ancient reddish rock. Your only real hope is to paddle hard toward the right while sliding down the Slither! Not so easy. A successful run puts you in Nirvana. What a feeling to have cheated fate and the big hole and to be sitting in the right eddy watching the Cross slip between the narrow walls.

I've walked "Slither" and seen lots of walks. I've run and seen a few good runs. I've seen excellent paddlers trashed in the hole. As the water gets higher, Slither Slide gets pushier and more fearful; lower flows are more of a match for mortals, but the other rapids start getting boney. Yet, once you've seen it or run it successfully, you really want to do it again. Do you see the dilemma?

Slither Slide can be portaged right on a simple trail that goes about 150 yards below Slither Slide to where the cliffs drop away. From here on out, be on your toes! Less than a quarter mile from Slither Slide, the Cross funnels into a constriction that lasts a hundred yards then bends left. This rapid, Boulder Sluice, is a IV filled with big boulders. It's good to scout it left as trees have lodged here from time to time.

The next half mile eases to II-III, but be on the lookout for down trees and broaching subsurface boulders. Look for a small channel breaking to the right, since you'll go left and then get out left in about a hundred yards. Don't get too close together here as the eddies you want are about two hundred feet above the Several Falls, which means these small eddies aren't altogether obvious. When you see a sloping class III-ish turn to the right with a low rock wall along it on the left, get out above this—it leads right into Several Falls.

The portage on the left is fairly easy; there are rock outcrops to walk on near the falls. I've heard boaters say the drops look runnable (while standing on the portage trail!). After a couple hundred yards of portage, you may put in just to run the last drop in the sequence, it's six or seven feet high and can kick your bow skyward, so be ready. Otherwise portage another 150 feet to a pool below the drop and rock walls and FERRY DIRECTLY ACROSS THE RIVER AND RESUME PORTAGING on a small trail on river right.

I write in capital letters because a death trap lurks downstream—the Black Canyon. The lead-in to the Black Canyon consists of steep runnable boulderbed curving tightly through the woods. You might not notice in the quarter-mile of whitewater that the right bank has turned into an eddyless gravel wall until a turn to the left shows you a horizon line leading into blackness. Don't find out too late about the last decent eddy one hundred feet above, and out of sight of, the blackness. You want to portage right so please ferry directly across the river after you portage Several Falls.

One paddler has entered the Black Canyon and survived, but now it's referred to as "Dumb Douglas Canyon."

Here's the story:

Pete Cary, Mark Gibson, Paul Douglas and myself were enjoying an October run on the Cross. Pete and I had paddled the Cross several times but it was new to Mark and Paul. After some "excitement" at Slither Slide (Pete chose the hole rather than the portage trail) and a boat chase down the Cross, our troops were regathered at the beginning of the Several Falls portage. It was about 3:30 in the afternoon as we decided that we had time to walk back to Slither Slide to fish Pete's pillars out of the hole. Three of us headed upstream leaving Paul to wait.

It took us awhile rounding up Pete's outfitting but we were mildly surprised to see Paul and his boat gone on our return. I'd told him about the upcoming portage and had said that first we'd portage Several Falls, then we'd paddle just a little and then portage an unrunnable gorge on the right. We thought he'd be waiting at the downstream end of the Several Falls portage, but he wasn't. Now I got a little worried—he's off on a wilderness run he's never seen by himself—hmmmm.

We ferried across and began portaging the Black Canyon along the small trail through the woods on the right. The portage is about a half-mile around a steep-walled black crack where the Cross thunders over one big drop after another at gradients averaging 400 ft/mile. We reached the put-in at the end of the portage, a spot where a ravine heads down to meet the river when it becomes visible again and bends sharply to the left. Still no Paul. Now we were very worried. As we put in we saw his red Dancer washed up on the right just below the Black Canyon, still no Paul. Now I was scared!

It has been in the back of my mind for some time that the North Shore rivers will take someone's life. So far there have been close calls, but no deaths amongst experienced paddlers. Foolish canoeists have died running the St. Louis through Jay Cooke State Park at flood and a tragedy occurred on the Brule to some locals. I thought this might be the first experienced kayakist to die on the North Shore.

We quickly organized a search. Mark headed downstream looking for Paul, Pete went up river right and I went up river left, dropping down low in the Black Canyon, looking and calling. With no sign of him for me or Pete we began a somber run of the last mile. We finished our run near the snowmobile trail about a quarter or half a mile above the falls at Highway 61. There we met Mark, Karen Jensen and to our joy, Paul, battered but alive!

They were glad to see Pete and me, too, since it was getting dark. Karen had been waiting for us at the takeout and had become alarmed at seeing a whitewater helmet lodged in the rocks near the takeout. She then began heading upstream along the trail on river right. In a few minutes she encountered Mark helping a dazed Paul limp toward the takeout. Now things were looking up. We had our whole group together again!

Once we were all in the shuttle vehicle we rushed to the Silver Bay Hospital. As we drove Paul told us what had happened. He had decided to continue with the Several Falls portage after waiting quite a while for us. He then put in and started

A final horizon line marks passage into the Black Canyon. ©2006 Dewey James

joerg
steinbach
second drop
devils track

41

to paddle, looking for the right hand eddy to start the Black Canyon portage, not realizing it's only a simple ferry. Paul was drawn in by the curves and gravel banks until to his horror the first horizon into the Black Canyon loomed.

No eddies left, Paul roared over the lip of a 20 foot falls and then faced cascade after cascade. He stayed in his boat through two more he thinks and then was trashed and swimming, going over big drops into deep plunge pools, rupturing an eardrum, getting banged and bruised, once almost passing out in the depths. It was that close to death.

The fury ended and Paul managed to catch a tree and pulled himself out and began hobbling downstream in a daze. Finally, Mark came on him and helped him to the takeout. When I saw Paul, I thought he'd broken many bones. Thankfully, at the Silver Bay hospital the doctor announced that Paul had no broken bones and would be okay.

Paul was lucky and we were lucky to still have our friend, "Dumb Douglas," who set off alone to unwittingly run the Black Canyon. The "Black Canyon" is now fittingly and lovingly remembered as "Dumb Douglas Canyon." I spent a lot of time on this story. It tells of what can happen. Please, please be sure to be as familiar with these runs as possible before paddling: look for eddies, eddy hop, hike, ski, buy my book. Wonders can be yours but there is also danger.

Returning to the river description, the last mile to 61 below Black Canyon/Dumb Douglas Canyon is excellent. This section includes steep class III boulderbed, a horseshoe drop of about five feet, and more boulderbed until the last third of a mile where slides and ledges come in rapid order just below a cabin on river left. The first few ledges are pushy, fun class III-IV, then turning IV-V as the river steepens, tightens and squirts left then right.

At moderate flows we've been able to run to just above the falls visible from Highway 61. A parking lot on river right at Highway 61 is a good place for the shuttle vehicle and also the start of the trail that heads up the right side of the river. It permits excellent scouting views of the last mile and could serve as access to run just the lower mile, an enjoyable run in itself that would be boatable even when the upper river is marginal. A spur of the Superior Hiking Trail also provides some access to the lower river.

As you can see, the Cross combines a lot of elements: easy water, tough challenges, dangerous sections to be portaged, the seductive Slither Slide. I think it's this mix of danger, challenge, lots of class I and a few portages that make the Cross what it is: an interesting river that paddlers don't hurry back to!

Temperance River

Here's a North Shore river suitable for intermediate paddlers. With its large drainage area and consequent size, it's not a "steep-creekin'" descent as are so many Lake Superior runs, but a bona fide medium volume river. In addition it has a very uniform gradient which while good is not in the 100+ feet/mile range until the last two-thirds mile plunge to the Lake. The even gradient, moderate size and medium size boulders create a river that reminds me of a typical Rocky Mountain run—mile after mile of wavy whitewater when high, and miles of boulder-dodging when low, with the water for the most part being class II.

There is one substantial obstacle on the run: Beerstein Falls. About four miles into the run the river changes from boulderbed to bedrock. The difficulty of the river changes from II to III as the bedrock breaks out. In this half-mile bedrock section, one 5 foot ledge stands out, Beerstein Falls, class III-IV. At moderate flows Beerstein is a fluffy leap: cush, exciting and fun. At high flows Beerstein becomes a voracious river-wide hole capable of stopping, trashing and recirculating even paddlers of baby gorilla strength such as Tom Aluni, whose boat and body suffered a pounding after not punching the hole.

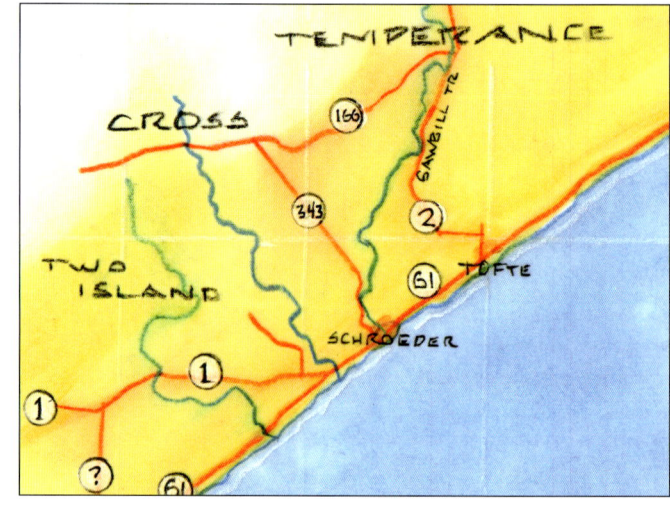

Beerstein is evident to the watchful and can be looked at or portaged on the right. The bedrock is soon over and the river returns to its bouldery ways until it pinches up close to Forest Service Road 343 and a big hill on river right. This is a good place for most intermediates to take out, and will have given you a pleasant class II-III run of about seven miles.

Just below this possible takeout point the river narrows and plunges over Fred's Falls, class V. A portage on river

TEMPERANCE RIVER

LENGTH: 6.5 MILES

CLASS: II–III

SUMMER: SOME

QUICK DESCRIPTION: MOST IS ENDLESS BOULDERBED, BEERSTEIN!

PUT-IN: SUPERIOR NATIONAL FOREST 166 JUST WEST OF SAWBILL TRAIL

TAKE-OUT: SUPERIOR NATIONAL FOREST 343 ON RIGHT ONE MILE FROM LAKE

right allows adventurous paddlers to slide into the Temperance off a rock shelf to enjoy a quarter mile of powerful and constricted class III-IV water. This little gorge is quite narrow and is said to be interesting even after the upper run is low and scrapey–there's even a place that can produce enders at the right level. The last drop in this sequence produces a couple of interesting surf waves.

This surf spot looks like a good place to get out as the Temperance appears placid just downstream. It is a good place to get out. A trail on river right leads in a hundred yards to a parking spot along Forest Service Road 343. It would be a mistake to think that the Temperance is flatwater below this point, however, since shortly after the mini-canyon the Temperance drops into a narrow rock cleft, thundering in unrunnable drops to just above Highway 61. The tail end of this canyon can be seen by looking upstream from Highway 61. There's a river gauge below the narrow rock cleft. It can be viewed by hiking about a hundred yards up from Highway 61 on the river right side and looking across the river.

The Superior Hiking Trail spur on river left can be used to portage to the parking lot on Highway 61 at the Temperance River bridge if you choose to continue below the surf spot. This same trail can be used to scout all of the last mile which includes Fred's Falls, the class III-IV section and the unrunnable cleft.

The majority of the river then, is a good intermediate run with the option of including heavier water. For those wishing a shorter run that includes Beerstein it's possible to run the last half of the river. To do this you must carry in a quarter-mile from the Sawbill Trail (Cook County 2). A pulloff along the Sawbill Trail roughly a mile north of the Britton Peak parking area is the starting point for the minor trail that heads to the river.

©2006 Dewey James

This section of the Temperance is just a short hike north of Highway 61.

©2006 dan monskey

joerg steinbach second drop devils track

43

POPLAR RIVER

LENGTH: 2 MILES

CLASS: II–IV+

SUMMER: RARE

QUICK DESCRIPTION:
MOSTLY CONTINUOUS CLASS III, CANYON

PUT-IN:
LUTSEN SKI AREA AT END OF COOK COUNTY 36

TAKE-OUT:
GOLF COURSE FOOTBRIDGE 0.25 MILE UPSTREAM FROM HIGHWAY 61

The Poplar is the one North Shore river to have suffered substantially from private development. First, a downhill ski area, Lutsen Mountains, scars the put-in area and causes erosion. Second, a golf course (!??!!), Superior National, was built in 1990 on both sides of the lower part of the run.

Fortunately, a thin strip of trees remains along the river corridor for most of the run. The Poplar has retained most of the beckoning forest that is its proper attire and is only denuded at the take-out where a footbridge was built and many ancient trees removed.

The put-in is reached by driving up Cook County 36 two miles to the Lutsen Mountains ski area. Here you drive to the furthest parking lot and carry down (or slide down on old snow—too exciting!) a ski run to the roaring Poplar below. Erosion, cast off junk and low footbridges over the river mar the put-in area. Be sure to look carefully here to see that no water pipes or wires are hanging above the river.

The Poplar then roars downhill away from the ski area at an even gradient of about 140 feet per mile which it maintains for the next two miles. At low flows there are many small eddies to catch behind the moderate size boulders. High flows bring lots of waves and racetrack speeds. Be on the lookout for strainers in the river, particularly in the first mile as the banks early on seem to slump and slide easily in places. The boulderbed rapids are class II-III at low water and exhilarating class III-IV at high water. The high water rush is great— the river is a winding, hissing snake of waves and jet speed current. Eddies are few—it's "guided missile boating."

After about a mile and a half of exuberance you'll encounter a distinct two ledge sequence followed by the river bending left. The drop is IV- in nature, but should be approached with care

John Kiffmeyer runs a drop on the class V section of the lower Poplar ©2006 Doug Nelson

for two reasons: first, there is at least one sticky hole here at high levels and second, and more important, you are 100-150 yards and one curve away from "Bielik's Surprise." The double ledge warns you to look for eddies as you are entering the Poplar's bedrock zone. There are eddies on left and right. The last one on the right is just above Bielik's Surprise and near a footbridge that crosses the Poplar here.

Don't be like Ted Bielik and paddle past these eddies, at least not before scouting. Bielik, who'd never run the Poplar, was running with a group well acquainted with the river. He flipped above Bielik's Surprise and rolled up with just enough time to "go for it." He had never seen the cascade which he was about to run, but it's a series of steep slides dropping at least thirty feet in perhaps 150 feet. Logs are sometimes lodged on the slides. Roostertails, piton rocks and other obstacles are everywhere. Ted's companions watched in horror as he slipped over the edge on the virgin run of this drop. They then sprang to shore to chase and give aid. Ted didn't need it! He'd survived unscathed! John Alt, probably the most unflappable river cruiser I've ever paddled with, studied the drop carefully for many minutes before performing the first intentional run. It was successful, but on the edge. I'd rate this drop class V+, honest! These are the only two runs of Bielik's Surprise to this day (that I know of).

Portaging is easy as a Lutsen hiking trail helps you carry on the right and then it's simple to put in at the base of Bielik's. Now the Poplar enters an exciting class IV canyon as the river slides over sloping bedrock in one chute after another. If you have no one along who has run the river you might scout the next third of a mile from river right. I suggest this because the Poplar Canyon is heavy and has only a short break before the finale of this canyon, class IV-V Amren's Stump.

Eddyhop the canyon until after snagging a right hand eddy you see a constriction and horizon line ahead as the Poplar drops between low crumbling rock walls. The horizon line is the beginning of Amren's Stump. Get out and scout on the right. The name commemorates an incident on a fine spring day when, after running the Baptism earlier, we were squeezing in a late afternoon run on the Poplar. Our party included John Amren, a C-1 paddler of great skill who in many instances was the first or one of the first C-1'ers to successfully negotiate our Lake Superior runs. I'll let my kayak prejudice show: I have never envied the C-1'ers I've seen on the North Shore runs. These rivers, while small, can be very powerful and things can happen fast—sometimes it's like a liquid avalanche. I've always been glad to have two blades to brace and stroke out with.

Al Sabean dodges falling golfballs in the Poplar Canyon.
©2006 Mike Cotten

©2006 dan monskey

joerg
steinbach
second drop
devils track

Amren had already survived running the lower drop of Two Step upside down that day, when he flipped towards the end of the Poplar Canyon. We watched from the safety of our eddy as he drifted past us, set up, rolled just before the horizon line and climbed out on the stump of a tree caught at the lip. He was safe, but couldn't really go anywhere, unless he climbed in his boat and ran the drop. We got out and scouted this tricky sequence of sharp, narrow drops. It has some "humdinger" holes, but the chutes mostly line up. To "reassure" Amren we ran it and survived—so did John!

This drop has not always been so kind. Another top notch exploratory boater, Tim Nelson, approached this drop in a brand new kevlar/epoxy/vacuum-bagged heavy duty cruiser. Second week on the river for this classy machine. He got nailed by the holes and brutally trashed—out he came, getting to shore fairly quickly but his boat was off on its own charging through the hundred yards of heavy III+/IV- runout following Amren's Stump.

I knew that the takeout was less than a half mile away and then the Poplar goes nuts, sinking into a narrow gorge that reverberates with thunder. I couldn't get it out in the heavy stuff, nor in the continuous II-III in the next quarter-mile. Then I reached the little island where the river splits. The takeout is just after the currents rejoin, for big ledges lie around the corner from the lower end of the island. One last try—and I had to let it go.

It's a weird feeling having to pull off and watch a boat go, headed for big stuff. We headed downstream from the takeout on foot. Tim saw his boat pummeled and broken at the base of a falls, then it disappeared with pieces showing up a few days later.

There have been other swims on the Poplar. Another memorable one ended with Henry Kinnucan paddling around a bend near the takeout to see John Wexler standing waist deep in the river with wetsuit pants pulled down by the motoring current. Mooned on the Poplar! All this talk of trouble isn't to scare you—it's just to let you know that this river at high water is an adrenaline blast and sometimes someone gets blasted! Much more manageable at lower flows, but at high flows it's oh-so-fun!

Today the takeout area is easily recognized: a pedestrian bridge for the golf course where the river banks have been cleared. Here money grubbers cut down the sacred groves that once shielded the Poplar from the outside world and lent a sense of peace and mystery to the river. No more! Carry out on the right to Highway 61 across the golf course or carry out left to the tiny Lutsen cemetery, just into the woods from the Highway 61-Cook County 36 intersection.

The gauge is on river left less than a quarter mile above the Highway 61 bridge. It's read by going up the river right to a pool which has a small closet-like building opposite the gauge. The numbers are a bit small so you may want to bring binoculars to read it easily.

If this run on the Poplar seems too tame, you can look at the additional half-mile of whitewater that just gets steeper and steeper as you go upstream from the normal put-in. The quarter mile above the regular put-in is fun class III-IV water which I'd recommend as worth the carry up on the right.

For a spectacular view of the start of the Poplar's whitewater, head to the Superior Hiking Trail bridge over the Poplar. To get there, follow a small dirt road out of the north end of the put-in parking lot at the ski hill. This will continue upstream and cross the Poplar at the exact spot where all hell breaks loose! Look upstream off the Superior Hiking Trail bridge and you see a peaceful, meandering stream, look downstream from the bridge and you'll see the Poplar falling away in cascades. When these cascades subside you hit the fun class III-IV water I mentioned earlier. A picture I'll always carry in my mind is a view of the rampaging river from this bridge on a sunny September day—sky so blue and hills cloaked in yellow and gold leaves, with a torrent below my feet.

John Kiffmeyer on the lower Poplar ©2006 Doug Nelson

CASCADE RIVER

The Cascade is without doubt one of the most difficult runs described in this book. I would warn those who'd like to run it that you should not expect a guidebook to show the way. Even the best of guidebooks is only a Zen-like "finger pointing." You must do the paddling, scouting, eddy hopping, sweeper dodging, portaging and enjoying. I will give you advice and a sense of what the rivers are like.

My first piece of advice–do NOT attempt the Cascade at high or even moderate spring flow. It's usually best to run this as the other Shore rivers near low to unboatable levels, near the end of spring run off. I'll tell you exactly how to determine proper level. Go to the upstream river left side of the Highway 61 bridge and look under the bridge. You'll see a flat concrete footing on which the bridge rests on river left. This is ZERO and good levels for running range from 3 to 9 inches below zero.

The Cascade has been run as high as +2 inches with the difficulty reportedly increasing by a half a class. Plus 2 inches is still far less than the Cascade's peak level in spring. At high levels it becomes a "portage-a-thon." At minus nine inches it's scrapey but enjoyable with little push. At minus three inches it's becoming pushy and developing

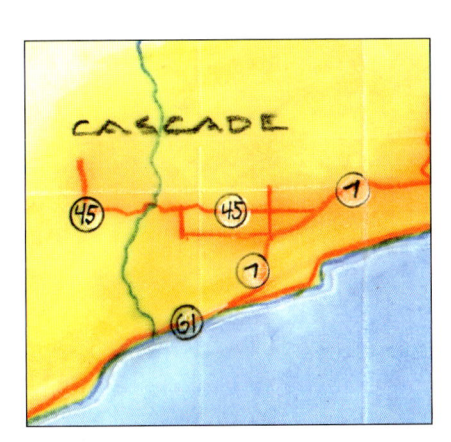

Northwood's hero John Alt runs Discretion Drop. ©2006 Doug Nelson

©2006 dan monskey
joerg steinbach second drop devils track

LENGTH: 3 MILES

CLASS: IV–V

SUMMER: RARE

QUICK DESCRIPTION:
TOUGH, MANY LEDGES, RUN WHEN LOW

PUT-IN:
COOK COUNTY 45 BRIDGE

TAKE-OUT:
0.5 MILE UPSTREAM FROM U.S. 61, CASCADE RIVER STATE PARK

47

Feisty Hidden Falls. It's just around a lazy bend from the put-in. ©2006 Mike Cotten

serious holes. Please attempt it first at low levels, then if you future paddlers think it's too easy or low, go for it. But for my sake and conscience start with a run with 3 to 9 inches of concrete showing.

Advice #2: Hike up the trail from the Highway 61 parking lot at the mouth along either river left or right for about a third of a mile and look at the Cascades—they're beautiful. They have in fact been run at low flow by a few boaters. Paul Everson was the first with a solo run early in October in 1994. As far as I know, this is the only complete run of the Cascades, with all other runs omitting the technically difficult last waterfall which flows into a sort of cauldron. There have been a few other runs, all at relatively low flow, and all have been filled with adrenaline and one near miss.

Maybe some of you "future boaters" will want to run them—I haven't done them and can offer no advice. Perhaps you'd be encouraged to know that Tim Nelson survived swimming over the last falls after slipping into the river from the bank. I have taken out on river right about a quarter mile above the footbridge that spans the Cascades. The river upstream from here holds so much good water that I'm always satisfied to take out safely well above the Cascades, but boaters always look and talk and ponder . . .

The run begins where Cook County Highway 45 crosses the river. This bridge can also serve as a takeout for a run on an upper section of the Cascade, one I haven't done but alleged to contain unrunnable falls, class II-III water and pretty scenery. The gradient above the Cook County 45 bridge is much more mellow than the gradient below Cook County 45 as the Cascade loses 650 feet in its last three miles!

There is a parking lot at the Cook County 45 bridge and you can also access the Superior Hiking Trail here. The Superior Hiking Trail essentially follows the river all the way to the takeout on the river left side. While the trail isn't always in sight of the river, it does help the unfamiliar scout and provides access in case of "problems."

About a third-mile below the put-in you'll encounter Hidden Falls. The portage around this imposing, sloping cascade is on river left. This drop had been run a number of times when the river was at a level of about -9 inches or so. I have witnessed one outstanding run here, when Ross Peterson ran it with the level between -2 and -3 inches. The river was furious and white, a real roller coaster. Through it all Ross stayed in control and made his move to the right at the end, just missing the big hole at the bottom. Ross has done some big runs and this was definitely one of them.

Just a hundred yards downstream of Hidden Falls is Discretion Drop, a complex class IV-V drop—scout or portage on the left. Beware getting too far to river right on the first drop here. John Alt, one of the Northwoods' finest paddlers, was entrapped here in his kayak during an October run. The whole boat was invisible, pinned underwater with the current pounding on John's back. Pete Cary and I hurried to river right while Tim Nelson manned the left. Pete and I each grabbed an arm and pulled and John pushed with his legs. After several minutes and rising alarm we gave a great pull and John gave a mighty push that got him out of the boat. The current washed him over the drop and hypothermia made John so weak he could barely walk in the shallow eddy water. After trying to get John to warm up for about fifteen minutes we were about to head back upstream when his boat emerged from the depths. We corralled his boat and called it a day.

This pin underscores for me the unavoidable risks even experienced paddlers must accept in steep creek paddling. Teamwork is necessary and it helps to have clear thinking and reliable companions such as John, Pete and Tim for aid in tight situations.

Jim Rada chooses river right through Long John. Robert Ruffner adds some color to the eddy.

©2006 Mike Cotten

7 Foot Falls, by Mark Gibson.   ©2006 Mike Cotten

Beyond Discretion Drop lies more of the same, but at low water levels every drop is runnable down to the takeout a quarter mile above the Cascades. Moose Rock Drop is one of the most intimidating as the Cascade charges down a hundred yards of ledges aimed right at Moose Rock, an island shunting most of the water to the right where the river just "keeps on truckin'" downhill. To the left, a narrow channel corkscrews down even more steeply. The left looks ugly to me, but George Stefanyshyn proved it's runnable. After rounding Moose Rock the action isn't over—watch out for the final hole as the river bends sharp to the left. Moose Rock Drop probably rates V.

The Cascade eases a bit after Moose Rock Drop, but the assault soon revives with Hanna's Hole—a steep sharp constricted drop (make sure you end up on the left!), and another intense section begins when the Cascade enters a small canyon, starting with a runnable eight foot falls. After pinching left to run this falls, you'll dash through heavy water right to slide down a 15-20 foot sloping incline. Catch eddies and scout.

More breathing room follows this intense section, then ledges erupt again—medium ledges followed quickly by Long John–an incredible banked turn screamer where you thread a narrow entry chute and then get twirled left by the curving wall. Those who get too close to the wall at the turn risk adding "gnar-knobs" to their heads. Next, a couple fun eight foot ledge leaps, another long slide over a wide sheet of bedrock that's usually a bit bony and a finale where the river pinches down and nozzles you through.

Have I forgotten any drops? I'm sure I have—it's a smorgasbord of class IV-V water and the last third-mile of easy boulderbed will allow you to reflect on the paddling excitement of the day. Just don't forget about the Cascades below the takeout . . . if you're like me, your adrenalin will already be gone.

©2006 dan monskey

joerg steinbach second drop devils track

49

DEVIL'S TRACK RIVER

LENGTH: 4 MILES

CLASS: II–V

SUMMER: RARE

QUICK DESCRIPTION:
STEEP, FALLS, PORTAGES, CLIFFS

PUT-IN:
COOK COUNTY 60 BRIDGE (GAUGE) OR GUNFLINT TRAIL BRIDGE

TAKE-OUT:
LAKE SUPERIOR, U.S. 61 BRIDGE

The name of this river, also called the Devil Track, raises a mood of mystery and foreboding in most. This river is fittingly named, as in the four to five mile stretch between the Hedstrom Lumbermill put-in at 1450 feet and the calm of Lake Superior, elevation 602 feet, you will enter a land of mystery, exhilaration and perhaps a bit of terror. I know of no paddler who has put in on this run that hasn't had a little uncertainty in the back of his mind.

For years during my early boating career this river was written off as largely unpaddlable. The reason? A canyon containing unrunnable falls and sheer cliffs–sometimes in close proximity. A group of Big Water Associates had run an upper stretch from Devil Track Lake to the Hedstrom Lumbermill and reported a fun class III run at high water. Then, Fred Young and friends had run from the Cook County Highway 60 bridge the mile and a half to the Three Falls and had then carried out. The Devil's Track Canyon remained unboated.

One November Tom Aluni, Henry Kinnucan, John Wexler and I hiked up the canyon from Highway 61 on frozen "whitewater." The beauty of the red cliffs towering two hundred feet over the river and the beguiling drops led us upriver to a real barrier–Pitchfork Falls, a forty foot falls flanked by cliffs. Here we were stopped. Then, on a summer's day a couple of years later, I waded the river at low water from Hedstrom's, past the Three Falls, climbing down a ravine into the sacrosanct canyon. On and on I went discovering wonderful eroded rock walls, slides and unearthly beauty. Entranced, I pushed on until my heart leapt. I was standing at the brink of Pitchfork Falls, gazing down on the pool below.

I don't mean to imply that the Devil's Track is an unexplored place. Small numbers of fishermen have found routes into the canyon for

Pitchfork Falls.   ©2006 Tom Aluni

years and cross country skiers have negotiated the run, rappelling at Pitchfork Falls. Ice climbers have discovered "Nightfall," a two hundred foot ice formation deep in the heart of the canyon. But I had a boater's eye, and noticed a route of escape from the canyon about a third of a mile above Pitchfork Falls, the spot marked by a big white boulder. This portage route and the ravine allowing portage around Three Falls meant the Canyon could be entered and left! The idea was planted to paddle the Devil's Track Canyon.

On a May day my dream reached fulfillment: John Alt and John Amren, on their way to do the Brule, dropped me off at Hedstrom's with boat, rope, lunch (of course!!) and a ten dollar camera. I successfully ran much of the Canyon before breaking my paddle, fortunately at a place where I could hike out with my boat. Over the next few years, accompanied by fellow adventurers and friends Tom Aluni, John Alt, John Amren, Pete Cary, Greg Breining, Henry Kinnucan and Tim Nelson, we gradually explored the mysteries of the Devil's Track. Here's what we found.

Putting in at the Cook County 60 bridge next to Hedstrom's Lumber, pay close attention to the downstream river left side of the bridge. There's a hand-painted gauge here—and a proper reading is critical for success. The run has been enjoyed at just over 1 foot, about 1⅛ feet, but there is a lot of scraping in the boulderbed sections (use plastic!!). One and a quarter feet is a good level for a first run, more cover on boulders, not too much "pushiness" and punchable holes. One and a half feet is getting serious. The highest levels run so far—around 1⅖ - 1⅜ feet—were an adrenaline rush. Fierce rapids, real momentum pushing, on the edge of "controlled descent." The river is frequently higher than 1¼ during spring peaks, so there's room for future generations to "up the ante." Look for the Devil's Track to be runnable when the Brule has fallen to about 1.5 feet. The Devil's Track's runoff is moderated by Devil Track Lake upstream, which makes it slow to rise and slow to fall. As there are rapids which must be run, take care.

The run opens with a brook-like appearance, skipping over or around cobblestones and boulders with trees hanging close giving a feeling of real intimacy. About a half or two-thirds of a mile of this enjoyable stuff brings you to the first ledge, a medium one set on a bend left and followed closely by another pinching drop, exciting seat-of-the-pants stuff. Be watchful for sweepers.

The general tone of the river will pick up to class III+, with medium ledges and poor visibility as the river snakes in tight curves—blind curves. You better eddyhop. When the "S"ing ledges begin to come almost continuously—prick your attention up to the top notch and proceed with caution—catch each eddy and look downstream. The "S"s will last about a half mile altogether—then from an eddy on river left you'll notice that in one hundred feet or less the river pinches a bit right, gray rock is on the left and the river appears to "drop off." Don't do anything stupid now—that's the first of the Three Falls and it can creep up on even paddlers who've been there before "like a thief in the night."

At low flows it's possible to run the first two drops of the Three Falls section; however, I'd recommend expecting to portage all three on your first trip down. The preferred portage at the Three Falls is on river right, so you must ferry across from left to right about a hundred feet above the first of the Three Falls. Land by jamming your boat into some rocks that form a marginal system of eddies—it's not so hard, and not

Jim Rada runs Second Drop. ©2006 John Alt

joerg steinbach second drop devils track ©2006 dan nemskey

A Devil's Track canyon. At right, John Alt, John Amron and Jim Rada scout Serpent Slide.

©2006 Photos by Henry Kinnucan

so easy either. Once on river right you head uphill, staying near the river. There's no trail, but the woods are relatively open. After about a third of a mile, you'll encounter a deep ravine—descend into it and follow it to the river. It joins the river just at the base of the third of the Three Falls, a spectacular sight, water spilling over red rock and spraying into the Canyon. When you put in, you'll notice that the riverbed now consists of slides over sheets of redrock.

Only a few hundred yards downstream from Three Falls you'll see a pine tree clinging to a high, rocky perch on the right. This tree is on a narrow peninsula of rock around which the river swings in a tight curve. It's a good move to get out on this peninsula and scout, because on the downstream side the river rockets through a rapid fit for an amusement park: Serpent Slide. As boaters round the peninsula, they'll find themselves presented with a steep slide which gathers the flow of the Devil's Track and sweeps it up against the cliff on river right. The water banks off and then veers to the left, a hundred feet later plunging over Boulder Falls, a class IV containing eight or nine feet of vertical drop.

Running Serpent Slide is a gas; you "go with the flow" and join the water banking off the right cliff—the acceleration is incredible, and often you'll be shot right into Boulder Falls. Serpent Slide has been forgiving, so call it a IV, but it ain't your ordinary run. Boulder Falls is best run near the left bank. By the way, Serpent Slide can't be portaged on the right, and it would be difficult to land and portage on the left, so count on running it.

Following Boulder Falls comes a steep stretch full of broaching rocks. The next 1.5 miles is very scenic—steep, continuous boulderbed typically running a hundred yards before a cliff forces the river to make a sharp turn. The Little Devil Track enters along the right in this section, but its confluence is partially hidden as it enters the Devil's Track at an angle. Be wary and look out for downed trees.

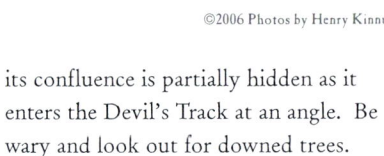

The pure boulderbed section will end when you encounter a series of medium size ledges (each 4-5 feet), III+, that requires quick thinking. An eddy below these ledges allows a break to regroup. You're now about a quarter-mile from two large ledges. The first, Dike Drop (IV), is evident as a horizon line and eddies exist both on the left and right. The name relates to an intrusion of whitish rock (quartz?) that shows up on river right just at the base of the drop. We often have a snack on the outcrops on the right here. Another hundred feet

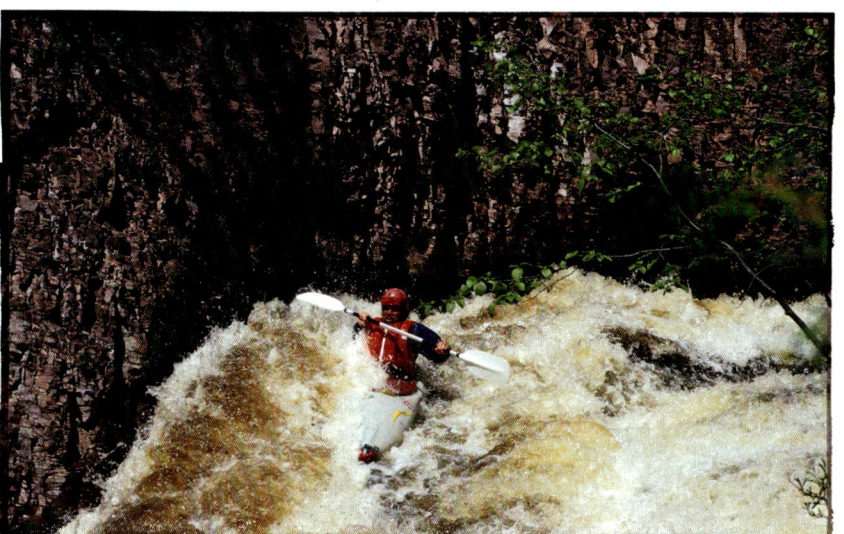

Jim Rada raids Serpent Slide. ©2006 Mike Cotten

Jimbo lances Pike Drop. John Alt and John Amron sit on a rock. ©2006 Henry Kinnucan

downstream is Pushover Falls, also a IV. You'll see the Superior Hiking Trail bridge crossing the Devil's Track just above Pushover Falls. Catch an eddy on the right just below the bridge if you want to scout. The best route over this sloping eight-footer seems to be on the right, preparing to go left at the bottom. Maybe you'll find out why it's called "Pushover," a double meaning.

Right after Pushover you enter a landslide area where trees have frequently slid into the river from the bluff on the left. In fact following a heavy downpour in July 1993 a large chunk of soil and trees slid into the Devil's Track, creating a small island just below Pushover Falls. After the landslide area the river careens over continuous small ledges and slides. You'll notice a place or two where low red rock cliffs flank you on both sides of the river.

Perhaps a half mile from Pushover Falls you'll run a section of rock sheets and then see an eddy and cliff on the right and an eddy and low bank on the left. The river turns sharply left here. You should get out on the left and look around the corner. A complex drop, Portage Down the Middle (class IV-V), greets you. There's no portage on the right; you can portage left only by hauling your boat up the bluff and then carrying down a ravine–brutal.

The ledge has a couple of offset holes–and the hydraulic at the base of the drop can stop and hold boats. I once got trashed in the hole, spit out with my boat and paddle into the cliffside eddy on river left. The water was ice cold and way over my head. Tom Aluni, John Alt and others then dropped me a rescue rope from the scree slope on the left. I caribinered my boat in and they hauled me, my paddle and boat (full of water) up out of the Devil's Track. I'll never forget Tom Aluni's booming "One, Two, Three, HEAVE" that coordinated the hoisting of me and my gear from the icy waters. Take a look at the spot on the left where they pulled from–I could just as well have pulled them all in! Tom still delights in reminding me that I'm the only

©2006 dan nenskey
joerg steinbach second drop devils track

53

person to have run Portage Down the Middle and then portaged it! The portage is so ugly that we've gotten used to running a "flying leap" route off the right lip and sliding/boofing just past the hole. Please note the funny angle the ledge cuts at the right lip.

With Portage Down the Middle behind, your thoughts turn to the exit from the canyon above Pitchfork Falls. About a third of a mile below Portage Down the Middle, you'll see a relatively large whitish boulder in the current–"The White Rock." The White Rock marks a critical area on the run. Not far downstream from the White Rock lies Pitchfork Falls, a forty footer that appears to be unrunnable. Pitchfork Falls is guarded on both sides by cliffs, so it isn't possible to paddle to the lip and then portage! You must get off the river and out of the canyon well above Pitchfork Falls!!

You can get out of the canyon on the right side at the White Rock. A nicer carry out is found if you follow the river bending left through heavy III and then take out right as the river eases and bends back right. This next spot is perhaps a hundred and fifty yards below the White Rock. This second takeout spot on the right offers an okay eddy and a steep but manageable carry up a gully on the right. The carry through the woods on the right side around Pitchfork Falls is hard to describe. You'll carry at least a third-mile, maybe even a half-mile downstream from your takeout. Your goal is to see Pitchfork Falls, a 40-45 foot beauty, and then find a gully two hundred yards downstream of the falls. The gully is steep, the rock crumbly, so it works well to work as a team and lower boats with long ropes. Entering the river below Pitchfork Falls from the right side is probably more dangerous than any paddling you'll do on the river, unless it's the drops shortly below Pitchfork you're scrambling down to run.

The combination of difficult put-in here and the heavy drops just ahead has led many to continue carrying along the right rim. If you do so, a much easier put-in can be made about two-thirds of a mile below Pitchfork. This is a long carry, but the paddle up to Pitchfork is great, and the scenery at the lower put-in is nice, leaving the paddler feeling well rewarded for his efforts. Those who want to have it all must suffer the awful descent to the pool below Pitchfork. The first gully ends in vertical "space," so you must traverse a hundred yards downstream to find a route to the river–still the route will be steep.

A third takeout exists above Pitchfork Falls about one hundred and fifty yards below takeout option #2. This third spot is on river left and has two major advantages: (1) You can carry up the very steep bank to the Superior Hiking Trail and then portage downstream on a trail and (2) When you encounter a small creek below Pitchfork Falls you leave the Superior Hiking Trail and follow the creek to the river. Putting in on river left below Pitchfork is much easier than coming down the crumbling cliffs on the right. Portaging on the left is easier but the takeout spot for this route is a one boat eddy and a bit hard to describe. If you are unfamiliar with the river it's easier to recognize the White Rock and portage on the right.

When you put in, you get to enjoy a tremendous view of Pitchfork Falls squirting between red cliffs. and then you're off in the true land of the Devil. As you paddle downstream from Pitchfork Falls, you have a real feeling of being in the canyon to its end. Getting up the cliffs and out would be difficult or impossible in some spots. The scenery for the third-mile below Pitchfork is incredible and the rapids easy.

Then comes one of the most thrilling whitewater experiences I've ever encountered. A third-mile below Pitchfork the current will accelerate as the river bends left. There's a lousy microeddy left and a somewhat better microeddy right. It is

Anett Trebitz boofs a perfect line on Portage Down The Middle. ©2006 Doug Demerest

possible—just barely—to get out and scout/portage on the right—don't count on it though; it's not easy. What you'll scout or have to run unscouted is an amazing torrent, "Ski Jump," where the Devil's Track accelerates down a steep, smooth slide losing 25 feet rapidly, by itself class IV+. If you don't snag the left or right hand eddy at the base of Ski Jump (and it's a 50-50 proposition), you're sliding down the next chute which also gains incredible speed and then blasts directly into the left hand wall, forcing the whole river to squirt back to the right. I call this "Up Against the Wall," and you'll feel like you're looking at a firing squad as you approach the humungous pillow where the water blasts into the wall. Your boat will bank with the water, tilting you way up on edge—it's the craziest, most insane feeling I've experienced in boating. My God, am I glad to be upright after that!!! Then it's delirium time—I'm SO happy, SO happy—I am always grateful for those rugged paddling companions who will come with me to collectively reach these heights.

Don't put in below Pitchfork Falls if you're not ready to take a chance on what might be the ride of your life. Up Against the Wall can be cheated with great difficulty by carrying Ski Jump or running Ski Jump and eddying out, then doing a seal launch on the right just below where the water hits the left wall. Neither carrying Ski Jump nor catching the eddy at its base is easy.

This can be a life-threatening area! While running the river with Mike Cotten and Paul Douglas during Memorial Day weekend, 1987, I blazed down Ski Jump, just caught the eddy, and looked downstream. A tree was across the river just above the wall in Up Against the Wall. To have missed the eddy (I've averaged about 2 for 3 catching the eddy) would've sent me into the tree and either broken my body or killed me—no ifs, ands or buts. Since Mike and Paul had never run the river, they would likely have continued over Ski Jump—and if they missed the eddy—same thing.

On the first run of this section, it was just John Alt and me. John didn't know what to expect at this spot. I'd hiked up the river during the winter on the ice. When he saw me miss the eddy and go into the frothy distance he thought I was gone. He got out and scouted, saw the rapid with me below and had a more controlled descent. Good old John, what a boater! Even John lost his paddle in Up Against the Wall once. He then rolled up off the bottom and eddied out. With no spare, I wondered what we'd do. No problem, John took a foam pillar out of his boat, broke it

Ross Peterson runs Ski Jump.
©2006 John Alt

in half and paddled the rest of the canyon with a chunk in each hand!! Humans are ingenious! I've also seen fishermen cooking up trout over a fire on river left just below Up Against the Wall, so it's possible to enter and leave the canyon here.

A spring party of boaters removed the tree blocking Up Against the Wall in 1988, with Mr. Alt doing the chopping. Since then the run has been made several times and as recently as July 1993 it's clean. If I've laid it on heavy—good, you will be impressed.

Below Up Against the Wall, you can relax and enjoy a mile of un-real scenery and class III water. Keep looking for sweepers, but the storm has passed. Finish up by going under Highway 61 and drifting out onto the Lake. The calm after the storm sinks in, and you can reflect on a day of truly being alive. This run is difficult, dangerous, beautiful and intoxicating—one of the best. If you are a careful, expert steep creek boater you will have a great time.

©2006 dan honskey
joerg steinbach
second drop
devils track

KADUNCE RIVER

LENGTH: 1 MILE

CLASS: IV–V

SUMMER: RARE

QUICK DESCRIPTION: TINY CREEK, BIG DROPS, SLOT CANYON

PUT-IN: SUPERIOR HIKING TRAIL BRIDGE ONE MILE FROM LAKE

TAKE-OUT: WAYSIDE ON HIGHWAY 61 TEN MILES EAST OF GRAND MARAIS

OK, here's one for the Topolino crowd! Bring a blunt boat and expect to do some banging on your boat and bod while power-snouting your way through a tight slot canyon. The scenery includes a narrow slot canyon complete with raven's nest, towering trees, overhanging cliffs and an intimacy that's fantastic. This little creek rarely has much water in it and so far paddlers have avoided the highest flows. The choice to date has been enough water to "lubricate" the drops and slides and little enough water so that it doesn't jam you into walls, undercuts or the possible logs.

The run was first done in 1993 or 1994 by John Alt and Chris Nybo so by the time I got the chance to do it in 1996 I'd already gotten some words of advice. "Wear leather gloves," said soft spoken John—bloody knuckles are a real possibility. Paul Everson talked about angling the boat just right to avoid what others called the "mandatory piton" at the drop I'll refer to as "Black Hole." Judging by the cantaloup cup dent he put in his Freefall LT just days after buying it from Cascade Kayaks, I listened attentively. It did help that I had good knowledge of the Kadunce garnered from several snowshoe trips and a wading trip up it with Pete Cary at low summer flow.

The run starts at the Kadunce River wayside rest on Highway 61, where the Kadunce flows into Lake Superior. Put your boat on your shoulder and start walking! Cross 61 and follow the hiking trail that heads upriver to the Superior Hiking Trail bridge, the put-in. During your one mile hike you can "rest" by scouting the river to determine the water level, presence of logs and routes. Some of the drops will be unscoutable/portageable at river level.

The run starts with two or three small redrock slides—fun! Then comes a pool where you line up for Gnar-thex, a steep twisting slide that drops 25 feet in a few microseconds. The key is to align yourself in the right hand slot and avoid bashing the wall or flipping. It was easier than I had imagined.

A quick eddy, then a couple curves and you're blasting into the "Black Hole." Here the river runs headfirst into the left cliff after dropping off a ten foot ledge. Your goal is to not do the same! Alt advised hitting the ledge on the right, angled right to avoid the worst bashing and it seemed to work pretty well—only a mild thump. Hey, if you're worried about your boat, use a "rock boat" on this run.

You're into the slot canyon now. It's narrow and beautiful and contains a couple fair sized drops which are pretty straightforward if there are no trees. The first had an invisible subsurface log on our run. Alt pinned on it and had to push himself up and over by pushing down on a rock shelf with his paddle. Fortunately, the log was gone when it was my turn. Another fifty yards brings you to a pretty curving falls that drops about 12 feet into a deep pool. EE-HAH!!

You've done the hard stuff now, so enjoy the cosmic view of a slit of sky overhead before leaving that wonderful pool. Your boat will say "ouch!" a few times as you navigate a couple hundred yards of scenic but barely navigable boulderbed. The next horizon line you see will be the last sizable drop—a clean double ledge followed by a cave and a sharp bend to the right. All that's left is a joyous bash to the Lake.

After running it Alt said, "So now you've run the much magnified Kadunce." I'd have to agree that the big drops seemed easier than expected and I almost felt ashamed at assaulting a river with so little water in it. It's such a small creek you just end up following the flow. And I didn't even wear the "leathers" on my hands—I didn't want any interference with the death grip I had on the paddle!

Kadunce canyon. ©2006 Paul Everson

BRULE RIVER

Rada steams into Sauna Bath rapid, Brule River. ©2006 Tom Aluni

LENGTH: 6 MILES

CLASS: II–IV+

SUMMER: SOME (MAINLY CANYON)

QUICK DESCRIPTION: LOTS OF BOULDERS, FALLS, LEDGES

PUT-IN: SAUNA BATH RAPID, HALF MILE HIKE IN FROM COOK COUNTY 70

TAKE-OUT: LAKE SUPERIOR, U.S. 61 BRIDGE IN C.R. MAGNEY STATE PARK

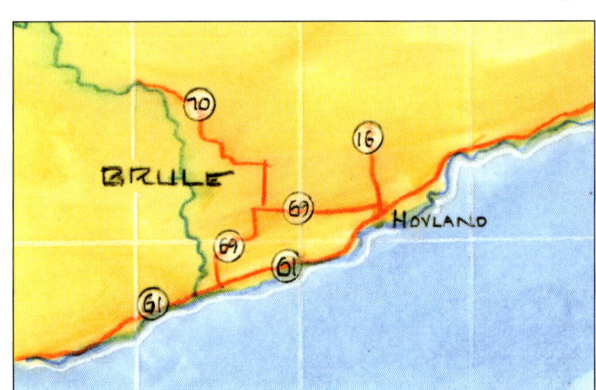

As the Baptism is a "must see" classic, so is the Brule. The Brule near Grand Marais, Minnesota isn't to be confused with the South Shore Brule near Superior, Wisconsin. The South Shore Brule is much more mellow and has earned the title "Bogus Brule" by comparison with its North Shore brother. I can heartily recommend a voyage down the Brule to an advanced boater seeking class II, III, IV (and V if desired) water amidst outstanding scenery. Of course there will be portages as well!

The put-in is a little hard to describe: starting at the Highway 61 bridge over the Brule at C.R. Magney State Park, head east on 61 about two-thirds of a mile to where Cook County 69 branches left off of 61. After about 3 miles of zig-zagging north and east on 69, you'll see Cook County 70 branching left off of 69. Follow this about 4 miles, in the process crossing over a couple of streams. After you've gone 4 miles on 70 you'll come to a road that branches left into a field with a planting of conifers and at this point County 70 seems to get a little smaller. There is a gate across the road to the left and you must make a decision here.

The gate is an indication that landowners of summer cabins beyond don't want people trespassing on their land. They are usually not around til after Memorial Day, but when encountered have often been angry and hostile towards boaters. Some of them seem more approachable than others. Should you choose to carry in to the river from the gate, don't tell them I said it was "OK," because I'm not telling you that. I'm telling you that for many years we did the following: Put your boat on your shoulder and take the road left into the field and follow to its end, in the process encountering a small creek, Mons Creek, with a rickety bridge. Carry

©2006 dan monskey

joerg steinbach second drop devils track

Pete Cary plunges through Sewer Pipe. ©2006 Mike Cotten

your boat across the little bridge and up a hill—you should see a cabin nearby. Go to it and just to its right you'll find a foot trail—got it? Great!! This trail will lead you down to the Brule at the site of an old sauna building perched on the edge of the river. This is the end of Sauna Bath, a magnificent class V rapid that is the starting point for the Brule run. We have used this access to the Brule for over twenty years and have had few problems until recently. When the ground is still covered with snow and the river is raging, it's very unlikely the cabin owners will be there. However, in recent years the Brule has seen increased use during the summer and there have been occasions when they were sunbathing in the nude when boaters arrived. This has made for some unpleasantness.

If you would like to access the river without risking a confrontation with the cabin owners, bring a detailed map and continue on County 70 past the gate. You will drive about 2-3 miles on a narrow but passable road and take a couple of forks to the left, passing just southwest of Lost Lake (it won't be in sight, though). The second fork should leave you in a clearing where there has been some logging recently and you'll probably have to park here because the road degrades into a trail with brush leaning in from the sides and down trees across the trail. Carry your boat about a third to half a mile on this trail and you'll come to the site of an old crossing of the Brule. This is the put-in. I've probably been inaccurate with the route because I've gone this way only once, with John Alt. Alt lives close to the put-in and maybe you'll be lucky enough to get better directions from him! Be prepared for a bit of searching—bring maps. As of 1996 this is one of the only access problems in the Northwoods and perhaps boaters will be able to continue to access the river at Sauna Bath if they take care.

However you got to the river, soon you are standing looking at a gorgeous example of heavy whitewater: Sauna Bath. Do you like to start your day with class V or at least IV+ action? If you came past the gate pull on the sprayskirt and carry upstream 150 yards from the Sauna Bath. You may have to push your way through deadfalls and brush since not many put in to do Sauna Bath. The steep, twisting path through large boulder blocks is one of the most picturesque thrills around. The crux move happens fast—my advice is to get right at the hole.

Putting in below Sauna Bath or portaging Sauna Bath allows you to warm up for about a hundred feet before hitting the juice. A sweeping left turn holds a surprise at the end—look for it. After the surprise, there's a brief calm and then the Brule charges one hundred yards downhill over moderate size boulders. At high water (2.25 feet and above) this verges on class IV, at moderate flows (1.5 feet) it's fun class III.

The next mile is beautiful continuous water varying from II to III as the gradient changes. In high water on a sunny day, the river is churning white everywhere. About a mile and a half from Sauna Bath, a major ledge, Second Island Falls (IV), breaks the continuous whitewater. Eddies on the right are small and scarce (and sometimes filled with ice shelves) so when you see the splitting of the Brule at the upstream end of the 150 yard long island, go right with the main current and look for scouting eddies on the right. You'll probably want to land.

Second Island Falls has a variety of routes—a double drop along the right side, an elegant S maneuver and others. Watch for the hole in the outrun on river right. At my high water run of 3.5 feet Second Island Falls featured towering waves and big water push. Below Second Island Falls, the boulderbed continues and is especially nice class III for the hundred yard straightaway below Second Island. Then the river bends gradually to the right. Be sure not to proceed around the gradual bend to the right. Take out on the right just above the corner as the water eases slightly.

This is the most dangerous spot on the river in my opinion. You're less than a quarter-mile from Canyon Falls, a VI at spring flows. Canyon Falls has only been run at low water (about half a foot) by John Alt, Chris Nybo and Mike Cotten. At half a foot the upper part of Canyon Falls was still tight but lacking in power. During spring Canyon Falls consists of heavy, constricted whitewater leading into a long steep slide as the river curves right and swings against cliffs on the left. The total vertical drop has to be at least forty feet. The quarter-mile between your takeout and the beginning of the heavy whitewater is innocuous class II, but the right bank turns into gravel and there are no decent eddies for a group to use. It's probably possible to land on the left, but a portage on the left would be hindered by the cliffs near the Falls.

In any case, the right side portage is moderately bad—through brush about a third of a mile in all. If you are lucky you will notice the portage trail cleared by John Alt in the fall of 1992. The trail is in keeping with John's personality—unobtrusive—you might not even see it! My hint is to stay about a hundred feet from the river as you portage until you climb a little hill where you can see the last slide of the falls. Pause and take in the grand view, then carefully follow the right rocks along the slide to its base. You can launch at the base and paddle a deceptively difficult rapid as the river twists left, or continue to portage another hundred yards on the right. It's a beautiful spot for a snack (bring COOKIES!!!), and the rapid at the twist has some play features.

Then onward!! The next three mile section is called "3 by III Flume" to denote that the continuous boulderbed rapids are of high quality and just keep on coming. Much is class II with bursts of III—it's a joy. The rapids hold a few playspots, but mostly it's boulder-dodging and eddy catching fun. When the Brule is over 2 feet on the gauge there's lots of white. One of my favorite vistas comes early on in 3 by III Flume: a high ridge with rocky cliffs towers along the right side just a quarter-mile from the Brule. Be sure to catch a few eddies and savor the view! When I paddled this run early in my boating career, I was blown away that this magnificent river and view could actually be in Minnesota, my home.

The end of 3 by III Flume is announced when, on a bend to the left, you see low rock cliffs on the right. Take out immediately in the large eddy on the inside (left side) of the turn. You are just above Devil's Kettle, something not to be stumbled over. The Brule at Devil's Kettle crests a horizon line and then there's a parting of the waters as the left side of the river plunges over a forty foot falls, while the right side falls into the "Kettle," a deep dark vertical cave with no obvious opening.

Devil's Kettle and the other falls and rapids that punctuate the Brule's final mile and a half are spectacular and rightfully showcased by hiking trails in C.R. Magney State Park. It's an easy hike (about a mile) from the takeout, the Highway 61 bridge, up the left side of the Brule to Devil's Kettle, with a spur trail going to Lower Falls. If you've never paddled the Brule before, the hike will give you an idea of the nature of the Brule's rapids and will allow you to scout (and possibly flag) the eddy above Devil's Kettle.

On your river run you'll portage both Devil's Kettle and Upper Falls in one fell swoop by carrying along the state park trail on river left—there's even a stairway to the pool below Upper Falls. You enter the Brule Canyon at this point, the most intense whitewater of the run, except for Sauna Bath. Only a quarter-mile from Upper Falls you encounter Lower Falls, V-. Give each other room as the good eddies on river right are at the lip of Lower Falls and are too small for many boats. Lower Falls is easily scouted or portaged on the right. Lower Falls is agonizingly simple—you have to get past the monster hole at the base of the eleven foot ledge. Finding a weak spot takes some looking and paddling finesse. Many times, particularly at levels over 1.5 feet, I've seen cold and weary boaters take the easy portage, saving their strength for what's left.

What's left below Lower Falls is a mini canyon with poor scouting that contains about a third-mile of heavy whitewater

joerg steinbach
second drop
devils track

culminating in Sewer Pipe, a IV+ tumult. This canyon, III+ to IV at high flow, forms a sort of oxbow, bending right around a pile of big boulders, past several ledges (The Land of a Hundred Holes) then swerving back left through hole-laden waters a hundred yards before Sewer Pipe. The lead-in to Sewer Pipe is simplified somewhat if you cut to the inside of the left turn and snag the eddy on the left.

Here you can get out and look at Sewer Pipe–a place where a protrusion of rock from the left shore pinches the river into a tight funnel against the right wall. The top of the funnel is guarded by a hole. It's a real challenge for even expert boaters to run Sewer Pipe in good form. Quite often the river runs boaters through: backward, sideways, rolling in the curler, backendering, graciously flushing all into the pool. If it wasn't so forgiving I'd certainly call it a V.

Rejoicing and smiles break out in the pool below Sewer Pipe. The rush is almost over–a couple hundred yards bring you to a nice set of surfing waves, then another quarter mile brings you to Footbridge Falls, the final drop on the Brule. Footbridge Falls rates III+ to IV- depending on flow.

The Brule river gauge is found on river right just downstream of the footbridge. It's a faint painted set of lines and numbers on the bare rock with foot and half-foot marks. Look carefully, and perhaps from the opposite shore to see it best. The Brule is runnable at half a foot, but the boulderbed in 3 by III Flume is very scrapey.

Carrying up to run from Lower Falls down is a pleasant run at this low level. A good level for a first run is about 1.25 feet: the boulders are fairly well covered, the river isn't so pushy and the holes aren't as strong. A strong intermediate can make the run at these levels with portaging and the watchful eye of more experienced boaters.

When the Brule gets over two feet the pulse quickens. 3 by III Flume is prime at levels of 2-2.5 and boaters start thinking twice about rapids like Sauna Bath. My run at 3.5 feet was an awesome experience. I only took a glance at the white hell of Sauna Bath. The rapids from Sauna Bath to Second Island Falls were magnificent and wild, 3 by III Flume was a wavy, mostly featureless flush, the water above Sewer Pipe heartpounding. Sewer Pipe was runnable where there's normally dry land. It didn't take long to do the run–there wasn't much goofing around.

I should note that the Brule's drainage is filled with lakes and swamps that moderate the flow and extend the Brule's season beyond many of the other North Shore runs. Since the Brule is also one of the largest North Shore rivers, this means that it's much more likely that the Brule will be runnable than any other North Shore river, with the exception of the St. Louis. Perhaps this would make the Brule a good first choice for the advanced paddler who wants to "get his feet wet" on a North Shore run.

The takeout is close upon Footbridge Falls, and you might start thinking of something to eat, maybe at the interesting Naniboujou Lodge, situated on the shore of Lake Superior a few hundred yards east of the mouth of the Brule. While you can take out right at the 61 bridge and load up your boat, I usually enjoy running the quarter mile of riffles to the Lake, there to meditate, perhaps surf and thank God for this river, my boat, my friends. A run down the Brule will repay the experienced boater for his efforts in many ways–a classic.

The Devil's Kettle in Judge C. R. Magney State Park. ©2006 Tom Aluni

PIGEON RIVER

Jim Rada watches as Mike Cotten runs the first descent of Middle Falls. ©2006 Ephram Holyoak

The **Pigeon River** is deeply rooted in the history of the Great Lakes. It served as a major highway for the fur trade and "voyageurs" of the 1700's and 1800's. These stalwart paddlers carried furs and canoes over nine miles on a portage trail to reach the stockade and trading post on Lake Superior, Grand Portage. Grand Portage also gave its name to the trail, which is now preserved by the National Park Service. Today's voyageurs in fiberglass and plastic kayaks first came to the river in the early 70's to find out what would make a real voyageur portage nine miles. What they found is an exquisite run that combines water suitable for intermediates with rugged wilderness country of pristine beauty.

The Pigeon is certainly not the prime whitewater run on the North Shore, but a pleasing combination of beauty and fun. It also isn't your typical steep small North Shore stream, but a fair sized river and the international border with Canada. In fact its size and whitewater seem more akin to the rivers of the Canadian shore than those of Minnesota's North Shore. The entire run of the Pigeon would be roughly 14 or 15 miles from Partridge Falls to the Highway 61 bridge (U.S. Customs station), but it's commonly broken into two sections.

UPPER PIGEON:

PARTRIDGE FALLS TO THE OLD HIGHWAY 61 CROSSING AT PIGEON RIVER.

I prefer this section of the Pigeon as it's totally wild for the whole length. Seeing moose

---

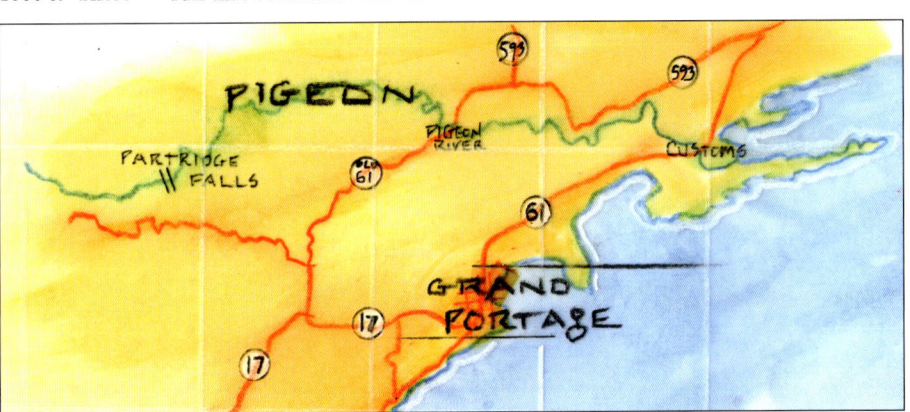

SECTION: UPPER

LENGTH: 8.5 MILES

CLASS: II–III

SUMMER: RARE

QUICK DESCRIPTION: WILD, SCENIC, LOTS OF FLATWATER

PUT-IN: PARTRIDGE FALLS AT END OF PARTRIDGE FALLS ROAD

TAKE-OUT: POPLAR CREEK ROAD NEAR OLD PIGEON RIVER CROSSING

©2006 dan monskey

joerg steinbach second drop devils trap

61

PIGEON RIVER

SECTION: LOWER

LENGTH: 7 MILES

CLASS: I–III+

SUMMER: RARE

QUICK DESCRIPTION:
FLATS, HORNE FALLS, SOME PLAY

PUT-IN:
POPLAR CREEK ROAD NEAR OLD PIGEON RIVER CROSSING

TAKE-OUT:
U.S. 61 AT CANADIAN BORDER CROSSING, OR UPSTREAM

Jim Rada vs. Middle Falls. ©2006 Mike Cotten

isn't uncommon. Also, the scenery and whitewater are better in the upper 8-9 miles than in the lower six.

The road to Partridge Falls is made of potholes and mud and requires high clearance. Four wheel drive is nice, but not essential. The put-in is on land that's part of the Grand Portage Indian Reservation and reservation wardens have on occasion forbidden putting in at Partridge Falls. My advice is to drive there (you probably won't see anyone) and be mellow. And remember to be careful putting in at the base of Partridge–Karen Jensen got pulled into the sharp drop just below the falls by the strong eddy currents. Not a nice way to start the day!

The next couple miles to the Cascades hold occasional class I and II rapids and the site of old Fort Charlotte (on the right bank). There's one nice broad surfing wave near Fort Charlotte when the water's up. A mile or so from the surfing wave will bring you to rapids that bend to the left, and it will be evident that the Pigeon is entering a canyon.

This is the Cascades, a beautiful gorge that begins with a falls and shortly roars over a couple more falls that are set between cliffs both left and right. A quarter mile upstream from the Cascades on the American side (right) is a small cabin with woodstove, bunk and diary that's open to provide shelter to the public. Halfway between the cabin and the first drop of the Cascades, a trail breaks downstream from a small clearing, finding its way to the rim of the gorge. Follow along until you see some way of climbing down and launching. The distance you carry will vary with your nerve and climbing skills. I'd say most people carry a third of a mile, maybe a bit more.

You'll put in on class II water that's quite fun, with playspots, eddies and low walls of slate-like rock. It may get to be almost III in places at high water, but it's quite benign and scenic. You'll probably enjoy about a mile of this nice stuff, and then the walls will fade away and the rapids diminish.

Swiftwater and class I will dominate now–keep an eye out for moose. A couple miles of winding will lead you to a set of ledges on a right hand bend. There are some nice play holes here.

Another mile or so and the Arrow River will enter on the left out of Canada, and between the Arrow and the takeout at the little locale of Pigeon River, there will be a few more bursts of whitewater. One is a class II-III spot where a very short gorge occurs and another noteworthy spot lies along the left less than a mile from the takeout, when a few nice waves break out at high flow.

Continue downstream about a hundred and fifty yards below the ruins of the old bridge crossing at Pigeon River and take out on the right (U.S.). Be careful not to park or hang out around the house at the U.S. end of the old bridge crossing. There's private land here and the owners have sometimes been present and unfriendly. The Upper Pigeon is certainly not a "heavy duty" whitewater run, but it is pretty, relaxing and fun for most boaters.

LOWER PIGEON:

OLD HIGHWAY CROSSING AT PIGEON RIVER TO HIGHWAY 61, U.S. CUSTOMS STATION.

The Lower Pigeon isn't quite the wilderness run the Upper Pigeon is. This is because Ontario Provincial Highway 593 comes close to the river in the lower half of the run and because of the Provincial Park at Middle Falls. What roads remove in terms of wilderness, they partially repay in access, so that you may avoid Indian lands, scout Horne Falls, see Middle Falls and camp by using the Ontario highway.

Following the put-in at Pigeon River crossing you'll encounter occasional easy whitewater, class II or less during the next 2-3 miles. It's mostly just swiftwater. When the river nears Provincial Highway 593, not obnoxious by the way, you'll encounter a good stout rapid, Horne Falls, class III+ to IV depending on water level. There's a good washing machine hole in the middle towards the end and a pop-up-ender spot on the left at the bottom at some levels.

Below Horne Falls the river meanders again for about two miles. When you encounter a good sized ledge and development on the left you'll be near Middle Falls. The ledge is a good class III-IV drop with a hundred yard runout before Middle Falls. Middle Falls drops about 20 feet and has been run. Mike Cotten got tired of skulking around the falls on the left amidst all the park visitors. His run on the far right inspired the rest of his troop, the Anokas, and myself to leap the falls. A variety of right side routes all ended well. The Anokas now laughingly refer to the falls as Cotten Falls.

Now the Pigeon bends sharply right away from the Provincial Highway, heading back into wilderness. It soon enters a short, pleasant class II-III canyon. I wish it were longer. The canyon opens and the Pigeon spreads out over boulders for a half-mile or less before cresting Pigeon Falls, a most impressive cataract dropping eighty feet or more.

A short canyon with heavy water follows Pigeon Falls, but it is difficult to put in. We have carried on the Canadian side along or on an old logging flume—be careful, my foot went through once on the flume! The portage trail continues to the end of the short canyon; put in where you choose.

The end of this last canyon is almost within sight of the U.S. 61 bridge and the customs station. The American shore here was recently acquired from a private campground by the state of Minnesota and Pigeon Falls has become the state's newest state park. There are trails to Pigeon Falls on the U.S. side that also pass a tree reputed to be the oldest paper birch in Minnesota. I like to take out a bit before the 61 bridge to avoid customs stares, but I've taken out at the bridge, too, and haven't been hassled. The Lower Pigeon is fairly mellow, but interesting—with a few playspots and a chance to leap "Cotten Falls."

STEWART RIVER

Dan Theis told me about this one. He and Dave Spencer did a short run on this and it's supposed to contain some nice tight slides and drops. Dan recommended it, and he has good taste. I gather that others of the Duluth crowd have done this one, too. It lies just east of Two Harbors; I'm not sure of the put-in and takeout.

SILVER CREEK

This one is another run just east of Two Harbors. Here the commonly run segment extends from the Lake County 3 bridge to Lake Superior, a little more than a mile. There is a small falls shortly after putting in and then a couple big slides down river I'm told. I've also heard mention of an upper canyon and have driven north on Lake County 2 from Two Harbors and then turned left on County 201 which quickly intersects Silver Creek. The creek here is beautiful and high gradient, definitely looks appealing for a run or at least a ski. I'm not sure if this has been paddled, but I've heard a few others talk about it.

TWO ISLAND

This flows through the "ghost" community of Taconite Harbor and is one of those runs which is short, steep and best accessed by hiking upstream from Highway 61. This is a pretty tiny creek which John Alt discovered made an enchanting ski and a challenging run. Apparently there are some very big and very tight drops mixed with others of more moderate size. Alt, Dusty from Duluth and one other boater were the first to paddle this in 1996, leaving some drops for "future boaters."

The high water spring of 1996 allowed runs on really, really tiny creeks some of which I'm not sure I'd recommend and which I'd probably skip, but for the record here are a couple of them.

FALL RIVER

Chris Broben and Paul Everson spent a day venturing down this one. They reported some drops that were runnable and some that weren't. Sounded like a bit of an ordeal. Don't be fooled by the name, this is not a river! I think I might check this creek out by foot first. There's probably lots of lumber in it.

KIMBALL CREEK

After knockin' his noggin on Two Step, Dag Grada from Chicaga became a true believer in North Shore whitewater. He and a companion spent a day descending Kimball Creek, near Grand Marais, reporting class II-V whitewater and lots of logs.

OTHER CREEK RUNS ON THE NORTH SHORE

The last few years have seen a lot of effort expended on finding new North Shore runs. As all of the larger rivers have been done this leaves only "creeks" left to be tackled, and they are only runnable for very short periods at any time. Because of this there are some North Shore creeks that have been done only once or a few times or by local paddlers only. Some of these I've been able to do and they've been included as individual runs. However, there are a few which I have yet to do and some I'm not sure I'd recommend. Here's a synopsis of some of these runs.

ST. LOUIS RIVER RENDEZVOUS

64 | A C-1'er enders under the Hwy 210 bridge.

Doug Nelson ©2006.

Downstream from the rodeo area lies the meat of the Lower St. Louis. This section is called The Wall.   Doug Nelson ©2006.

Bright lights, frothy hole at the Night Rodeo. Tyler Hillstrom (top) and Steve Stratman compete.   Doug Nelson ©2006.

Paddlers of all ilks converge on the St. Louis River for the St. Louis River Rendezvous. These paddlers compete in the freestyle event underneath the Highway 210 Bridge, where others run a slalom course through the canyon. The night rodeo usually wraps up the weekend.

65

WATER AND GRAVITY

Right: John Kiffmeyer buries himself in Illgen Falls. Below: A boater submarines through a drop on the Lower St. Louis river.

Holy Shit rapid, Lester River. ©2006 Mike Cotten

Dan Monskey ponders The Thumb on the Sucker River. ©2006 Paul Everson

The St. Louis below Finn Falls rages at 28,000cfs. ©2006 John Alt

67

SPRING MELT

Springtime brings dangerously high water. Above is Long John Rapid on the Cascade River. To the left is the Kadunce River and far left is Upper Falls on the Brule River at 3.25 feet. North Shore hero John Alt takes these pictures rather than run rivers on a first day of April.

All photos by John Alt, ©2006

Above is Sauna Bath rapid on the Brule River at 3.25 feet. On river left sits the sauna bath itself. To the right shows a fine view of Sauna Bath's rapid from inside the sauna bath. It no longer stands, as spring waters have since coaxed it downstream.

LOWER CASCADE

Class V-V+

Destination hairboating anyone? This steep little gem on the Cascade River consists of five interesting waterfalls which have been run from minus 18" up to minus 6". This is a good option when the rest of the river is too low to run. At levels above minus 13", the last two falls are quite horrendous.

Carry up about 0.4 miles from the highway past the footbridge putting in river right about 150 yards upstream. A twisting class III-IV rapids precedes the first drop, a 12 foot vertical falls with a sneaky "Chicken Chute" river left. Next comes "Deep Throat" about 13 feet, run left or right depending on the level. Third is "Chastity/ Sodomy" the most technically challenging, and probably the most dangerous drop on the river. This 20 footer is preceded by a tricky twisting boiling lead in.

You really would probably prefer to stay chaste in the left chute when you run this one! At lower flows (minus 18" to minus 13"), missing the left line could result in being spun backwards over the right side to back-piton on sharp rocks near the base of the right wall.

It may be helpful to use your hand on the left wall, shoving your paddle into the middle rock to help attain the launch slot.

At lower flows (minus 18" to minus 14"), be sure to seal launch out of the left notch with some momentum and good control to clear the base of the cliff. Don't get distracted by tourists, you may get caught in the "Chastity Belt," a sticky pour-over directly under the footbridge.

Takeout is possible and advisable at levels over minus 13" river right just prior to the fourth drop, "Libido," a 15 footer. At higher flows, five out of five Pro boaters required rope assistance to be pulled clear from the base of "Libido" in order to approach the fifth and final drop, 30 foot+ "Cascade Falls." Here it would be great to have a safety rope set up river left below the cauldron. A swim in this cauldron could be dire, so don't blow your sprayskirt and don't piton the right wall! Ya-Ya-Hoo!!

— Paul Everson

You can find the Lower Cascade in Cascade River State Park, just south of Grand Marais on Highway 61. See a map and river description on page 47

Joerg Steinbach runs Deep Throat.

©2006 John Linn

Jilted by Lover's Leap. ©2006 Doug Nelson

Tim Hebrink runs Chastity falls ©2006 Doug Nelson

71

The Canadian shore of Lake Superior is markedly different from Minnesota. First, while there are high hills, the general slope of the land toward Lake Superior is less pronounced. This reduced gradient makes for more lakes which feed the rivers, moderating them and extending their seasons. The runs also tend to be larger, full blown rivers as opposed to the many "steep creek" runs of Minnesota. These rivers tend to be technically easier, with quite a lot of class II, III, some IV and a little V whitewater. This means most of the runs can be of interest to intermediate and advanced paddlers.

Ice-out usually occurs later than in Minnesota, at the end of April or early May. The delay in runoff and larger size of the rivers often means enjoyable runs can be made through Memorial Day into June, although the good peak water will have passed. In some ways the land seems more rugged with hills rising like mesas (they're called "questas") and the woods have a feel of being far north. The term "the bush" seems a distinctly Canadian way of describing the primitive landscape of many lakes, endless forests and few roads.

You'll also certainly notice a change in culture as you cross into Canada—it's fun to experience the difference in language, food and mindset that Canada offers.

This book just touches on the whitewater of Lake Superior's Canadian shoreline between the Minnesota border and Nipigon. There's more whitewater, I'm sure, but I haven't been able to investigate it as much as I'd like just yet! For all these reasons, I think Northwoods paddlers will find great enjoyment in exploring Canada's North Shore.

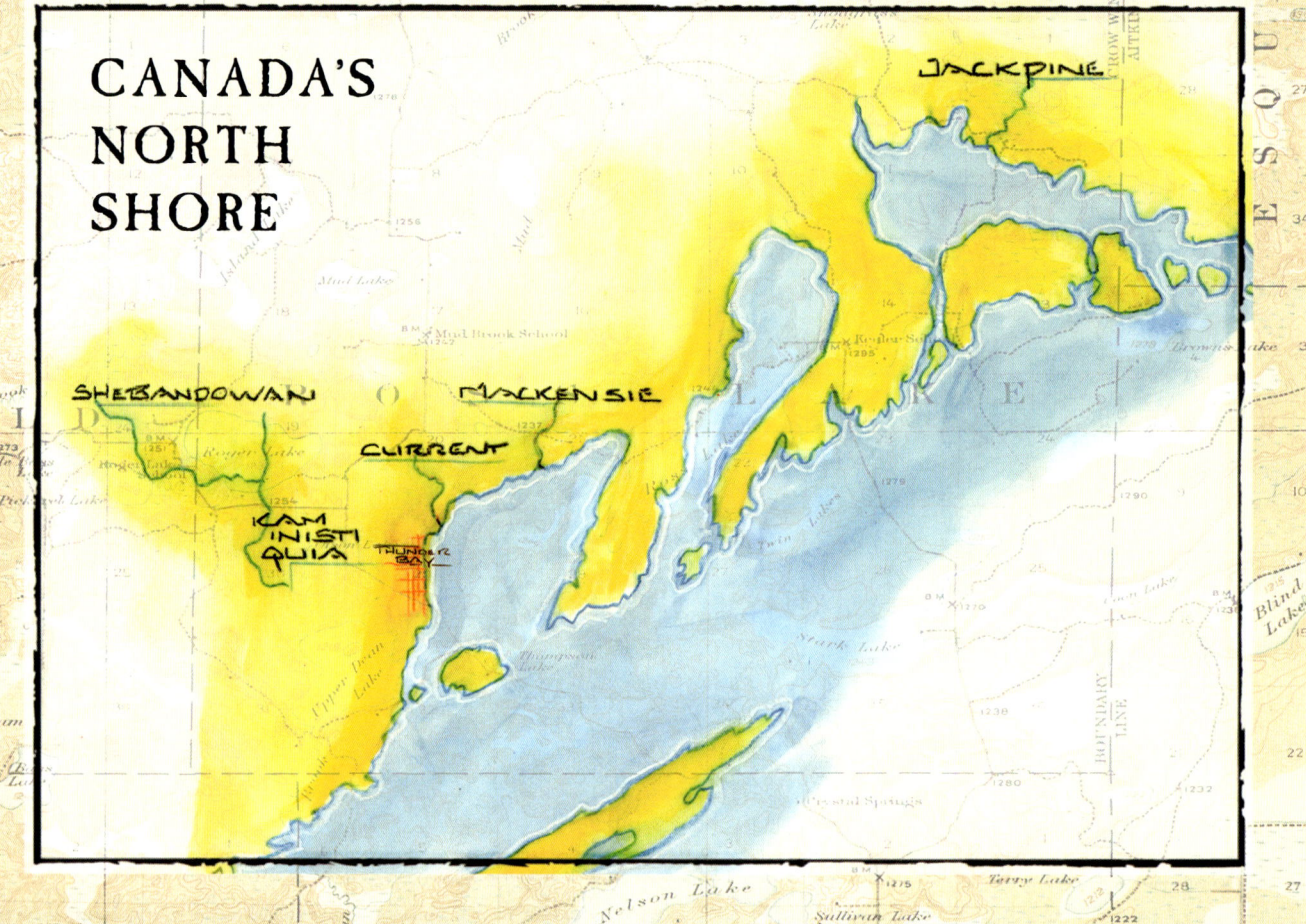

CANADA'S NORTH SHORE

CANADA'S NORTH SHORE

John Alt's well-worn homemade helmet lies along side the forest road to the put-in of the Jackpine River.

©2006 Doug Nelson

KAMINIS TIQUIA RIVER

LENGTH: 4.5 MILES

CLASS: II–III

SUMMER: YES

QUICK DESCRIPTION:
BIG RIVER, PLAYSPOTS, NICE GORGE

PUT-IN:
MOKOMON ROAD OFF HIGHWAY 11/17, 5 MILES N. OF KAKABEKA FALLS

TAKE-OUT:
HUME, AT END OF ROAD 2 MILES N. OF KAKABEKA FALLS

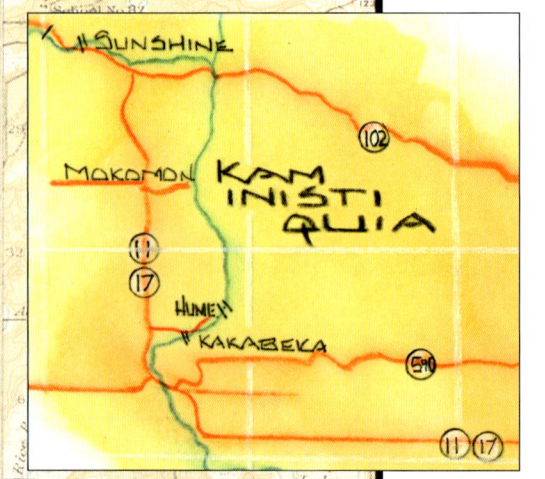

A kayaker surfs a hole in Hume Falls on the Kam. ©2006 Kevin Hill

The "Kam" is a big river that provides Thunder Bay paddlers with "action" even during the summer. My single visit to the Kam showed me the spectacular Kakabeka Falls and allowed me to paddle "The Gorge" one time at moderate flow. The run contained pool-drop rapids of class III nature, except the last drop of the 4-5 mile run which was a steeper ledge that could be run on a side channel on far right.

My memory of the run is a bit foggy as I ran this section only once five years ago. The centerpiece is a quarter mile long rapid with bedrock cliffs, scattered pines, nice playspots and easy access to the railroad tracks should a boater wish to carry up to this rapid a half mile from the Hume takeout. The run has been compared to Section I of the St. Louis in Minnesota, a common summer run that suits experts, intermediates, playboaters and squirt-men and women.

I think this comparison is a good one. Both display some nice rapids, scenery and playspots and both run during the summer. This section, however, is currently threatened by a hydropower proposal. The Thunder Bay Kayak and Canoe Club and the Friends of the Kam are two organizations currently fighting this destructive proposition.

The put-in is reached by driving about 5 miles north of Kakabeka Falls on Highway 11/17 and then turning right (east) on a road that goes into a tiny locale called Mokomon. Take the road from Mokomon that follows Brule Creek to the Kam. You'll reach the railroad tracks and the river in about a mile and a half.

The takeout is at a railroad wayside called "Hume" on the 1:250000 series Canadian topo map for the Thunder Bay area. This would be a good map to have for paddling the Thunder Bay runs. Hume is reached by going about two miles north of Kakabeka Falls on 11/17 and then taking the dirt road that spurs east off 11/17. This road will dead end at a parking spot about 2-3 miles from 11/17. That's Hume!

I will add here that there's another whitewater "point of interest" on the Kam: Crooked Rapids. Crooked Rapids is about nine miles upstream of the put-in for the Kam Gorge or about five miles south of Dog Lake. It can be accessed by a dirt road that goes to Dog Lake on the river left side of the Kam. Crooked Rapids is a dam controlled rapids about a quarter-mile long that has a couple of ledges at the beginning and end and flows between low cliffs in the middle. There are some informal camping spots here that are convenient for paddlers doing the Kam and Shebandowan runs. Crooked Rapids were "dry" when I was here but the Thunder Bay club has a slalom or two here each summer. Apparently Crooked Rapids can be a fun playspot as well when the dam is releasing.

74

SHEBANDOWAN RIVER

SECTION I
Mabella Section

The Mabella section is to my mind the finest of the three Shebandowan runs mentioned in this book. From just below Mabella to the takeout near Shabaqua, the Shebandowan sneaks away from roads, railroads and development. Here, in a boreal setting, you'll find the best rapids that the Shebandowan has to offer.

The takeout is on river left where the Oskondaga River enters the Shebandowan. Two hundred yards up the Oskondaga from this juncture is a road that used to cross the Oskondaga, but now the bridge is gone. This leaves a parking spot on either side of the Oskondaga. The easiest way to find this old bridge crossing is to enter Shabaqua going west on Highway 11/17 and turn left on a dirt road. For identification, this road is only a block or two east of the Ontario Provincial Police building. Go down the road a bit less than a mile and take the right fork near an electrical station. This fork will quickly bring you to the old Oskondaga bridge site.

You may put in either in Mabella, a cluster of cottages just south of Highway 11 four miles west of Shabaqua, or an additional two miles west where Highway 11 comes quite close to the Shebandowan. This upper two miles holds lots of flatwater, a couple of hundred-yard long class II stretches and a joyous leap over a 7-8 foot falls. When you reach Mabella you'll encounter a dam that's runnable on a natural channel on the left—a fun rapid. Then a long pool before the Shebandowan enters the woods.

Below Mabella the Shebandowan is a necklace made of flatwater pools and whitewater pearls. The first stretch of rapids begins with a nice class III ledge, but be ready, as a hundred yards later the Shebandowan roars round a corner and dashes over a turbulent lead-in to a small falls, class IV. This can be scouted from the left. The rapids continue below the ledge and then a pool. The next few sets of rapids are rather long, narrow and continuous. I believe it's the second series below the initial ledge sequence that's best. Here the river necks way down and drops fast, class III-IV. This piece reminds me of the Tablerock Canyon rapids on Minnesota's Vermilion.

The river continues to alternate pools and narrow channels of whitewater. Below the "intense" continuous section comes a piece with a beautiful surfing wave and another piece where the Shebandowan splits around an island. The left side carries more water, but it's a big drop either side of the island, class IV. Soon the Shebandowan mellows and you'll think the whitewater's through. As you pass under a railroad bridge you find the Shebandowan has a last trick up its sleeve, at least a half mile of fun class II boulderbed. As rapids tail into riffles you'll see the Oskondaga enter on the left. Time to take out.

The Mabella section is a fine run containing good whitewater and choice scenery. It's rapids are, as I've said, reminiscent of Minnesota's Vermilion, with lots of III and a bit of IV. This river will be attractive to many paddlers, particularly as it tends to

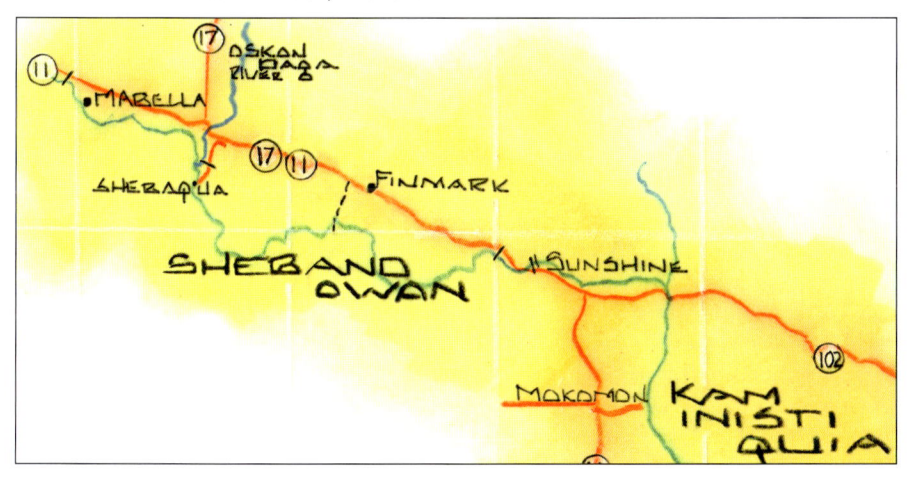

SECTION: I, MABELLA

LENGTH: 4-6 MILES

CLASS: III–IV

SUMMER: SOME

QUICK DESCRIPTION: LONG GOOD CONTINUOUS, LEDGES, POOLS

PUT-IN: HIGHWAY 11 NEAR R.-6 MI., OR MABELLA-4 MI.

TAKE-OUT: OSKONDAGA R. JUNCTION WITH SHEBANDOWAN, PARK 1 MI UP

SHEBANDOWAN RIVER

SECTION: II, GLENWATER
LENGTH: 4 MILES
CLASS: III–IV
SUMMER: SOME?
QUICK DESCRIPTION:
ALTERNATE POOLS, RAPIDS, CAN BE BIG
PUT-IN:
DIRT RD. BRIDGE 1 MILE WEST OF FINNMARK OFF HI. 11/17
TAKE-OUT:
HIGHWAY 11/17 NEAR RIVER 1.5 MILES WEST OF SUNSHINE

SECTION: III, SUNSHINE
LENGTH: 3.5 MILES
CLASS: II–III
SUMMER: RARE
QUICK DESCRIPTION: EASY RAPIDS, PRETTY FALLS, SMALL
PUT-IN:
HIGHWAY 11/17 BRIDGE OVER RIVER AT SUNSHINE RAPID
TAKE-OUT:
HIGHWAY 102 BRIDGE OVER KAMINISTIQUIA RIVER

run into early summer, due to dam regulation of the level of Shebandowan Lake upstream. Paddlers looking only for the nicest rapids probably should start in Mabella, but the eight foot falls and the couple other rapids do make the upper two miles worthwhile, too.

SECTION II

Glenwater Section

You can take out for the Glenwater run at the Highway 11/17 bridge over the Shebandowan at Sunshine but it's possible to eliminate a couple miles of flatwater by taking out west of here where the highway comes close to the river.

The put-in for the Glenwater section isn't so obvious. Go a bit over four miles west on 11/17 from the Sunshine bridge and take a road that veers left toward the Shebandowan. In about a mile to mile and a half you'll reach the Shebandowan. This gives you a 4-5 mile run.

It's like the lower Sunshine section in that it's pool-drop with long stretches of flatwater and a nice longer section of good water after the midway point. It was quite high the day Dan Theis and I did this, and I have recollections of surprisingly powerful big water, class III and IV.

SECTION III

Sunshine Section

This is the easiest of the Shebandowan runs and has good access at both ends. The put-in is the Highway 11/17 bridge over the Shebandowan at Sunshine and the takeout is about four miles east where Provincial Highway 102 crosses the Kaministiquia, which has just received the Shebandowan's water upstream from the bridge.

There is a ledge at the put-in but this rapid may have been changed due to the construction of a new bridge at Sunshine during 1991. The next couple of miles holds mostly flatwater with a couple of short rapids. After the halfway point the Shebandowan enters a pleasant stretch of more or less continuous class II-III that extends for the next mile and a half. Another mile of flatwater will bring you to the Highway 102 takeout bridge.

Mackenzie River

Writing this book during the winter was good for me, as it made me think about the runs I'd heard of, but hadn't done. So far this spring I've managed to get down three of the runs that had eluded me and I've been pleasantly surprised to find all three runs nice in different ways. The Mackenzie is the nicest of these three. As more paddlers trek north to visit the Jackpine and Thunder Bay, maybe more people will visit the Mackenzie, too.

The Mackenzie is located about 15 miles northeast of Thunder Bay and may be easily viewed from the Trans Canadian Highway. This "view" probably scares away a few boaters as the Mackenzie races into a fifty yard tunnel filled with whitewater only to spill over a nine foot drop as it exits. It looks mighty as does the drop a hundred yards downstream, but you should know that this is not what the run is really like; it's mostly nice class III with enough IV to be fun. Yes, there are a couple of easy portages, but these only add to the scenic nature of the run.

Access at the takeout is easy—simply run to Lake Superior and carry out right along the Canadian National railroad tracks. This brings you to a dirt road in two hundred yards. The dirt road branches off the alternate route to Thunder Bay about a half mile west of the Highway 11/17 crossing over the Mackenzie.

To reach the put-in, drive one mile west of the Mackenzie on Highway 11/17 and turn north on the dirt Mackenzie Station Road. In two miles you'll cross railroad tracks and enter a small cluster of homes, Mackenzie. On the north side of Mackenzie go right (east) at the crossroads. Follow this crossroad to one of two places: a pipeline (and road) about a mile east of Mackenzie or go another half mile to a one-lane bridge over Walkinshaw Creek. Walkinshaw Creek is a tributary of the Mackenzie and you can paddle down this creek a mile to get to the Mackenzie.

However, I'd recommend my choice—taking the pipeline road to the right off the dirt road. If you have high clearance and four

MACKENZIE RIVER

wheel drive you just might be able to ford Walkinshaw Creek and drive an additional mile along the pipeline to the Mackenzie, otherwise carry your boat on your shoulder for that mile. Using the pipeline road lets you see an extra half mile of the Mackenzie, and it's quite a nice piece!

I carried in on the pipeline to the Mackenzie. You reach the river just as it divides into two channels, the right channel being the larger. Both channels drop about fifty feet in a third of a mile. I was on the river at low flow and took the right channel—the big boulders and medium ledges created a tight, narrow steep-creekin' feel like you'd find in the Appalachians—nice class IV water! The neat thing is that the left channel is probably just as good.

When the channels combine the Mac calms down and you'll soon see Walkinshaw Creek enter on the right. It looks kind of fun itself, but not as nice as the "Island Section" of steep creekin' that you'd miss. With the added flow, the good sized Mackenzie heads toward the Lake, two and a half miles away. Though the water was low, the large boulders and small ledges created interesting water between low, blocky rock walls. Nice cedars, too. I think at high flow these rapids would be excellent III-III+ water. There are some constrictions, too, which would amplify the juice. These rapids build and maintain for perhaps a mile.

When you notice the left rock wall rising high, maybe forty feet, get ready for the first portage: Mackenzie Falls. You should eddy out right (easy) and scout and/or portage the two runnable ledges that immediately precede Mackenzie Falls. The Falls itself is interesting and picturesque. There are two channels, the main one being a narrow cleft left of a rocky point, the right being a broad and nearly dry portage route at my level. At low flow the left looked like a scary class V, launching off the lip and falling 15-20 feet into a fifteen foot wide boiling notch. It looked like you'd squirt through. At high flow Mackenzie Falls is probably just a no-think portage. A beauty spot, though, and easily portaged.

The two-thirds of a mile from Mackenzie Falls to the Trans Canadian Highway is more good water—just fun, and it includes a short mini-gorge with twenty feet of rock on either side, an old cedar hanging over the river and mellow water slipping between the walls. Enjoy this scenic spot and then be ready because next the river turns left and the Trans Canadian Highway comes into view. Take out left or right to end the run, portage the tunnel or scout. At low flow it looked feasible to run the tunnel, boofing the final drop far right, but I portaged.

Below the Trans Canadian Highway lies a half mile to Lake Superior, and this section is dominated by three large ledge drops. The first is the most complex, a multi-channeled slide lying a hundred yards below the Highway, IV-IV+ depending on flow. Next comes a seven footer—boofable—class IV. The final drop is a fun, curving slide with a hole at the end. This drop occurs just before the takeout on the Lake and is class III-IV. All of these three ledges are easily scouted or portaged.

The way I see it, this river should appeal to lots of paddlers of advanced skills. Most of the water is enjoyable III up to the Trans Canadian Highway and scouting and portaging are easy. Access is pretty good, and the river quite scenic. Expert boaters will enjoy the steep creekin' Island Section and the ledges below the Highway. "Hardened hard men with Bavarian blood" will enjoy running the Tunnel and maybe Mackenzie Falls at low flow, or at least they'll enjoy a good "gumping." In a word, the Mackenzie is a "gem."

I know that I look forward to seeing this run at higher water. I think there may be more whitewater gold in the Mackenzie's hills—topo maps show excellent gradient on both the Mackenzie and little Walkinshaw Creek several miles above this section, but road access looks poor. Time for an exploratory!!

LENGTH: 3 MILES

CLASS: II-IV

SUMMER: SOME?

QUICK DESCRIPTION: VARIETY, GOOD CONTINUOUS, LEDGES

PUT-IN: PIPELINE CROSSING 2 MILES EAST OF MACKENZIE STATION

TAKE-OUT: LAKE SUPERIOR, CARRY OUT RIGHT TO DIRT ROAD ON RAILROAD TRACKS

CURRENT RIVER

SECTION: I
LENGTH: 1 MILE
CLASS: III–V
SUMMER: RARE
QUICK DESCRIPTION: LEDGES, SLIDES, SOLDIER'S HOLE
PUT-IN: TROWBRIDGE FALLS CAMPGROUND, NEAR FOOTBRIDGE
TAKE-OUT: HIGHWAY 11 / 17

SECTION: II
LENGTH: 1.5 MILES
CLASS: II–III
SUMMER: RARE
QUICK DESCRIPTION: EASY BOULDERBED, SLALOM SITE
PUT-IN: HIGHWAY 11/17
TAKE-OUT: BLACK BAY ROAD AT SOUTH END OF CENTENNIAL PARK

The Current is the main "town" run of the Thunder Bay area, but this doesn't mean it's overly developed or industrial. The river corridor is largely protected by parks and is pretty nice for being in a town.

SECTION I

Section I, from Trowbridge Falls to the Trans Canadian Highway, has some good stuff and there's camping available near the put-in. Putting in at Trowbridge Falls gives you several class III-IV ledges and slides right off the bat, followed by nice continuous water.

Do take care to eddy out on the right when the continuous stuff slides out of sight. Ted Halpern didn't and got to run through class IV-V Soldier's Hole without ever having seen it. It should be noted that Ted was the fifth boater to try to make a four boat eddy!

Soldier's Hole can be portaged on the right if desired, and you'll then begin the regular Current run (Section II) as you pass under the Trans Canadian Highway bridge.

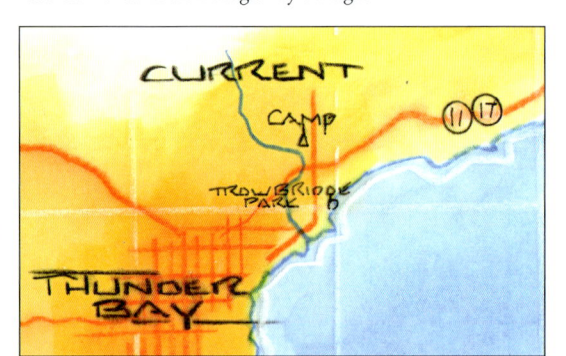

SECTION II

This commonly paddled stretch contains class II and III water and is about a mile and a half long starting at the Highway 11/17 bridge.

You will paddle through Centennial Park and under a bridge there that marks the best rapid on the lower run. There's parking near the bridge and this is the site of the annual Current River slalom, usually held during Memorial Day weekend. The rapid here has a couple of holes and a few nice waves—it's possible to get enders here at some levels on the waves.

Another two-thirds mile of class II brings you to the takeout on river left just above the Black Bay Road bridge. To reach the takeout from the Highway 11/17 put-in, go east over the Current and turn right on Highway 11B/17B (also called Hodder Ave.) and then drive south on Hodder Ave. to the first four way stop. That's Black Bay Road which you then take right to the Current. The road to the Centennial Park slalom site turns right (north) off of Black Bay Road just before you reach the Current on river left.

A group of boaters scout just below Soldier Hole. ©2006 Doug Nelson

Another section of whitewater exists on the upper Current, from where the Current leaves Onion Lake to a couple miles south of Stepstone. This section apparently contains intermittent class II and III rapids, but I have yet to see this run.

Thunder Bay Rivers

I'm certainly no expert on the Canadian rivers in the Thunder Bay area. Yet the brief forays I've managed so far make me plan to return. There are several reasons for giving thought to paddling in the Thunder Bay area. First, it's close! If you paddle the Pigeon, you're less than fifty miles from Thunder Bay and even closer than that to the Pine River. Second, the idea of chasing the snowmelt north applies. Peak runoff in the Thunder Bay area is behind that in Minnesota. Third, the Canadian rivers are in some cases larger or dam-controlled and this extends their season for paddling. Fourth, visiting Canada is an interesting change of culture—really!! Cookies are "biscuits" in Canada—you should know that much to boat here. Fifth, there are outstanding rivers in Canada, examples being the Jackpine and the Mackenzie.

I've described those runs with which I'm best acquainted in my usual format, but there are a few others which I'd like to at least mention briefly.

PINE RIVER

Put in off Ontario Provincial Highway 597 approximately four miles northwest of Cloud Lake and take out on Highway 597 about four miles west southwest of Cloud Lake. I've done this run once at low water. There were some longish sections of ledges and boulderbed that were class II-III, a series of scrapey, rapidly dropping shelves and a nice eight foot ledge. In addition to this run, the Pine below Provincial Highway 61 appears to have scattered ledges and a long stretch of continuous boulderbed during the last mile to Lake Superior.

MCINTYRE RIVER

I haven't done this run yet, but it's supposed to contain quite a good run right near Thunder Bay. The rapids sound as though they're frequent ledges of moderate size and that they extend right to Lakehead University, the takeout, at the Highway 130 bridge. To put in, a couple of possibilities are a road that goes west from North McIntyre, branching off of Highway 102, giving a run of about 5 miles, or putting in at one of the other secondary bridges closer to town, resulting in a shorter run. The river is a small one, and runs for only a short time.

BLACK STURGEON

Another river I've only heard about, it's supposed to contain a nice section with playspots. I have, however, spent much of a dreary day checking out possible put-ins and takeouts. I saw a surprisingly big river, but little whitewater. On returning home, a map check showed that the most likely candidate for the run I'd heard vague compliments of was a four mile section running from Black Sturgeon Lake to Nonwatin Lake. The Black Sturgeon drops about a hundred feet over this section and this could produce some nice rapids. Road access is convenient for the put-in at the outlet of Black Sturgeon Lake and at a takeout on Nonwatin Lake just south of where the Black Sturgeon enters the lake. The put-in is about 30 miles up the gravel "Black Sturgeon Road" from the Trans Canadian Highway, probably 70 miles from Thunder Bay.

Here are a few runs for which I have even less information, in some cases just the name!

SLATE RIVER

Small intermediate run west of town.

WHITEFISH RIVER

Intermediate run twenty miles west of Thunder Bay.

MOOSELAND RIVER-GULL RIVER

A multi-day wilderness whitewater trip that apparently starts where Provincial Highway 811 crosses the Mooseland River about eighty miles north of Thunder Bay. The run continues on the Gull River to where Provincial Highway 527 crosses the Gull just west of Lake Nipigon. This run is supposed to contain sections of class III+ whitewater, which I can believe after looking at a topo map of the area.

THUNDER BAY RIVERS

From my limited experience, I can only provide a somewhat sketchy glimpse of the whitewater of the area. For more information I'd recommend contacting the following very active club and store:

LAKEHEAD UNIVERSITY CLUB OF KAYAKERS

WEBSITE:
http://flash.lakeheadu.ca/~luck/

WILDERNESS SUPPLY COMPANY, LTD

244 PEARL ST. S.
THUNDER BAY, ONTARIO
P7B 1E4
TEL: 807-684-9555
FAX: 807-344-9457

623 FERRY RD.
WINNIPEG, MANITOBA
R3H 0T4
TEL: 204-783-9555
FAX: 204-779-4922
WEBSITE:
http://www.wildernesssupply.ca/

JACK PINE RIVER

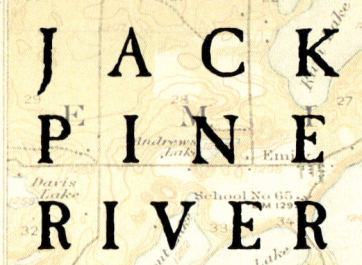

LENGTH: 14 MILES*

CLASS: III–IV

SUMMER: RARE

QUICK DESCRIPTION: LAKES, SCENIC CLIFFS, GREAT RAPIDS

PUT-IN: CENTRAL L.-BY DIRT ROAD LEAVING 11 / 17 2 MI. E. OZONE CRK

TAKE-OUT: HIGHWAY 11 / 17 BRIDGE OR LAKE SUPERIOR, DIRT RD. TO MOUTH

* May be broken into shorter sections

Al Sabean, Jackpine River.   ©2006 Mike Cotten

OK, OK, I don't know a lot about the Canadian Shore rivers–I need to return and paddle some more here, and I will, gladly. I do know of one river that should be talked about–the Jackpine. I had heard tales of the Jackpine for several years; comparisons were made with the Presque Isle. That was enough for me–I had to see it, as I consider the Presque Isle a great run.

During the spring of 1986 Dan Theis and I finally got to this gem hidden in the "bush" east of Nipigon. It was worth every effort we made to do the run. I've been back many times since, and it's one of those rivers I'd like to see every spring. What makes it special is the exceptional combination of wilderness, fine and varied whitewater and spectacular scenery. I'll describe it in some detail, as I think you'll very much want to see it.

The Jackpine run is about 14 miles long extending from a put-in at Central Lake to a takeout on the shores of Lake Superior's Nipigon Bay. As with many runs in this book access is available to break the run into two segments. This access can be used to eliminate some flatwater paddling as well.

Putting in where the dirt road first comes close to Central Lake, you must paddle about a mile to the south end of the lake. The lake may still have substantial ice on it, even when the river is running high. There's a runnable dam as you leave the lake. You then paddle more flatwater, then another ledge, more flatwater, then another ledge. These enjoyable class III/IV drops take you about a half-mile below Central Lake.

After this last ledge, very enjoyable class II-III boulderbed runs through an intimate forest. It appears that some of the larger boulders here were long ago removed from the riverbed and placed on shore. I believe this was done to make floating logs downriver easier. About two-thirds mile of this nice boulderbed leads to a pretty thirty-foot falls tucked into the woods. You can eddyout and carry on the right side, but be cautious; the eddy isn't huge.

Returning to the river, a little playspot follows the falls; then the river begins meandering. The Jackpine comes close to the shuttle road shortly below the falls, making it possible to do a short run on the upper section. The next three miles include swiftwater, lakes and two or three short class III gorges before hitting a two mile long lake. The road is close to the river for a couple of miles before this two mile long flatwater stretch, but then pulls away from the river, now a lake. The complete upper run takes out before doing this skinny lake.

The lower section contains the better whitewater and is frequently run by itself. You may drive in on the shuttle road until you're next to the lower lake and put in or even better, park closer to the south end of the lake and carry down a quarter mile path that eliminates quite a bit of paddling on the lake.

However you get to this lake you must paddle to the end of it and again encounter a dam which is runnable. In fact, on a spring trip in 1996 we found this spot to be an incredible ender site, though I don't remember it being so good on previous trips. Perhaps it was altered by the flood of '96. High rock "questas" (mesa-like formations) rise on your right. These spectacular plateaus, the Kama Hills, will parallel the river for many miles now. Below the lake, the rapids are easy for about a mile, then comes a half-mile burst of good class III-IV whitewater.

Once again the river calms and you are able to enjoy the beauty of paddling a conifer-shaded river with high cliffs towering a half- mile to your right. Numerous pristine creeks spill down from the Kama Hills to enter on the river right—sometimes you can see waterfalls or icefalls tumbling off the high plateaus. The rocky cliffs reach as high as 700 feet over river level.

After you've gone about four miles below the long lake, you will probably see a somewhat larger waterfall or icefall high on the right. When you are even with this waterfall, you will have reached The Portal.

The Portal is a class V constriction in the Jackpine where huge boulders have rolled down from the cliffs and blocked the river. It pours over a couple steep drops and then squirts through a door-like slot, a stunning view. The lead-in to this slot is heavy so it's best to get out on river right about a hundred yards above The Portal. A portage/scouting trail of sorts exists over and around the big boulders on the right shore. If you choose to portage The Portal, lower your boats carefully and put in below The Portal—now comes the whitewater I've been waiting for!

The Jackpine has changed its gradient radically at The Portal and charges headlong toward Lake Superior. For the next two miles to the Trans Canada Highway it roars around and over big boulders and ledges to create continuous III-III+ water, with stretches becoming continuous IV at high water. The quarter mile below The Portal is one of the best sections, but there are many other places where high water brings a nonstop blizzard of waves and holes. It's outstanding!! I've caught it high twice, moderate several times and low a couple times: high is definitely great and moderate is nice, even low is fun, but the push is gone. High water requires expert skill; moderate has less push, more eddies and allows advanced paddlers to have fun—there's even some playing. But at high flow, running the river is all you need.

Al Sabean eddies below The Portal. ©2006 Mike Cotten

In the spring of 1996 an incredible flood altered the last mile or so of the Jackpine. The river right bluffs just upstream of the highway show the effects of a landslide initiated by this flood. Most of the rapids escaped without radical change, but the mouth of the river was reworked and a new channel opened. It was very impressive to see a river so changed.

As all good things must, it ends. As you near the Trans Canada Highway, the slam bang river eases a bit. Some people take out at the bridge, but it's fun to continue to the Lake, a half mile away. The mouth of the Jackpine is a magical place—you'll see islands out in Nipigon Bay, birds picking over the Jackpine's waters as they slip into Lake Superior, maybe even some ice on the bay.

When I heard of this river, it was compared to the Presque Isle—I find that a good comparison: similar in size and length, both include rustic swiftwater, big ledges that stand by themselves, fine scenery and both rivers are crowned by a couple miles of "hog wild" continuous whitewater fun. And what can beat camping on the beach at the mouth of either run after a great day of paddling?

SOUTH SHORE OF LAKE SUPERIOR

Stretching from Duluth to Marquette the shores of Lake Superior show lots of diversity. In general the South Shore seems more "mellow" and not as spectacular as the North Shore. Not so many cliffs, but lots of sand beaches. Not so many pine and spruce, but more maple and other hardwoods and hemlock. Not so many spectacular falls and state parks, but fewer tourists and more secret beauty spots. Many times in spring it's even ten degrees warmer on the South Shore than on the North Shore! Both shores, however, share the unique and unifying mystery of Lake Superior.

The South Shore runs usually break up a couple of weeks earlier than the North Shore rivers and are scattered in "pockets" of whitewater rather than being laid out uniformly along the coast. Many rivers that enter Lake Superior along its South Shore are pretty flat, and much of the whitewater even on the better runs is a few miles from the Lake. The main "pockets" of whitewater are around Superior, Mellen, Ironwood and L'Anse, with the better runs being in Michigan's Upper Peninsula, the U.P.

Most, but not all, of the South Shore runs are less intense than the North Shore runs. The bedrock often includes stretches of conglomerate that erodes into bizarre, beautiful and bodacious rapids. Another feature of the South Shore that I like is brought about by the absence of a "coastal highway" such as Highway 61 in Minnesota. This means the rivers are off the beaten track and less "touristy."

The communities are more backwoods and simple. It's fun to eat pasties and talk to "Yuppers" (not Yuppies!!!) in the U.P. and there are lots of little parks to camp at for free. The North and South Shores are an interesting and complementary pair of wonders.

SOUTH SHORE OF LAKE SUPERIOR

Manabezho Falls, Presque Isle River, in Michigan's Upper Penninsula. ©2006 Doug Nelson

NEMADJI AND BLACK RIVER

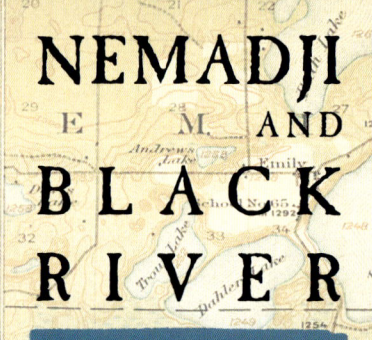

NEMADJI RIVER

LENGTH: 9 MILES

SUMMER: FREQUENT

QUICK DESCRIPTION: BOAT BUSTER'S DREAM STREAM

PUT-IN: COUNTY W BRIDGE, 1 MILE S OF COUNTY C NEAR OMBERG ROAD

TAKE-OUT: WISCONSIN HWY 35 NEAR OMBERG ROAD

BLACK RIVER

NEAR SUPERIOR WISCONSIN

LENGTH: 3.5 MILES

CLASS: II–III

SUMMER: RARE

QUICK DESCRIPTION: EASY RAPIDS, PRETTY FALLS, SMALL

PUT-IN: BASE OF LITTLE MANITOU FALLS, 0.25 MILE EAST OF WISC. 35

TAKE-OUT: RAILROAD TRESTLE HIKE OUT TO STATION ROAD

Don't let the sluggish, marshy appearance at the put-in fool you. This run is a serious test of physical and mental endurance, not for the faint of heart or weak of spirit. After an epic ordeal involving the solo first descent of "Beaver Dam Falls," long time friend and all around river rat "Buff Joe" returned home to his wife sporting bandages on his cerebellum and bruises on his sizeable ego. Do not underestimate the difficulty of the Nemadji! Tricky currents and logs abound. Best to first attempt this run at low summer flows, where you can boat scout many of the features.

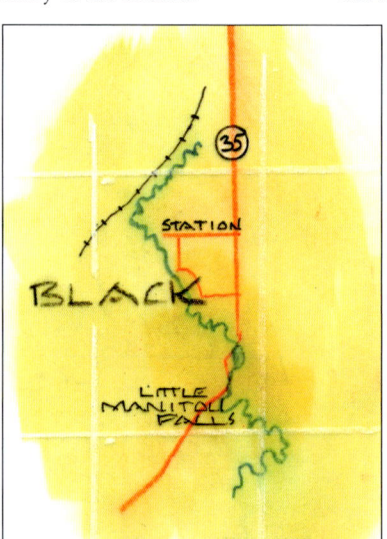

While you won't be able to see much from the road, the fun starts soon enough, just around a few bends, beginning with "Mud Slide," a smallish drop which kicks off a multi-mile extravaganza of interesting water continually increasing in fun and difficulty. The climax comes at beautiful "Beaver Dam Falls." The lead in to this maelstrom comes abruptly, so it is best to get out to scout on the left before the clay banks become too high. After a respite, the bedrock surprisingly emerges from the clay and some abrupt ledge-like drops follow. All but one of these have been run at lower levels. For my sake, please use caution, and scout carefully for downed wood.

You know the action will soon be over when you pass the Black River confluence. Perhaps now, a quiet evening of reflection camping out on the pebble beaches of historic Wisconsin Point. If you have time and energy left, be sure to visit 165 foot Big Manitou Falls in Pattison State Park just south of the put-in.

Upper Nemadji: The mysterious eight mile Upper section from Hwy 23 to County W still awaits exploration. It is rumored to have one sizeable falls.

The tiny Black,

fifteen miles south of Superior, boasts the tallest waterfall in Wisconsin, Big Manitou Falls. Big Manitou drops 165 feet into a short, enchanting gorge, the centerpiece of Pattison State Park. An interesting run can be done by putting in about a mile upstream of Big Manitou Falls at the base of Little Manitou Falls, a twenty footer also in Pattison State Park.

A trail coming in to Little Manitou from Wisconsin Highway 35 allows easy access. The half mile from Little Manitou to Interfalls Lake contains some class II and a class III ledge. Paddle across Interfalls Lake a half mile to the Highway 35 bridge, take out on the left and portage Big Manitou on the left.

As you wander along the left gorge rim you'll find a trail that descends into the gorge. The closer you can put in to the base of Big Manitou, the better water you'll get to run. A little III right below Big Manitou quickly fades to class II and then I. The whitewater here is by no means exceptional, but it is a pretty place to explore and can easily be included with a run on the Amnicon, which certainly is runnable if the little Black is boatable.

To reach the takeout, drive north on Wisconsin 35 just under two miles from Big Manitou and turn west on "Station Road." In a mile this road will lead you to a railroad track, which will be your takeout. On the river, proceed 1.5-2 miles on the Black downstream of Big Manitou Falls. You'll encounter a few small class I-II ledges along the way. Climb out of the valley on the right side at the railroad trestle and follow the tracks to your car.

Don't confuse the Black near Superior with the Black in the Upper Peninsula or the Black in southern Wisconsin. This Black is not a primo whitewater run, but a cute little river and a chance to do some exploring relatively close to home.

The Amnicon

is a river that caught my attention during the awful drought of 1977. Every weekend we'd go boating on the Vermilion in northern Minnesota or at Taylor's Falls on the St. Croix, and every week the rivers

AMNICON RIVER

LENGTH:	2 MILES
CLASS:	II–IV
SUMMER:	RARE
QUICK DESCRIPTION:	EASY ABOVE AMNICON FALLS STATE PARK
PUT-IN:	U.S. 53 BRIDGE
TAKE-OUT:	AMNICON FALLS STATE PARK–YOU CHOOSE WHERE!!

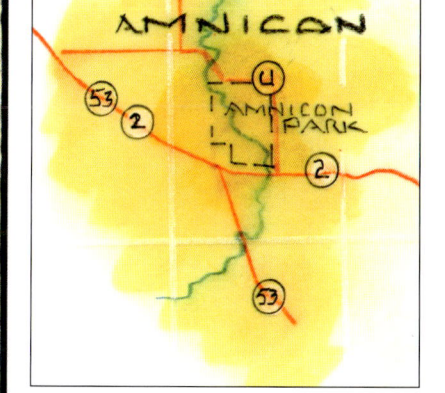

would be lower, scrapier and rockier. It seemed like a better time to hike rivers than to boat them.

Looking at topo maps took Greg Breining, John Wexler and myself to the Amnicon about fifteen miles southeast of Superior, Wisconsin. Greg and I were mesmerized by the falls and rapids in Amnicon Falls State Park and kept wandering downstream. John, on the other hand, wandered upstream. When he returned we made up our minds to return and paddle some day. The rapids and falls in the park plus the "falls" John reported upstream prompted a return when the river was running.

Putting in where U.S. 53 crosses the Amnicon, you can paddle about two miles, taking out in Amnicon Falls State Park. The park authorities have seemed a little unfriendly to boaters and will ticket vehicles parked here that don't display a daily or annual permit. However, during spring runoff there seem to be few people around.

The mile and a half between U.S. 53 and U.S. 2 is easy class I and II boulderbed with the exception of "Wexler's Falls," a good class III. Wexler's Falls is found about a third-mile upstream of U.S. 2 and consists of multiple sloping ledges that produce a drop of maybe 8-9 feet over fifty yards. After passing under U.S. 2, small ledges begin to appear and the whitewater picks up.

The small highway bridge in the park marks the first significant drop, III+ to IV at high flow. This drop can generate a good hydraulic at high flows, as Tom Schellberg discovered. He quickly swam to shore but his boat floated on downriver. Being only a quarter-mile from the falls, I was encouraged to see Pete Cary run his boat up on shore and SPRINT downstream while I helped Tom. He came back smiling and said Tom's boat had washed up on rocks above the falls and that he'd pulled it in. I complimented Pete on his speedy action and he replied, "I didn't think I could save it, but I did want to see it go over the falls!" So things happen in a hurry below the bridge drop.

There's a little calm and then a couple hundred yards of beautiful tight class III as the Amnicon twists and drops over continuous small and medium ledges. This section has some tiny eddies and makes excellent "slalom" practice.

When you see a small footbridge as the Amnicon splits into two channels get out for a look or to take out. Some of the water goes left into the "Snake Pit" to form a tight twisting steep creeking run that contains 3-4 drops in a few hundred yards. If you follow the bulk of the current at the split you'll take the right channel and immediately jag downward over a sharp drop of 15 feet. A tight class IV+ at low flows, this drop becomes an awesome sight at high water, making a portage look mighty good.

Two hundred feet below the footbridge, the Amnicon rumbles down a steep flume that flies off a vertical dropoff. Total elevation loss: 20-25 feet. This has been run at low flow, but the rock shelf downstream of the plunge pool becomes a factor at high flow–so far no one has tried it then. A "swimming hole" below this falls lets boaters regroup before the last "falls," a sloping slide of perhaps nine feet. This is where we've taken out, although I think there could be a bit more I and II water below.

The Amnicon's watershed frequently gets rain at the same time as the Kettle. This circumstance can make for a nice weekend: the fine play water of the Kettle paired with a short, technical run on the Amnicon.

BOIS BRULE RIVER

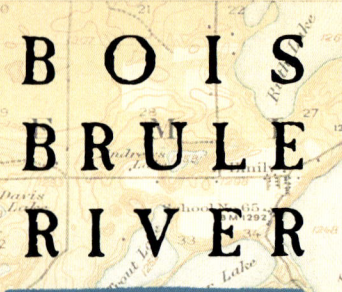

LENGTH: 2.5 MILES

CLASS: I-II+

SUMMER: YES

QUICK DESCRIPTION:
PRETTY, EASY STREAM –
MAY'S LEDGES NICE

PUT-IN:
COPPER RANGE CAMPGROUND
OFF DOUGLAS COUNTY H
NORTH OF BRULE

TAKE-OUT:
CANOE ACCESS ON RIGHT
0.5 MILE DOWNSTREAM FROM
COUNTY FF

The Bois Brule River thirty miles east of Superior, Wisconsin is a favorite of open canoeists, intermediate and beginning kayakists and trout fishermen. During spring one can see a lot of fishermen on this intimate and woodsy run. The run has many possible access points between the Douglas County S bridge over the Brule and Lake Superior, thirty-five miles away.

The put-in for the best whitewater is Copper Range Campground, about four miles north of Brule, Wisconsin on County H. The river between Copper Range Campground and the County FF bridge includes numerous class I rapids and Lenroot Ledges, a good class II. The distance from Copper Range to FF is a couple of miles.

Just downstream of the FF bridge comes far and away the best rapid on the Bois Brule, May Ledges. This series of sharp ledges of medium height rates II+ to III depending on water level. May Ledges can provide some playspots to knowledgeable kayakists and safe thrills to those without a lot of whitewater experience. It's possible to take out at a deluxe landing on river right shortly after May Ledges or you may continue downstream an additional three miles to a landing just south of Wisconsin Highway 13. For those interested in other sections of the Bois Brule, more information can be found in the book, CANOEING THE WILD RIVERS OF NORTHWESTERN WISCONSIN, a guidebook centered on rivers of interest to canoeists.

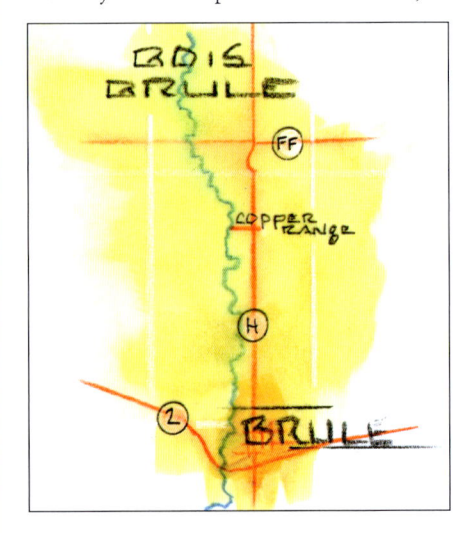

It should also be mentioned that the Brule ("Bogus Brule" to some who are acquainted with the Minnesota version of the Brule near Grand Marais, MN) has headwaters in boggy country which moderates flow noticeably, providing a long season for boating and preventing flooding. This even-tempered nature is evident in the hydrograph found elsewhere in this book. Since the Brule can be run during summer months, canoe and kayak rental is available in Brule, although the kayaks aren't "high performance."

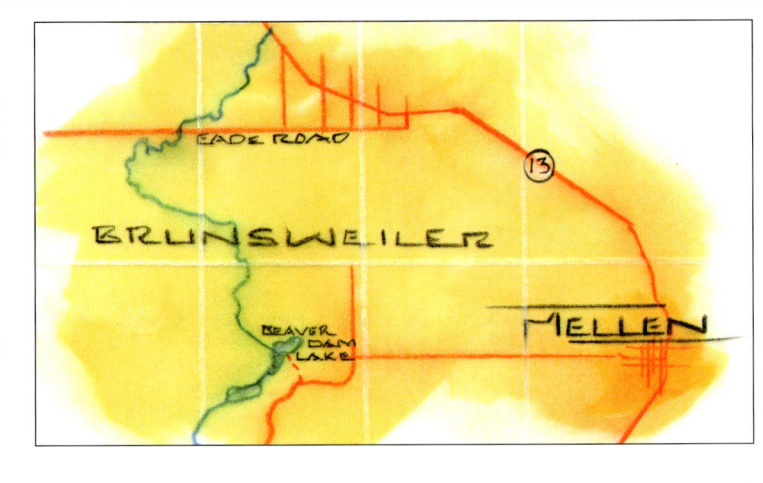

The Brunsweiler River is a

small stream tucked away in the Chequamegon National Forest nine miles west of Mellen, Wisconsin. It's so inconspicuous that there was quite a time lag for me between first hearing of the river and being able to find it on a map. I view the run as one which offers variety to South Shore paddlers, worth doing occasionally, but not the cream of the crop.

Starting at Beaverdam Lake, you portage a small, manually controlled dam on the north side of the lake. Now that you're on the Brunsweiler you won't have to wait long for action because a very narrow gorge appears about a quarter mile from the lake. There are several drops in this short gorge, the largest being a very technical seven foot drop. Some easy boulderbed follows this little IV-IV+ gorge and then the Brunsweiler becomes swiftwater again. About a mile below Beaverdam Lake Forest Road 189 crosses the Brunsweiler. This can make a good alternate put-in for those not wishing to paddle the tight, rocky gorge upstream.

Below the FR 189 bridge, the Brunsweiler heads into a pleasant unpopulated woodland for four miles before reaching a ford crossing on Eade Road, the recommended takeout. During this stretch the Brunsweiler is primarily class I-II boulderbed and swiftwater, punctuated three or four times by sloping ledges which create some class III water. You also pass a few rustic rock outcrop knobs tucked into the peaceful forest. One of the class III ledge drops consists of a series of steps that lasts perhaps sixty yards, the others I recall as being quite short. It's possible to add an additional two miles to the run by continuing to the Ashland County C highway bridge over the Brunsweiler. No additional ledges are encountered in this stretch, but the boulderbed seems a little steeper here.

Taking out at Eade Road may involve carrying your boat a few hundred yards up the hill on the right side, as the condition of the road near the river is poor. Continuing to C allows you to take out at a highway bridge, but the last two miles becomes brushy and the already small Brunsweiler sometimes divides into even smaller channels. If you're looking for a day of solitude on your own little whitewater run, the Brunsweiler will be happy to oblige.

BRUNSWEILER RIVER

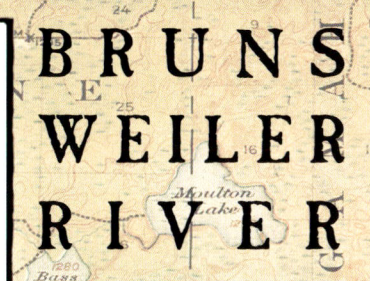

LENGTH: 6 MILES

CLASS: II–IV

SUMMER: RARE

QUICK DESCRIPTION: CANYON EARLY THEN SCATTERED LEDGES

PUT-IN: BEAVER DAM LAKE SIX MILES WEST OF MELLEN

TAKE-OUT: EADE ROAD FORD CROSSING, ASHLAND CO. C – 2 MORE MI.

Henry Kinnucan drops his glass boat down a seven-footer in the canyon. ©2006 Maria Toivio-Kinnucan

Tom Aluni, glad to be past it. ©2006 Maria Toivio-Kinnucan

MELLEN AREA STREAMS

Mellen, Wisconsin has a number of little runs in its vicinity that while not major runs can provide some interesting paddling. I'll describe these runs briefly and leave the reader to investigate further.

Bad River

Several sections exist on the Bad. The one with the most whitewater is reached by going south of Mellen on Wisconsin 13/77 four miles, then turning right on Chequamegon National Forest Road 184, or Conley Road, which comes to the Bad in 1.5 miles.

This section runs about 3.5 miles to a take-out on Ashland County GG where the river approaches close to GG two miles west of Mellen. There is one big drop of note: "Rocket Railroad Falls," a two step ledge drop that rates IV and several smaller sloping ledges. Rocket Railroad Falls is preceeded by a short stretch of rather nice continuous water.

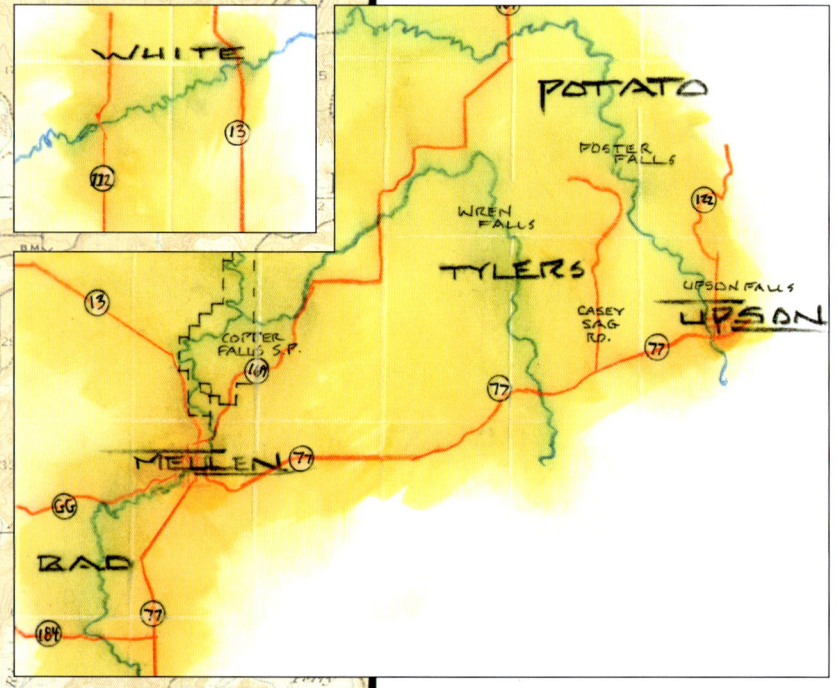

Another section can be done by putting in at the Wisconsin 169 bridge a mile northeast of Mellen and running to Copper Falls State Park. This run contains quite a bit of flatwater and two sections of major (class IV-IV+) water. The first section comes about a mile from the put-in, and is called Red Granite Falls. Red Granite Falls can be reached by a trail from Copper Falls State Park. In a third- mile the Bad races over about five distinct but very closely spaced drops. This can be enjoyed by expert boaters, but results in a portage on the railroad tracks on river left for others.

Another mile or two brings you to Copper Falls, a very picturesque 25-30 footer. Below Copper Falls the Bad squeezes through a narrow and beautiful gorge for a quarter-mile, a gorge made even more scenic by the Tyler Forks River entering the gorge on river right by a waterfall, Brownstone Falls. I haven't paddled the gorge, but looking from the cliffs it appears to be solid class IV water up to where Brownstone Falls spills in. It appears that there is a sharp drop and constriction about two hundred feet above the Tyler Forks juncture. It also appears that you could portage around Copper Falls on the right and then run the gorge. I've heard that park officials frown on climbing in the gorge. Portaging is a different story, right?

Below Brownstone Falls is another quarter-mile of easier water, which appears to have a couple of playspots at small ledges and a spectacular ending as the river emerges from the gorge through Devil's Gate, a drop where the Bad eats its way through high flanking cliffs. Just below Devil's Gate is a footbridge and you may carry to the Copper Falls parking lot on either river right or left, it's probably shorter on the left.

According to another whitewater guidebook, WHITEWATER, QUIETWATER, it's possible to continue on beyond the footbridge to enjoy an intermediate run in a sort of wilderness. I haven't paddled this section. I would like to note here that the book WHITEWATER, QUIETWATER is a good guidebook. It contains runs in the Wolf/Peshtigo area that I haven't included and details on some easier runs that I have omitted.

On the other hand, the guide you are now reading, NORTHWOODS WHITEWATER, is aimed at kayakists interested in the best water in our area, which is generally found near Lake Superior. NORTHWOODS WHITEWATER is an attempt to describe the many fine runs of the Lake Superior area, most of which have received little or no attention. It also is an attempt to preserve some of the lore of our whitewater heritage. So WHITEWATER, QUIETWATER is a good book and can complement my volume, but if you can only afford one, buy mine!

White River

Put in at Wisconsin Highway 112 five miles south of Ashland. The next two-thirds of a mile contains some nice class II-III water according to reports I've had. I haven't done this section. You should look at county maps to take out as soon as possible, as the "White" water comes right at the beginning and then the White meanders.

Tyler Forks

Another small run I haven't done. Put in about 9 miles east of Mellen on Wisconsin Highway 77. After 2-3 miles of easy water, you'll come to Wren Falls. Wren Falls is a very picturesque little falls and runnable. It's about eight feet high and reminds me of a miniature version of the Baptism's Illgen Falls. Wren Falls is followed by about a half-mile of class I-II water before encountering Vogues Road, the takeout. Vogues Road is a moderate quality dirt road accessible from Wisconsin 77 or Wisconsin 169.

Potato River

The Potato is mostly falls, some unrunnable ones near Guerney, a boat banger near Upson at the town park and Foster Falls, located about five miles north of Upson that may be reached by dirt road from either Wisconsin 122 to the east or Casey Sag Road (dirt) to the west. I have scouted some of the river below Foster Falls, and there seems to be some class II whitewater and some rocky drops to portage in the mile below Foster Falls. It looks like a kind of pretty run, but nothing great.

Erik Strahler blasts through Rocket Railroad Falls on the Bad River. ©2006 Erik Strahler

©2006 dan menske

zack banne rge fal ack riv michig

MONTREAL RIVER

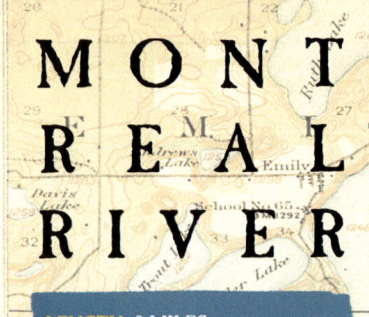

LENGTH: 3 MILES

CLASS: II–III

SUMMER: NOT NOW

QUICK DESCRIPTION: GREAT PLAY WATER IN FINE CANYON

PUT-IN: SAXON FALLS POWERPLANT, OFF IRON COUNTY B

TAKE-OUT: WISCONSIN 122 BRIDGE INTO MICHIGAN

MONTREAL RIVER, GOOD INFO!
DAM 1-715-893-2213
400 CFS MINIMUM! 1000 IS OK.
5000 IS AWESOME!
You can also get West Branch info here!

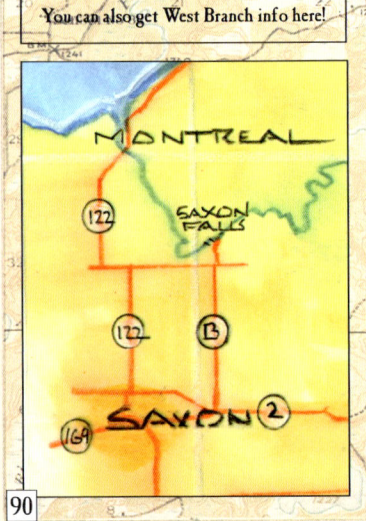

This run is one of the most prized in all the Northwoods. It's short, but beautiful. Generally class II and III, but loaded with fine playspots. It runs during spring snowmelt, but can also run during summer IF Northern States Power (NSP) will release water from the Gile Flowage twenty miles away. To date, the power company has seen fit to do this only on a couple of rare occasions.

The situation is this: the powerplant at Saxon Falls has a limited generating capacity and the reservoir above Saxon Falls is also of small capacity. In spring water spills over the dam, largely coming from the East Fork of the Montreal, as most of the West Fork's water is held back in the Gile Flowage near Montreal, Wisconsin. The West Fork's water is doled out during the low water months of summer, fall and winter to permit the Saxon Falls and Superior Falls hydroelectric plants to generate a small amount of power year round.

Unfortunately, the FERC relicensing on the Saxon Falls dam occurred during 1989 and boaters lost the leverage that this process provides. I still believe that releases for boaters can be obtained IF boaters act in concert and show their appreciation, as large numbers did during releases in 1984 during the Memorial Day weekend and during a Pan Am Cup wildwater race in August. Once you've paddled this river during spring snowmelt you, too, will want to paddle it during summer!

A beautiful day on the Montreal River.   ©2006 Tom Aluni

The run begins with a carry of your boat down a humungous stairway that leaves you deep in the canyon, looking upstream at the Montreal thundering over Saxon Falls, a tiered falls flanked by tall pines. The next two miles will present the paddler with opportunity after opportunity to surf as the Montreal slides over intermittent sheets of bedrock, often sculpted conglomerate.

The first part of the canyon is dark, the rock old and weathered in appearance, the banks cloaked in cedar and pine with an occasional tiny creek spilling in. Then conglomerate begins to show, with especially nice formations in two places: the "Big Ear" on the left side (Wisconsin) early in the canyon and the "Devil's Throne" spires on the right (Michigan) which signals that the canyon will soon open up.

In addition to the abundance of surfing waves, a good hole is found at the base of the Big Ear and another more serious hole is found about a quarter mile below the Devil's Throne, on the left. This second hole has resulted in a few swims at high flows and you may want to avoid it then. The run-out below this hole contains a huge eddy on the right, a jet speed surfing wave next to the eddy and then an ominous narrows where the water is still but swirly and deep.

WEST FORK OF THE MONTREAL

LENGTH: 3 MILES

CLASS: II–IV

SUMMER: NOT NOW

QUICK DESCRIPTION: DAM-CONTROLLED, FINE RAPIDS, RARE

PUT-IN: ROCK CUT FALLS- ACCESSED BY POWERLINE 2 MILES N. OF MONTREAL

TAKE-OUT: U.S. 2 BRIDGE

Here the Montreal squeezes out of the confines of its canyon and begins a transition as the river leaves the narrows, splits around a small island and heads into a broader and shallower canyon. Below the little island the river steps down many regular ledges of small to medium height; the largest is probably four feet high. No more conglomerate, but now there are many holes to sidesurf, with a nice one just below the small island, more on the left below the island. A couple of "blocks" below the island you'll encounter one of the largest steps, if you run it on the left–I prefer this route. Then a bit of peace, but soon some lovely sidesurfers on the left and in the center, then a swinging drop set on a curve to the left with a nice wave at the end, a last burst of ledges and the riffles break out.

It's all over now except for a swift two-thirds of a mile to Wisconsin Highway 122 bridge into Michigan, where you take out. Downstream lie the Superior Falls dam, powerplant and the falls itself, a beauty. These are best checked out by hiking along the right (Michigan) side.

There are a few general comments I'd like to make. First, this is a fine play river with water that all intermediates and experts will enjoy in a scenic canyon. Second, the more or less continuous whitewater can make boat rescue a lengthy process in the event of a swim. This, combined with the steep walls, has gotten boaters separated from their craft. It's not always easy to walk downstream two hundred yards to your boat. This means only that it's good to have a group mentality here, perhaps watching over less experienced boaters more than the difficulty of the water would suggest. Not a good run for teams of novices to practice synchronized swimming!

Third, think about how to convince the power company to have a release or two during the summer!! A last suggestion, and one that I'm being generous to make, is that you might enjoy camping at Little Girl Point, a Gogebic County Park in Michigan. It's easily reached from the takeout by driving across the Montreal into Michigan and continuing for about six miles. It's a simple place, a few pulloffs with picnic tables, outhouses, a sand beach and a picture perfect view of Lake Superior and the hills east, towards the Black. Camping here is a nice end to a fun day on the Montreal.

The West Fork of the Montreal

originates, for all intents and purposes, at the Gile Flowage a half mile south of Wisconsin Highway 77 in the town of Montreal. It's mostly a curse and rarely a blessing, as most dams are, that the power company (Xcel Energy) regulates the flow. Once this river ran in accord with the seasons, but now it's screwed up. Yet, the run is so fine that it was used as a Pan Am Cup wildwater course in 1984, is so fine that it holds the record for my earliest river put-in (about 5:30 a.m. in predawn fog as we knew the river would be dry by 8:30), is so fine that I jerk my head whenever I cross it on U.S. 2 or Wisconsin 77 to see if it's boatable, but usually all I see is the steady flow of about 100 CFS that trucks water down to the Saxon Falls powerplant.

There are two times when you stand a better than average chance of seeing it running: peak of snowmelt and October. If the snowmelt is really heavy, the Gile Flowage may rise to levels that threaten to flood U.S. 51 on its east flank and they'll spill water, also a little water will come in from the banks. In October there's sometimes a drawdown of the Gile Flowage to prepare for the next spring's runoff–this can mean a chance to boat it, as I did one Columbus Day with Tom Schellberg, beneath a canopy of yellow, orange and gold sugar maples blazing against a blue sky. In fact, my cruise during the August 1984 Pan Am release was equally memorable: bathtub warm, shaded by those same maples, green and lush. If boaters succeed in getting water releases for the Montreal Canyon, the West Fork will run, too, so let's work on getting scheduled releases.

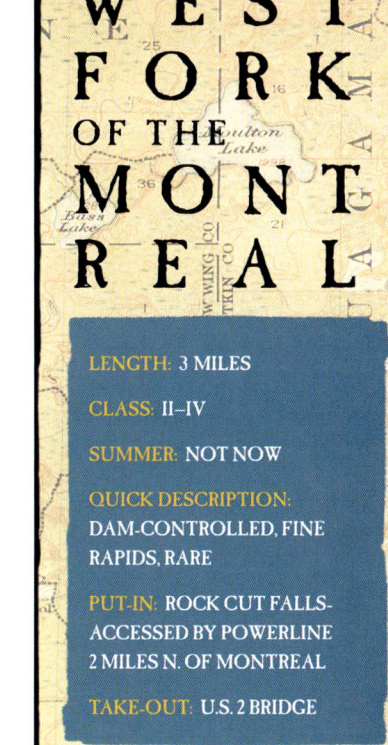

As for the run, if you start at the Gile Flowage, you'll be treated to a short, narrow mini-canyon holding one drop with a powerful, recirculating reversal. There's a ski trail that goes up from Wisconsin 77 to look at

91

it–park at the Montreal Town building near the Highway 77 bridge. However, from Highway 77 the next two miles is simply flatwater, so I prefer to carry in just where the West Fork runs into the Penokee Range hills, about one and a half to two miles north of Montreal. Walk in to an old farm clearing or along a powerline cut from the small dirt road that runs about a quarter-mile west of the West Fork. This will bring you to the crux rapid of the run, a steep, constricted flume as the West Fork pinches up against a rock wall on its left and goes under an old railroad bridge, now a four wheel drive trail (the Iron Horse Trail).

Some paddlers refer to this wonderful two hundred yard long class IV as "Railroad Rapids" because of the bridge, but I prefer the locals' name for it, Rock Cut Falls. Whatever the name, several sharp narrow drops in quick succession make the paddler churn his way through some hefty holes–wildwater indeed! A hundred yards of confined "holy water" eases slightly at the railroad bridge, then takes off for a few more shots–I love it!

Following Rock Cut, the river broadens a bit and hurries down some pretty steep boulderbed–don't broach. Okay, now be lively because about a half mile from the railroad bridge you'll encounter a nifty double ledge, class III-IV, scout left. This ledge snared an open boat from Missouri once, which we left stranded, coming back to retrieve it an hour or two later when the river was dry again.

The next couple miles are easier, picking up with some nice little ledges after you pass under a small bridge where Center Drive crosses the river. About a mile after this bridge, you'll see another bridge, this one leading to the Kimball Town Park on river left. I recommend scouting here as the drop just below this bridge, Maple Sap Falls, changes from class III to IV+ as the water level goes up.

At low flows Maple Sap Falls is just a scrapey sloping double ledge; at moderate flow there's a good hole right and a narrow tongue tight left. At flood, which I've seen, there's an awesome hole at the bottom and I was glad to portage. You have only about a half-mile of river left after Maple Sap Falls, so relax as you approach U.S. 2 and look forward to surfing in the culverts under U.S. 2 and then take out, feeling quite lucky to have found water in the West Fork!

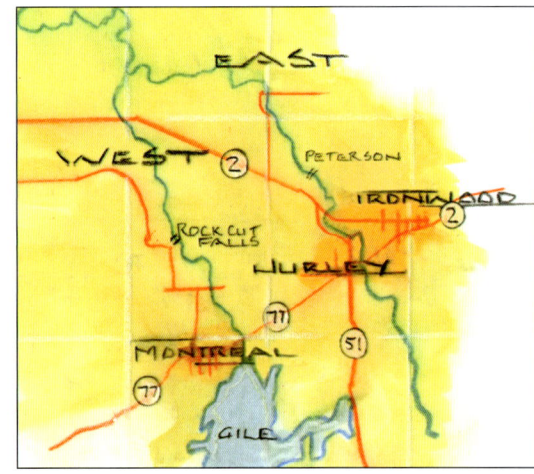

The mini canyon upstream of Hwy 77 on the West Fork.   ©2006 Thomas O'Keefe

UPPER MONTREAL

EAST FORK OF THE MONTREAL

LENGTH: 3 MILES

CLASS: III+

SUMMER: RARE

QUICK DESCRIPTION: CONTINUOUS FINE WATER, TREES, FALLS

PUT-IN: U.S. 2 BRIDGE INTO IRONWOOD

TAKE-OUT: ERICKSON ROAD BRIDGE

So it's spring, the snow's melting fast and you want to do something other than paddle the Montreal canyon yet AGAIN. Well, how's about the Upper Montreal? Get on U. S. 2 and drive to the border between Michigan and Wisconsin and put in!

Don't forget to park your car, though. The Michigan Visitor Information Center just a block into Michigan makes a great parking spot and they have lots of FREE maps. So put in, paddle the winding creek between the trees (your constant companions on this run), past the sewage treatment plant and in about a third of a mile portage around rocky Peterson Falls on the left. Sounds bad, huh? Well if you don't like trees it gets worse, but if you take a liking to natural slaloms you may get into this run.

After portaging the falls the fun starts, high gradient with small ledges and outcrops through the trees. This is just a big creek, so if the runoff isn't cranking it'll get scrapey. If everything's in flood this "big creek" can get mighty white and exciting with some real holes and current rushing through the trees. Yes, exciting. And it gets even more exciting when you know that about a half-mile below broken down Peterson Falls the river leaps over twenty foot Interstate Falls.

There's a house just below Interstate Falls on the right and a portage can be made. The action is nonstop up to the lip. You'll know you're very close when the river broadens and goes over a 3-4 foot ledge–grab an eddy quick!

I've never run Interstate, but I hear tell it has been run. Once past Interstate, the river mellows a bit, but the next two miles it keeps throwing medium and small ledges at you as it winds through the trees. Do eddy-hop; the danger of sweepers is very real, as you've surely noticed.

Claustrophobic types may not like this run, but there's actually quite a bit of fun here.

I'd rate the rapids above Interstate as continuous III when low, pushing IV when high. Below Interstate the river is II with bursts of III when moderate, with the "bursts" getting to be III+ when the river's high.

The takeout is a small bridge (Erickson Road) about three and a half miles from the put-in at U.S. 2. So are you going back to the Montreal Canyon AGAIN?

Eric Platenburg barrels over Interstate Falls. ©2006 Thomas O'Keefe

©2006 dan monskey

zac banne
gorge falls
black river
michigan

93

BLACK RIVER
MICHIGAN'S U.P.

LENGTH: 8.5 MILES

CLASS: II–V

SUMMER: RARE

QUICK DESCRIPTION: EASY TO CONGLOMERATE, HARD BELOW

PUT-IN: NARROWS PICNIC AREA ALONG BLACK RIVER ROAD.–GOGEBIC CO 513

TAKE-OUT: LAKE SUPERIOR, BLACK RIVER HARBOR

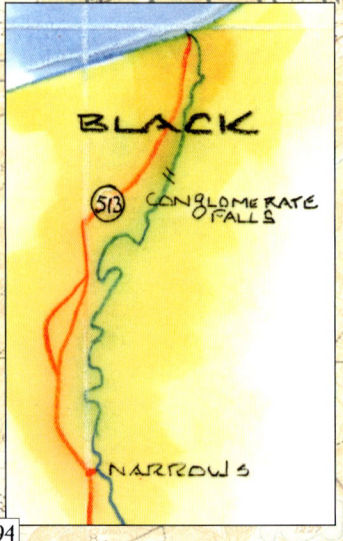

The put-in for mortals is here, just below Gorge Falls. ©2006 Steve Corsi

This has to be one of my favorites on the South Shore for beauty and it can be one of the most exciting rivers around. I think the Black is something of an under-used asset for boaters. With the Montreal and Presque Isle nearby, most boaters find their weekend gone, and the Black just doesn't fit in. That's too bad because it holds a nice intermediate run and a heartpounding expert section in the nine miles from the wayside at The Narrows to the scenic park at Black River Harbor.

Putting in at The Narrows you'll almost immediately encounter a quarter-mile long delightful class III, structured by large boulders. The Narrows at high water made me think of the big boulderbed water found on the Poudre in Colorado or the Cheat in West Virginia. The next couple of miles below The Narrows is swift and easy, becoming class III again as you come even with the Copper Peak ski jump, where the river curves broadly over Chippewa Falls, an open low gradient drop.

Between a half and a quarter-mile past Chippewa Falls, a ford crossing occurs. Carrying out to the Copper Peak Road a third-mile to the left allows a short intermediate run of about three miles from The Narrows. I'd recommend continuing on for intermediates interested in more of the same whitewater.

Beyond the ford crossing the Black becomes very picturesque to my mind, the banks shaded by beautiful hemlocks and pines, the swiftwater broken occasionally by ribs of bedrock creating low ledges and class II-III rapids. A few of these rapids have some rather nice playspots. All in all, the three miles from the ford crossing to Conglomerate Falls is beautiful, friendly and carefree fun.

At Conglomerate Falls the nature of the Black changes to one of power and adrenalin. While I can recommend the six miles from The Narrows to Conglomerate Falls to intermediates, below this point it's experts only, so others should hike out the trail on the left to the nearby Black River Road.

While I would also recommend the Narrows-Conglomerate section at high flow, I would not recommend continuing on the Lower Black at high flow. I've "paddled" the lower section at medium-high flow with John Alt and found it to be mostly good exercise for the legs, carrying my boat. While the Narrows run is good high, the Lower Black is best saved for days when the Montreal and Presque Isle are still runnable, but tailing off. In this manner the Black plays a role similar to the North Shore's Cascade, which also is a good last gasp run as the runoff fades.

I'd urge all paddlers, though, to hike in from the Black River Road to see one or more of the falls of the Lower Black—it's a beautiful hike in through big hemlocks to views of an enchanting river.

If the water levels are right and your skills are good—here's the Lower Black: Conglomerate Falls is a sloping slide that loses twenty or more feet of vertical before smashing into a serious hole—hope you break through, class V. Then, after perhaps a third of a mile you'll encounter a wide sloping bedrock sheet that ends by dropping off sharply—Potawatomi Falls. Portage on trails on the left around this and Gorge Falls, a 20-25 foot falls that's beyond pretty, set next to sculpted cliffs on the right, plunge into a dark and ominous pool.

Potawatomi Falls has been run, by some Hoofers and by Rick Klade and Paul Everson among others. Paul ran sort of in the center and Rick dropped off unintentionally into a narrow cleft on the extreme left, now known as Klade's Coffin.

Gorge Falls has been run as well, with Paul twice having slid into the river just above it in order not to be messed up by the tight constricting hole a hundred feet above Gorge Falls. This falls is one of the most beautiful I've ever seen. I love the smoothly sculpted conglomerate and there's usually an icefall clinging to the river right during the early spring runoff.

For those uninterested in running Potawatomi and Gorge Falls, a very popular option is to park at Gorge Falls and then climb down the steps to the river below. By doing this you get to enjoy a two mile run packed with class IV-V whitewater and an easy portage or two.

Climbing down the stairway below Gorge Falls brings you to a never-never land, the waters momentarily calm and swirling down a conglomerate canyon with caves carved into the sides, creeks and icefalls spilling in. The calm lasts about a third- mile, and then the Black twists right over a class IV- slide. This begins a mile and a half of delightful pool-drop water, containing 6 drops of

John Kiffmeyer wrestles the business end of Gorge Falls.   ©2006 Doug Nelson

zack bannow
gorge falls
black river
michigan

Ed Holladay rides Roller Coaster. ©2006 John Linn

Andy Lovering puts in below Sandstone Falls. ©2006 Steve Corsi

class IV-V nature before you encounter Rainbow Falls.

These half dozen rapids provide lots of excitement. In order they are:

(1) Rollercoaster—a narrow screaming acceleration that terminates in a wave/hole—for a backender go left.

(2) Sandstone Falls—a mighty 15 foot drop followed by undercuts that force the Black to the right while going over small ledges. The "sneak" route is to eddy out on the right and slide down in front of the right undercut on a narrow tongue, while the "man's" route is to go over the big drop. I've seen Marcus Witt and Ross Peterson do the manly run at high flow and watched the mighty power of the Black blast them under the hole at the base of the drop to emerge ten feet downstream.

(3) Surprise—taking the main right chute at an island leads to a nine foot ledge which is cut at a surprising angle.

(4) Under-The-Falls—once again the conglomerate forms an island where most of the river goes right but quite a bit goes left. If run to the left, you descend a fairly straightforward 15 foot slide, but if run to the right you get to choose between blasting three serious holes in succession or going "under the falls" of water spilling back into the right channel from the left channel. Going under the falls is quite a feeling!

(5) Bump and Thump, where the river spreads broadly over a series of small ledges and then constricts at the end.

(6) Jill's Delight is a rapid that again splits at an island with most water going right. The left side is a tight twister and the right side an easy 12 foot slide.

If I didn't get the order right on those, forgive me; you're supposed to be scouting! The last drop, however, is hard to get out of order: Rainbow Falls, a 35 foot slide of dizzying speed that is now run by a growing cadre of brave souls.

Paul is quite the guy—he wanted to run Illgen the first time he saw it. But he listened to good old Mr. Conservative, me, when I said that maybe he should save that for his second run of the Baptism. Ah me, Paul got an early "edition" of this book and wore out the pages. He was the first one who really seemed to enjoy the book and made me feel like I'd accomplished something by putting together a guide to the wonderful rivers our little corner of the world has. I believe he especially noted every place where I said that something hadn't yet been run or where something waited for "future boaters." I digress, but part of this book is to record something of the history of paddling on these rivers, and such a history would certainly be incomplete without Paul. The future boaters are here! But don't worry, the Northwoods will have challenges enough for future "future boaters."

The reason I mention Paul now, when talking about Rainbow Falls, is that of all the falls that Paul has first descents of, this is the one I would most like to do for myself. For many years I've loved the sweet sensual lines of the water accelerating and curving as it slides towards home. This falls looks as though it would be outrageous fun if all went well. With the help and encouragement of some future boaters, maybe one day I'll do it, too. Do take a look at it and see if you aren't hypnotized by it, too. Rainbow Falls is easily portaged on the right down the trail, or the left, the route I've always taken. Both routes offer superb views of the falls.

I've completed the inventory of whitewater on the river, but it is so much more than this. The two miles below Gorge Falls is one of my favorite pieces of river anywhere. With towering hemlocks and white pines, eerie eroded islands of conglomerate, and solitude amidst the roar of rapids, it's a great place to be. And to make matters better, it doesn't take much water to be enjoyed, because the water is channeled through the drops. I've done it a few times solo when you'd think the whitewater season had ended. It's nice if it's sunny and warm to have a little lunch and soak up the day. Ah, again I digress from the guidebook mode.

Below Rainbow there are a few small ledges and then the Black is still as it winds below ponderous pines to Black River Harbor. Check out the beach, you'll like it, or the forest primeval surrounding the Black. Camping at Black River Harbor is relaxing, either on the beach or in the National Forest campground overlooking Lake Superior. With the whitewater, scenery and camping the Black provides, it's a treasure for boaters.

Andy Lichtenheld bears down on the rarely run, and awe inspiring Rainbow Falls. ©2006 Steve Corsi

zack bannow
gorge falls
black river
michigan

PRESQUE ISLE RIVER

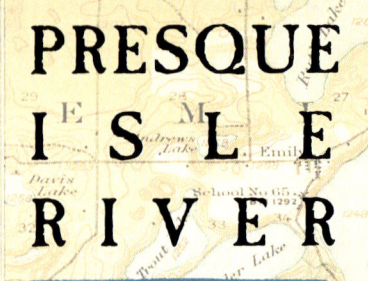

LENGTH: 14 MILES

CLASS: II–IV+

SUMMER: RARE

QUICK DESCRIPTION:
LONG STRETCHES OF III, LEDGES

PUT-IN:
DIRT ROAD ONE MILE WEST OF MICHIGAN 28 BRIDGE

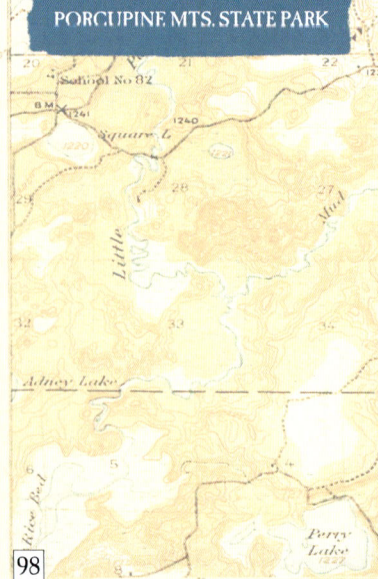

TAKE-OUT:
SOUTH BOUNDARY ROAD, PORCUPINE MTS. STATE PARK

Paul Everson runs Manabezho Falls.   ©2006 Doug Demarest

"Running the Presque Isle is one of the rites of spring," says Dan Theis, one of the Northwoods smoothest kayakists. "What a river!" exclaimed Steve Horn, one of the Northwoods toughest as he finished his initiation, running the Presque Isle at 8.7 feet (that's very high!) as part of the infamous "Death Run."

During the Death Run a group of approximately ten expert kayakists and C-1'ers was ripped apart on the famed "Conglomerate Staircase," a two mile stretch of continuous whitewater that at that level contained continuous class IV blazing between huge stopper holes. That day the river carried a few boats away, left swimmers to hike out and disorganized the rest so much that each paddler reached the South Boundary Road takeout thinking he was either the first or last paddler to finish! There have been so many boats lost on this run at high flow that the logjam near the end will probably become an archeological site for anthropologists studying kayak shards from the Early Kevlar and Middle Rotomolded Polypropylene Age.

Boats have been lost, some destroyed and there have been many swims by competent paddlers. Got your attention? Good, now I can tell you that the danger drops significantly at flows under 8 feet on the gauge, and that gauge readings are very important on this run. The kicker is that the gauge washed away!

The gauge used to be located on river right about 150 feet downstream of the South Boundary Road bridge. The original USGS gauge was washed away by a flood a couple of

98

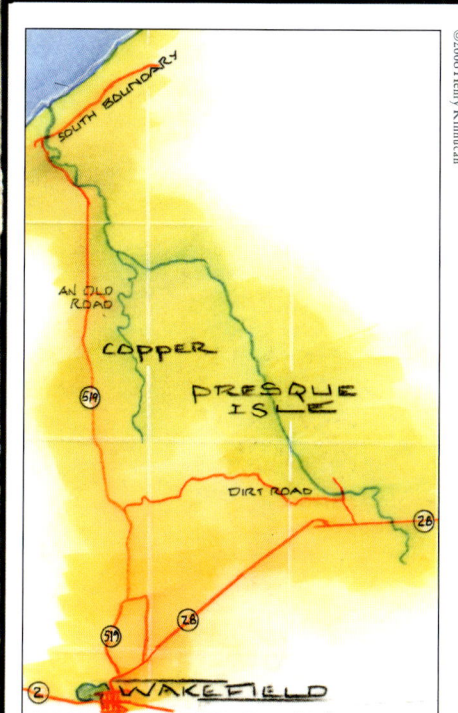

Tom Aluni, Jim Rada and John Alt warm up at the Presque Isle put-in. April, 1980.

years ago, but was replaced by one of the Hoofers. According to Mike Hermann, the new gauge was positioned with the aid of scratch marks in the rocks that recorded where the 8 or 9 foot level was. This gauge seemed to read about the same as the old one. Unfortunately, floods blew out the gauge again and for a couple of years there was no gauge on the river.

During the summer of 1996 I decided to remedy the situation by painting a gauge on the downstream river right pier of the South Boundary Road bridge. I was in a quandary as to how to mark the gauge so I did it two ways: On the upstream end of the lines are numbers giving the depth of the river at the pier and on the downstream side are numbers giving the best match I could make with the old gauge. I'm probably a sentimentalist but I think it sounds better to say I ran the Presque Isle at "eight feet" than at three feet. It probably won't match the old gauge, but it preserves some history. In any case, there's no history for the new gauge and all flows mentioned in this description refer to the old gauge, which is part of history. Boaters will just have to gradually switch over.

Editor's note: Add 1/2 foot to South Boundary Road's Boat Buster Guage. This equals the levels Jim mentions in his description. Also, Check the AW or USGS site for the U.P. Black's level; it's just next door to the Presque Isle.

The highest run I'm aware of was at approximately 9 feet on the old gauge by John Alt and myself, aided by John Wexler doing a moped shuttle. The river was amazing, portages many and the Conglomerate Staircase a big rollercoaster, with many holes washed out. At the Death Run level of 8.7, which I've done a few times, there are ferocious holes hidden among big waves. At 8.3 the pressure has dropped and the river becomes more manageable, at 8.0 the Conglomerate Staircase is fun but straightforward III, below 8.0 people can't imagine the adrenalin of a Death Run. Boating can be enjoyed on the river with some scraping down to about 7.3. These were all numbers from the old gauge and now new experiences will have to record what numbers match these conditions with the new "Boat Buster" gauge.

Parts of the river were first boated in the mid-70's by groups led by Fred Young. Fred described the river at high water as "nothing but six foot deep holes." In 1977 I got my first taste of the Presque Isle with Tom Aluni, Pete Cary and Lorene Vedder and was hooked, returning weekend after weekend. Now it's one of the three Northwoods rivers I try to do every spring along with Minnesota's Devil's Track and Canada's Jackpine.

A classic all day run starts either at the Michigan 28 bridge or at a broken down bridge reached by going one mile west on Michigan 28 from the Presque Isle, then turning north on a dirt road that comes to the river in about a mile. Putting in at the broken bridge can save two miles of flatwater, but in early spring the dirt road can be totally covered with snow. It's about 15 miles from Highway 28 to South Boundary Road, 13 miles from the broken bridge to South Boundary Road.

There are three other access points for shorter runs. One is a logging road that splits east off Highway 519 about five miles north of Thomaston. This road

zack bannow
gorge falls
black river
michigan

Jimbo passes a hole on Triple Drop. ©2006 Karen Jenson

A brave C-1'er runs Nokomis Falls. ©2006 Mike Cotten

then meanders for another five miles before crossing the Presque Isle at the "Steiger Bridge." The Steiger Bridge is the usual lunch stop for paddlers doing the whole run. Putting in at the Steiger Bridge places you six or seven miles from the South Boundary Road takeout. Packed into these miles are the Presque Isle Canyon, the Conglomerate Staircase and a playboating finale. I've used this logging road put-in several times, and if it's open it makes for a lot less flatwater.

However, I'll note three things about this access: the road may be snowed in during peak flow in April, the road can be muddy and require high clearance and there's a gate that might be locked. Until lately, the gate has rarely been locked. The key for the gate was allegedly available from Steiger Building Supply along U.S. 2 on the east side of Bessemer. I think that Steiger's closes at noon on Saturdays. However, now word has it that due to some type of lawsuit involving a snowmobile or ATV accident, Steiger's has been locking the gate and no key is available.

Another means of access is to paddle in on Copper Creek, which joins the Presque Isle towards the end of the Conglomerate Staircase. I'll describe the Copper Creek run separately, but this requires a carry-in through the woods.

The last access point is a road branching east off Highway 519 just after the road passes a big wooden sign for Porcupine Mountains State Park. This little side road is about two and a half miles south of South Boundary Road. Here you can carry in to the river by walking about a mile on the road. This is a fairly popular option, because it allows a boater to paddle the fun playwater below Lepisto Falls, giving a 3.5 mile run.

Now let's talk about the river itself, starting from the top. Putting in at the broken down bridge, the first 2.5 miles will be swiftwater, with a few class II rapids thrown in along the way, some containing playspots. This nice warmup readies you for the first rapid of significance, S Curve, a III. S Curve is identified as a rapid that starts easy, then bends left, narrowing and dropping sharply. There's a pop-up/ender spot at the narrows.

Below S Curve the Presque Isle is calm again for a couple hundred yards before splitting into two channels. Take the right channel and then look downstream. See a horizon line? That's Minnewawa, a IV-IV+ that should be scouted from the right bank. The first drop of Minnewawa flushes through pretty well, but pushes boaters right. I've seen a boater or two stuck in the eddy on the right. The second stage of drop forms the finest ender spot I know of in the Northwoods. Too bad the water's usually ice cold!

La Pisto. ©2006 Mike Cotten

Jim Rada surfs the last wave of Zoom Flume before Lake Superior. ©2006 Doug Nelson

A quarter-mile beyond Minnewawa, whitewater breaks out again and the river divides. Generally work right, so that you're in the right-most channel eventually. The intensity of the water will change from II to III. Eddyhop, looking for Nimikon Falls, class IV-IV+, about 200 yards downstream from the beginning of this stretch of whitewater. Nimikon is about a 9-10 foot drop, broken down on the left. There's a small eddy on the left just above the drop so you can get out and scout on the left. Be sure to take note of the hole fifty feet downstream from the drop–it's sticky!

Now it's 2.5 miles of swiftwater and class II from Nimikon to the logging bridge and lunch. After the logging bridge you encounter continuous easy boulderbed rapids that gradually escalate from I to II in the next mile. The intensity continues to build in the next half-mile to class III as the river narrows, a few backrollers appear, rock outcrops appear on the banks and suddenly a rocky island shunts most of the river right. Follow this main channel, grabbing eddies. This island marks the entrance to the Presque Isle Canyon.

There are no towering cliffs here, but low rock walls, high bluffs, ancient trees and excellent whitewater. There are enough low regular ledges and slides here to create continuous heavy III-IV water when the Presque Isle is over 8 feet. Plenty of holes and waves and some convenient eddies.

You should also be aware that the entrance island marks the beginning of a third-mile of heavy water leading up to Triple Drop, IV at low flows, V at moderate flows (up to about 8 feet) and always portaged when higher, it seems. Your clue that Triple Drop is near occurs when you pass the bow of Battleship Island, a long skinny rock island crowned with trees. The name commemorates the view Alt and I had of this island at 9 feet: jet speed current slammed into the upstream edge of the island and then rolled off as a huge curler; it looked like a battleship steaming upriver!

The left channel at Battleship Island is wider, easier and sets you up better to grab the left side eddy one hundred yards from the bow of Battleship. Catch the eddy!! It's a good one, but it's the last

©2006 dan monskey

zack bannow
gorge falls
black river
michigan

101

Ed Holladay runs the last of Zoom Flume.   ©2006 John Linn

one before Triple Drop. Now get out on the left and scout Triple Drop, the very picture of difficult, dangerous class V.

The first drop is easy, about eight feet sliding around either side of a huge outcrop, then after a hundred feet, the second drop, the crux. This drop is complex and changes dramatically with water level. At about 7.9-8.0 there's a hole (punchable) the outwash of which charges downhill into another hole that's vicious. You want to be moving "full speed ahead" here.

Remember all the lost boats and swims? Quite a few happened right here. The author got stopped here at 8 feet after eddying out above drop #2. Should've kept my speed up! The violence of this hole is immense. I swam, kept my wits and made for the right shore. It was a sweet feeling to put my feet on terra firma again, a feeling which sank as I watched my boat and paddle float by. You see, I was running solo, but despite my poor judgement, the river gods were kind enough to return my equipment to me . . . eventually. Oh what a feeling to get through #2! Fifty feet to exult and drop #3 is on you–watch out for pitoning, it'll go fine. Yes, sirree, fine run.

If it's portage time, you should go up the bank from Triple Drop to find a sort of flat bench and rough road. Hike along this for a half mile, keep looking down for Nokomis Falls. If you're portaging Triple Drop you'll want no part of Nokomis. Even if you ran Triple Drop, there's a good chance you'll want to portage Nokomis.

I must say here that the intensity of the Canyon varies tremendously with water level. At low flow you eddyhop down, Triple Drop can be boat-scouted and Nokomis is a cheap thrill. There's no power or push at low flows (in the middle sevens on the gauge). Above 8 feet the push and excitement rise exponentially. Of course all the numbers in this guide refer to the old gauge which doesn't exist anymore! We're in for a period of "calibration" as we learn how the numbers on the new South Boundary Road bridge gauge correlate to whitewater "action."

In any case the approach to Nokomis should be handled with care. Get out well ahead of it and look the situation over. Basically, Nokomis is a slide that drops 15-20 vertical feet into a sort of a V-hole. The question is whether or not you can punch through. At high water punching is unlikely and a swim would be awful. Nokomis is preceded by a very regular four foot ledge that has extracted adrenalin from those who took it lightly.

The carry is difficult, too. A steep bank, rock outcrops and a violent outwash make a left side portage tough and the right side is worse. You may have to go high up and around to portage past Nokomis. Frankly, the portage high starting at Triple Drop is the rule above 8 feet. The upper portage follows an old road covered with deep snow and/or mud. When the road peters out, you continue ahead about a hundred feet and then slide down a muddy gully to put in a hundred yards below Nokomis.

Now comes the big fun. The Canyon isn't over—there remains a half mile of constricted heavy III-IV water that's just superb. Then the banks get smaller and the river spills into the open, roaring away as continuous whitewater.

The next 1.5 miles leading up to Lepisto Falls is the Conglomerate Staircase. This is fun class III at about 8 feet, with numerous sidesurfing holes and lots of nice waves—fun. At about 8.3-8.5 the waves are great and visibility still pretty good, but the holes are getting powerful. At 8.7 you've got big waves, stopper holes and fun for the jaded, in other words the Death Run. Too much fun for some! At 9 feet the waves seemed more rolling and some holes were washed out—it seemed easier.

Your next major obstacle is Lepisto Falls, a set of three major drops in a half mile. The first one is the one usually thought of as Lepisto—a 9-10 foot sloping ledge made of conglomerate, it looks like a concrete dam and has a hellacious hole at the base. Class IV at moderate water, it's V at high flow. This is the scene of many swims. Easily portaged on the right, sometimes there's enough water to sneak it on the extreme left.

A couple hundred yards and a cable crossing appears. This is one of the access points I mentioned earlier. In fact I should mention that there is a logging trail on river left which might be useful to someone hiking out or someone interested in looking at the river that heads upriver from the cable crossing. The cable car can also be used to cross the river. I skied on this logging road for a ways during winter and it looked as if it might go all the way to the exit of the Canyon.

A hundred yards below the cable crossing is Second Lepisto—about seven feet of drop, best skirted far right with a hole backed up by rock in the center. Another hundred yards and an island forms two choices at Third Lepisto, broad ledges to the left and an intimate seven footer on the right. I usually run right since I like the sharp drop better.

All the named rapids are behind you now, and what remains is excellent play water for a mile and a half, then a mile and a half of scenic swiftwater. If we ran from Michigan 28 it's always late as we leave Lepisto and my energy is always fading in the late afternoon sun (I sure hope it's sunny!). Yet, who can resist a quarter mile of sidesurfers or the great surfing waves that roll one after another? A good plan is to do the whole Presque Isle on Saturday, camp at the mouth and then Sunday carry in to the cable car and play the section below Lepisto. After the playspots the river winds down, snaking through the woods. Check the logjam for lost boats, look for the eagle who lives near the logjam and then look for the friendly South Boundary Road bridge.

South Boundary Road is the takeout for the usual Presque Isle run, but there's obviously a mile left to the Lake. It contains three falls and a supreme wildwater rapid. The first two falls, Nawadaha and Manido are somewhat broken down and of approximately 15-20 feet vertical drop. The last falls, Manabezho, is a 20+ footer that looks as though it could be shallow in the pool.

According to myth all of these falls were run by Fred Young and Associates at low summer flow. I don't know if I really believe this, but I do know that everything, and maybe even Manabezho, has been run under spring conditions with high water. The two broken down falls preceeding Manabezho are actually fairly straightforward if approached on the extreme left: Nawadaha is a straight out high speed slide and Manido involves a sharp turn to the left half way down.

Portaging Manabezho is easily done on the left, but everyone has to first look at the falls and attempt to judge the depth of the plunge pool for themselves.

Although Manabezho is run from time to time, I've never done it nor seen it done, but it looks as though the left side might be deep enough. At low summer flow the extreme right looked like it might present a deeper pool.

A couple more moderate size ledges occur shortly after Manabezho, but the mighty Presque Isle has one more rip-snorter: Zoom Flume. The Presque Isle breathes a fiery last gasp before dissolving itself into Lake Superior. The hundred yards of wildwater that lies just upstream of the footbridge near the mouth is always a wild ride and at very high levels has produced a couple mighty swims. When the water is up, there are usually two fine surfing waves just before hitting the Lake. At last the Presque Isle is quiet, but it has left memories that will ripple for years.

tim hebrink
manabezho falls
presque isle river
michigan

©2006 dan monskey

COPPER CREEK

LENGTH: 2+ MILES, 4 MILES ON THE PRESQUE ISLE

CLASS: II–IV

SUMMER: RARE

QUICK DESCRIPTION: HEMLOCK SHADED LEDGES, SMALL

PUT-IN: HIKE IN OLD ROAD 4.5 MI. S. OF S. BOUNDARY ROAD OFF 519

TAKE-OUT: SOUTH BOUNDARY ROAD, PORCUPINE MTS. STATE PARK

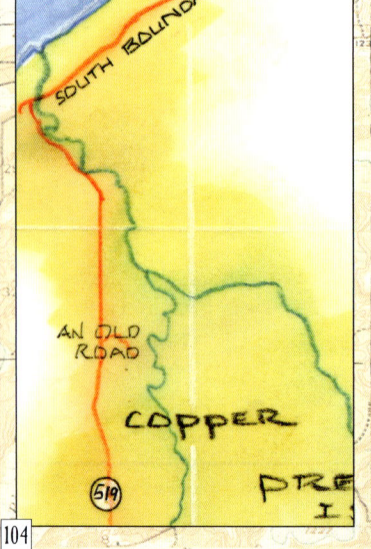

Copper Creek, a large tributary of the Presque Isle, is an interesting run in itself. To put in on this creek, go south on Highway 519 a little less than two miles from the wooden Porcupine Mountains State Park sign that marks the "cable car access" road to the Presque Isle. You will see a small road here heading east. You'll have to carry your kayak through the snow taking whatever forks in the road you need to in order to travel as nearly due east as possible. When the road ends, keep going due east.

You'll be overjoyed when you finally come to a deep valley–it's Copper Creek! Paddling Copper Creek is not a lot of fun at first. It snakes around and there are down trees to portage, but things get better. The hemlocks arch over this little river, which provides three bursts of ledges: Ogima, Ogimakwe and Abinodji Falls. Each of these "falls" consists of a series of medium ledges occurring in rapid succession, class III-IV. None of these bursts lasts more than 100 yards; each is very beautiful with tree-shaded bedrock, sort of primeval.

One of the three has the ruins of an old cabin up above it on the right, back in the woods. The last half mile of this two and a half mile run is more or less continuous class II+ water as Copper Creek trips over small ledges and dodges between boulders. Then suddenly, you'll notice that the water looks heavy up ahead and you'll realize that you've reached the Presque Isle!

The conclusion of the run will be paddling the last two-thirds mile of the Conglomerate Staircase, the Lepisto sequence and all the nice play water below before taking out at South Boundary Road. It seems a good deal, trading a mile carry-in for the chance to enjoy Copper Creek's falls plus the bonus of some nice Presque Isle water.

Maybe you'd enjoy a little fable concerning Copper Creek? One Sunday as we ate breakfast at the Presque Isle campground, people talked of their paddling plans for the day. The campers included myself and some Minnesotans and a bunch of "Hoofers" from Madison, Wisconsin. All of us had paddled the Presque Isle on Saturday in the "rites of spring" mode.

We Minnesotans were headed for the Black or Montreal and asked the Hoofers what they were up to. "Oh, we might look at Copper Creek," they said, thinking it had never been run. "Yeah, it was a good run when we did it last year," we said and watched their faces visibly sag. I love kayaking in general, but there's a special joy to paddling where no man (or woman!) has gone before.

I worry sometimes that this book might take away from the adventure for some boaters. Yet, my hope is that this book will lead new friends to the rivers. I was fortunate enough to be boating during the Northwoods' days of exploration, a heady time.

Are there still exploratories worth doing in the Northwoods? I think there are, but I'm not telling the world about them! Explorers, get out your maps and head for the woods, and don't forget your "Moosepuller." You'll need it when you're up to your hubcaps in mud in the "bush!"

Jim Rada on Copper Creek. ©2006 Mike Cotten

ROCK RIVER

I have NOT run this river, but have received good reports on it from both the Hoofers and the Anokas. My account here is based on their stories and Matt Kuckuk's article in the Sept.-Oct. 1981 issue of the AMERICAN WHITEWATER JOURNAL (Vol. XXVI, no. 5), "Best of the South Shore-Part II." As an aside, let me say that the American Whitewater Affiliation, which publishes the JOURNAL, is the best whitewater organization in the U.S. by far, concerned with conservation of our whitewater resources and exploring them.

The Rock, by all accounts, is a small and intimate river that boasts a few miles of continuous high quality and high gradient boulderbed. I've heard it referred to as "a miniature Savage," a comparison to Maryland's World Championship Wildwater/Slalom course.

I've run the Savage, and the thought of continuous class III water splashed with tinges of IV sounds very appealing, a contrast to the ledgy runs on most of Lake Superior's drainages. The last three miles to the Sturgeon are supposed to be the best, featuring 100 ft/mile gradient, being easier (class II) from Vermiliac Lake (also known as Worm Lake) down to this high gradient conclusion.

The small size of the river means that trees are a concern and that the "pushiness" of the Rock varies greatly. At low flows it loses some of the zest boaters love at higher levels. Matt also says that the drainage includes enough lakes to moderate the flow considerably and help keep it up a bit longer than other rivers in the L'Anse area.

I'm looking forward to seeing this one soon. You must paddle about two miles of flatwater on the Sturgeon River to reach the takeout bridge, Baraga County 231, which crosses the Sturgeon about three miles north and 1.5 miles east of Watton, a small community on Michigan 28.

The run can be extended to include Tibbett's Falls, a healthy sequence of drops on the Sturgeon, three quarters of a mile downstream from 231. Tibbett's can be accessed by low quality dirt roads and trails. The put-in could be either at the Michigan 28/U.S. 141 bridge over the Rock, which would include the last three miles of steep boulderbed, or at a bridge just north of Vermiliac (Worm) Lake. This put-in would add about two miles of class II water.

To reach this put-in turn right on a road that breaks east off of Michigan 28/U.S. 141 just less than a mile east of Covington. You'll drive 2-3 miles east on this road to reach the Rock.

Jim Rada. ©2006 Mike Cotten

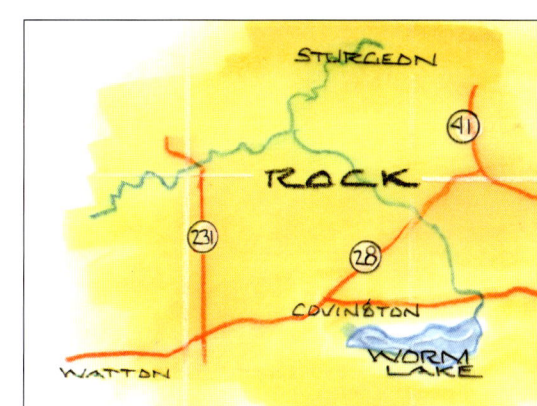

tim hebrink
nonabezho falls
presque isle river
michigan
©2006 dan monskey

LENGTH: 4.5 MILES PLUS 2 MILES ON STURGEON RIVER

CLASS: II–III+

SUMMER: SOME

QUICK DESCRIPTION: BOULDERBED, CONSTANT, BEST BELOW M-28

PUT-IN: BRIDGE AS ROCK LEAVES NORTH EAST CORNER VERMILIAC (WORM) LAKE

TAKE-OUT: BARAGA CO. 231 BRIDGE OVER STURGEON, 1 MILE ABOVE TIBBETT'S

STURGEON RIVER

STURGEON CANYON

LENGTH: 1 MILE

CLASS: IV-V

SUMMER: SOME

QUICK DESCRIPTION:
TIGHT CANYON FILLED WITH DROPS

PUT-IN:
U.S. 41 BRIDGE

TAKE-OUT:
WALK BACK ON TRAIL ON RIGHT TO PUT-IN

STURGEON CANYON

This run is accessed via a parking lot and trails that allow sightseers to glimpse the canyon, which lies just downstream of the U.S. Highway 41 bridge about ten miles south of L'Anse, Michigan. The Sturgeon here is considerably smaller than in the Sturgeon Gorge, twenty miles downstream. However, the Sturgeon makes up for this smaller size with a hefty gradient and a narrow riverbed contained between twenty-foot high cliffs. The river exhibits at least a half dozen class IV-V drops as it roars through this very intimate, scenic canyon. The run is short, about a mile from the bridge to the end of the canyon.

There are two drops of special pizzaz, the ten foot falls entering the canyon, which at some levels can be portaged on the left, and another sheer drop flanked by cliffs in the middle of the run. With the steep gradient and walls, it can be intimidating and I would recommend waiting til after the U.P. rivers peak to run this, as a couple of the constrictions can develop awful hydraulics. I'd also recommend using the trails on river right to carry your boat back up to the parking lot when the canyon ends. There's nothing but bends, down trees and beaver dams below the canyon for miles—don't ask me how I know that! A short, intense and very scenic run, that's the Sturgeon Canyon.

STURGEON GORGE

I've only paddled the Sturgeon Gorge once, but found it to occupy a unique niche in Northwoods whitewater. Viewing the broad, deep valley of the Sturgeon from the Sturgeon Gorge Road (Ottawa National Forest Road 2200) one has a feeling of being in the Appalachians – it just looks too grand in scale to be a Northwoods run! The whitewater, too, is atypical of North and South Shore rivers—it's big boulder-bed, with one notable exception—Sturgeon Falls. We put in by sliding down the steep bluff from Sturgeon Gorge Road to put in about a mile above Sturgeon Falls. The put-in is

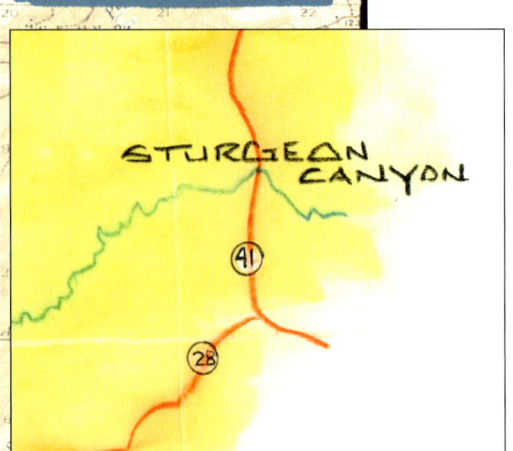

Boaters scout a log below Canyon Falls in the Canyon section. ©2006 Kelly Fountaine

STURGEON RIVER

Evan St. Peter runs Unnamed Falls in the Canyon. ©2006 Kelly Fountaine

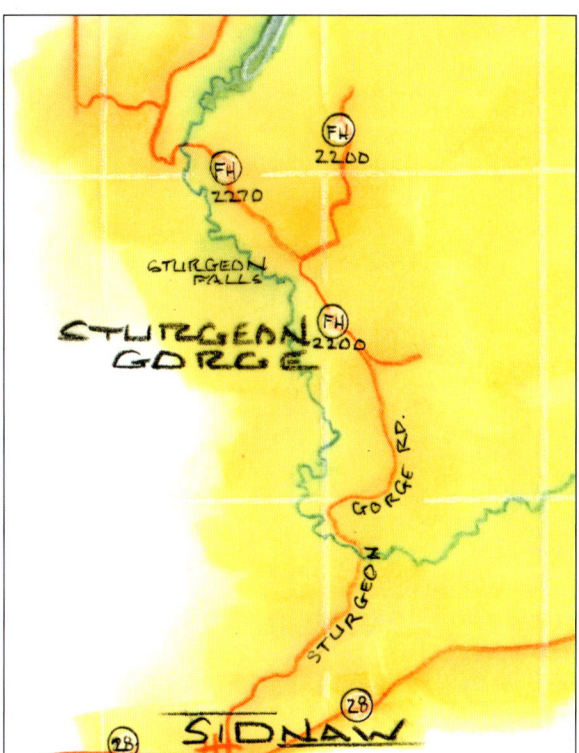

STURGEON GORGE

LENGTH: 3.5 MILES

CLASS: III-

SUMMER: RARE

QUICK DESCRIPTION: FALLS, BOULDERBED, DEEP VALLEY

PUT-IN: OTTAWA NAT'L FOR. 191, NEAR HOUGHTON/BARAGA LINE

TAKE-OUT: OTTAWA NAT'L FOR. 193 BRIDGE

reached by taking Michigan 28 to Sidnaw and then turning north on Sturgeon Gorge Road, and following this until you're near the Baraga/Houghton county line. There's no consequential whitewater until you get near the falls, a magnificent twenty-five footer which is easily portaged on the right.

Steve Corsi and Tom O'Keefe recommend to be sure to get out early as there are significant hydraulics before the falls that have caught at least one boater unaware and caused a swim that resulted in loss of life. In fact, a walk down to the falls on the trail system to scout before your run or even just putting in below the falls is a good option.

Below the falls come stretches of nice class II-III boulderbed with big boulders. These stretches are best near the falls and diminish as you approach the takeout, a bridge over the Sturgeon about a mile south of Pickett Reservoir. The considerable drainage area of the Sturgeon at this point creates a Western feel to the boulderbed on this four mile run. A word of warning about the roads: they seem prone to rutting and "quagmiring" in the spring and they're not heavily traveled during boating season.

tim hebrink
manabezho falls
presque isle river
michigan

©2006 dan nonskey

FALLS RIVER

LENGTH: 2 MILES

CLASS: III-IV+

SUMMER: RARE

QUICK DESCRIPTION: RUNNABLE TEN FOOTERS, OTHER LEDGES

PUT-IN: DAM AT END OF POWER DAM ROAD IN L`ANSE

TAKE-OUT: LAKE SUPERIOR, PARK IN CELOTEX PARKING LOT

This or the Huron has to be the **hardest river to catch** "up" in the Northwoods. Many's the time the locals have told us, "Shoulda bin here Tuesday." If you can catch it with water, you'll find a two mile run that lives up to its name, lots of ledges and small falls and some rapids to boot.

Takeout is on Lake Superior's Keeweenaw Bay just west of downtown L`Anse. The put-in is reached by going 1.5-2 miles south of L'Anse and turning west on Dam Road, then a bit less than a mile to the river. Other put-ins further upstream also exist.

There's a portage around an old dam early on and less than a mile later a sharp drop followed by a huge boulder–there might be room to miss it, but I have portaged. As you approach the Lake the river falls over sloping sheets of rock, sort of broad runnable cascades. To see if there's enough water for a run, check the river from the U.S. 41 bridge–if there's sufficient water to scrape over these broad ledges–go for it; the upper river is generally narrower and not so rocky.

You may expect to do a little scraping and boat abuse–you'd be a white-haired old man if you waited for "optimum" conditions.

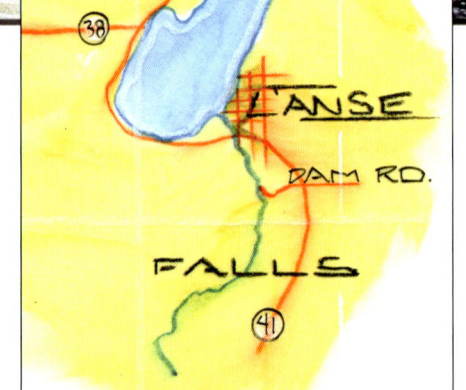

Rada on the Falls River.   ©2006 Mike Cotten

Paul Douglas, Falls River.   ©2006 Mike Cotten

SILVER RIVER

Silver River's Hail Mary rapid. ©2006 Mike Cotten

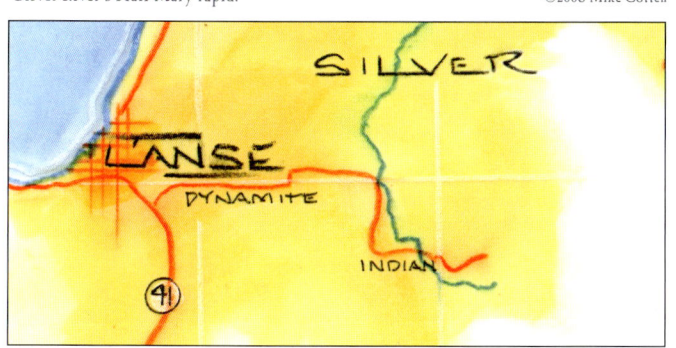

One of **the U.P.'s finest** runs stairsteps down to Lake Superior from Mount Curwood, Michigan's highest point (well, nearby Mount Arvon might dispute that according to recent USGS statements).

As the Silver slices through the woods five miles east of L'Anse, it throws ledges and slides of every description at the boater. The run is divided into two segments: the Upper Silver–from the Indian Road bridge to the Dynamite Road bridge and the Lower Silver from Dynamite Road to the picnic area at Silver Falls. Silver Falls is reached by a dirt road that branches south off of Skanee Road for a half mile.

It's possible to run both sections back to back, but it's also convenient to run the sections individually. The Lower Silver is easier from a technical standpoint by a hair, IV-IV+ on the Lower and IV-V(p) on the Upper.

The first run on the Lower Silver was done by the Hoofers and Fred Young. Word of their success reached us here in Minnesota. The word was that "all the drops were runnable," and that in fact a C-2 piloted by Dave Murphy and Joanne Artz ran everything.

When our Minnesota contingent of Dave Blinde, Jim Pedginski, Jerry Giru, Tom Aluni and the author launched on the Silver, we had it in the back of our minds that everything had been run. We put in at the Indian Road bridge, since looking at the topo maps showed good gradient downstream.

As we ran the Silver we were amazed as we came to drop after drop that a C-2 had apparently run. Reassured by knowledge of the successful Hoofer run, we ran drops and slides galore, until we got to what's known as the Cabin Section. Here we portaged, bummed that a C-2 mixed team would run what we chose to portage! On reaching Dynamite Road bridge, Jerry, Dave and PJ called it quits—only Tom and I continued. We reached

SECTION: UPPER
LENGTH: 2.5 MILES
CLASS: III-V
SUMMER: RARE
QUICK DESCRIPTION: STEEP CREEKING AT ITS BEST
PUT-IN: INDIAN ROAD, 6 MLESE OF L'ANSE
TAKE-OUT: DYNAMITE HILL ROAD BRIDGE

SILVER RIVER, GOOD INFO!	
LEVEL	USGS AW WEB SITE (FT)
TOO HIGH?	10.5
HIGH (NICE!)	9.5
MODERATE	8.5
LOW-MODERATE	8

tim hebrink
manabezho falls
presque isle river
michigan

©2006 dan monskey

Three Falls rapid on the Lower Silver River. ©2006 Mike Cotten

Mark Gibson hits Bridge Abutment rapid on the Lower Silver River. ©2006 Mike Cotten

Silver Falls in darkness and began hiking towards L'Anse by starlight (the shuttle vehicle had gotten stuck in mud).

Later, when we described our run to the Hoofers, we found that they hadn't run the Upper Silver—just the Lower, and our pride rebounded; we weren't wimps after all! It's pretty interesting how you act when you believe something has been run before.

UPPER SILVER

The Upper Silver is only 2-3 miles long but a lot of action takes place. I won't describe it all but give the highlights of this class IV-V run.

The first two-thirds mile is fun class II-II+ stuff, the river tiny, narrow and tight. This nice warmup ends when you come to a horizon line where the Silver slips quickly over a series of ledges, then turns sharp left (90 degrees!!) into a constricted little gorge pocked with holes.

Scouting or portaging this 150 yard long class IV-IV+ rapid on the right is easy, but don't think the river's going to let up. There's a fifty foot pool after this rapid; then a footbridge spans the Silver. There's a cabin on the left and a small statue of the Virgin Mary on the right. Although the statue is now broken, the class IV drop under the footbridge is called "Hail Mary." The runout of Hail Mary offers a couple of small eddies which you should use to set up for the next IV-V drop fifty yards below Hail Mary. This drop is a big ledge which funnels water into a powerful reversal. The water encounters undercuts along both shores, so a good line is necessary, scout right.

A little breathing room and you'll encounter three big slides squeezed into no more than a fifth of a mile. I'm sure you drop at least forty feet as you careen through this sequence, quite amazing, class IV-V. Now the Silver "calms" for perhaps a bit less than a mile. In this section you can relax and enjoy quite a few medium height (4-7 foot) ledges, some sloping, one a nifty little bubblebath falls.

Most of these class III-IV- ledges are boat scoutable. The end of the "calm" comes as a healthy horizon line appears and a large cabin looms downstream on the right. Get out right for a look at the famous "Cabin Section."

The first drop is about 15 feet and not quite vertical, class IV by itself, but it feeds out immediately into a sharp twisting drop that ends in a strong hole. This drop, "The Commander Shuffle," in honor of Commander Mike Sklavos, requires some deft paddlework to dance through. Next, a short pool, followed by the capstone of the Cabin Section, "First Man Falls." First Man Falls, V-V+(p), starts with a sloping seven foot ledge, trivial in the Cabin Section, then a short pool, a twist to the left and the whole Silver narrows and screams downhill, blasting into an awful looking hole, finishing by racing madly into heavy water between sloping rock shores for fifty yards. It's a doozy! All of this can be scouted or portaged on the right.

The name commemorates the day this rapid was first run. The drop was reached almost simultaneously by a group of Hoofers and a party of Minnesotans. "Silver Season" is short, usually a week or two around April 15-20, so the river was getting its visitation. The right bank was crowded with scouting parties checking out the big hole in First Man Falls.

I was the first man to run it, honest! I ran it approximately two minutes after Hoofer Superwoman Denise blasted through the hole!! I suppose some sexists would call it First Woman Falls, but I doubt that Denise bragged about it so much. Somehow, "I was the first woman to run it!" doesn't sound as bold as "I was the first man to run it!" Oh, oh–better shut up or even my girlfriend won't buy this book.

It's pretty much over for hairball and hijinks when the Cabin Section's through. In about a half mile you'll be at Dynamite Road bridge. This bridge marks the end of the Upper Silver and the beginning of the Lower Silver. The Dynamite bridge is also a nice place to check out the level before running. Does it look scratchy? Is it pumping? Usually, it's just too low to boat, but on those magic days when it looks like you could scrape by or better–go for it! The river is usually a bit higher than it appears at Dynamite bridge. If there's good flow at Dynamite, you're in for fun . . . if it's flooded–beware!! The Silver can display a skull and crossbones nature when in flood, but it's an interesting hike.

LOWER SILVER

The Lower Silver shoots most of its bullets in the first mile to mile and a half below Dynamite Road. A little boulderbed first, then a couple very technical and tight slides with sharp turns and sharp rock.

These first few ledges are IV-, but can do some boat damage if you piton. Shortly below these you'll see the river bend sharp right, complete with horizon line. Scout on the right, as the Silver goes around the corner with a Bang!–Bam!–Boof!–three big drops in quick succession. Each of these drops rates about a IV/IV+ on its own.

Shortly after this sequence you encounter a string of three falls, all runnable and with the slots actually lining up! This is the "Silver Bullet," a major pleasure of life for a steep-creeker. It's not difficult to run these, but it is quite a thrill to descend more than forty feet in a flash. Looking back upstream is something else, the Silver spilling over those falls beneath a canopy of Northwoods greenery.

Now that the premium mileage of the Lower Silver is behind you, put the muscle into the flatwater for a couple of miles. You'll have to snap to attention again when you hit a big, scrapey IV/IV+ ledge that slides past the abutments of an old bridge. Another mile of meandering brings you to the Silver Falls picnic area. You can take out left or enjoy one more class IV as the Silver rips through a narrow mini-canyon. A hundred yards below this drop is Silver Falls, yet to be run, and then three miles of flatwater to the Lake. If you like steep-creekin' ledge-leapin' you'll like the Silver!

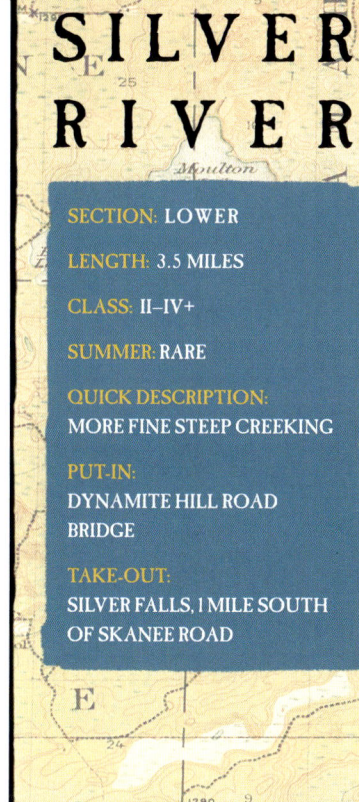

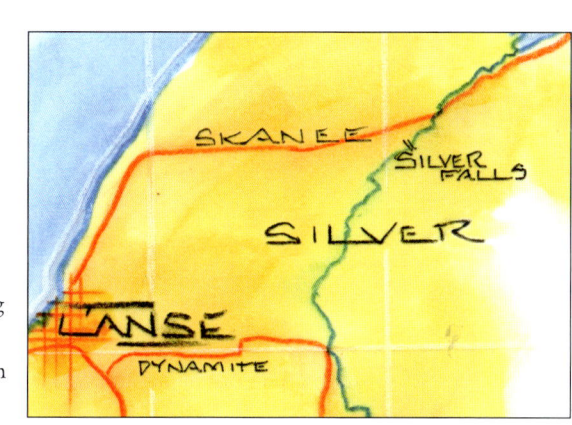

SILVER RIVER

SECTION: LOWER

LENGTH: 3.5 MILES

CLASS: II–IV+

SUMMER: RARE

QUICK DESCRIPTION: MORE FINE STEEP CREEKING

PUT-IN: DYNAMITE HILL ROAD BRIDGE

TAKE-OUT: SILVER FALLS, 1 MILE SOUTH OF SKANEE ROAD

tim hebrink
nanabezho falls
presque isle river
michigan

©2006 dan monskey

SLATE RIVER

LENGTH: 4.5 MILES

CLASS: IV

SUMMER: RARE

QUICK DESCRIPTION:
SLIDES AND LEDGES, SLIDES AND LEDGES, SLIDES AND LEDGES

PUT-IN:
ARVON ROAD 4.5 MILES SOUTH FROM SKANEE ROAD

TAKE-OUT:
BRIDGE AT SKANEE ROAD

By Steve Corsi

As stated on the American Whitewater River Tools web page, the Slate River "is considered by some boaters to be **one of the U.P.'s finest** days of spring boating. It has excellent back-woods scenery, a real small creek feel, and a bunch of great drops."

The takeout is at the bridge about 11 miles Northeast from L'Anse (4 miles northeast from the Silver River bridge) on Skanee Rd. Here is where you can get an indication of water level. Measure down from the lower edge of the beveled surface on the upstream side of the road directly in the center of the bridge (this is about 1" below the road surface). Minimum level is 10'6" down. A small change in water level here makes a significant change in whitewater intensity above. At 10'3" down, you have a very nice run ahead of you.

To get to the put-in from Skanee Road, drive up the west side of the river on Arvon Rd. After about 3 miles you'll come near the Slate and a number of cabins, one of them the "Heartbreak Hotel," locale of a recent Elvis sighting. Continue up Arvon Road another half-mile and you'll encounter a road that leads to a bridge over the Slate River. Continue another half-mile down Arvon Road to a point where the River comes within 50' of the road to the put-in. The road is a bit questionable on this section, so drive as far as you dare, and walk the rest.

Now you're ready to encounter a class III-III+ rapid that's nearly a half-mile long. The slate careens and twists this way and that over perfect sheets of smooth slate with Black Slate Falls, an 8' ledge, as the finale. It's non-stop, dropping 75 feet in a half-mile, with the maximum gradient pushing 300 feet per mile, and it's all runnable! Now float for a hundred yards under a bridge and a little further to Quartzite Falls (also known by boaters as Banana Peel). The river pours over a 5' ledge but continues on down a slide over 50' in length with another 15' of vertical descent. The river mellows for a while after this as it passes by the cabins that you drove past on the shuttle. This is an alternate take-out if you want to make it a short day or a possible spot to start the double shuttle option if you want to avoid the mile of flatwater below the cabins.

Now the real fun begins. Sections of continuous rapids and ledges eventually lead to Ecstasy Falls where you can scout on the right. This is a stunning series of ledges and slides that drop 50 feet of vertical in less than 150 yards. Truly spectacular! Continue on down eddy hopping your way to the next 10' ledge, and eventually to Kuckuk's Plunge. This is a 15 footer into a short pool with a quick turn left followed by another 5' pitch. A few more rapids and meanders before approaching a left hand turn into an amazing, perfect, silky smooth slide that is unreal in its perfection. Smooth Creamy Thigh is an 75 foot slide dropping 15 feet over immaculate slate bedrock. The river right eddy directly at the bottom of this slide is the point where many boaters choose to take out and walk the half mile around Slate River Canyon to put in below Slate River Falls.

Then again, some expert boaters choose to venture into the canyon. Falls here are aplenty! Sheer falls of fifteen feet, stairsteps of six to eight feet, and big steep slides. Unfortunately for the river runner, all these things are contained in a steep sided canyon with towering pines shading the gorge. It would be very difficult to exit this class V (VI at times) gorge in certain places due to steep, crumbly rock banks that can make portages within the canyon difficult or even impossible in spots. Plan your escape routes and carefully evaluate the water level before committing to this part of the run.

This section has been run at least a few times, and more frequently since the logs in Slate River Falls were blown out in high water during 2003. If you plan to run this section, it's well worth the walk up to this 25 foot falls that exits the canyon, both to check the falls for logs and to scout a spot to eddy out for another look at Slate River Falls while running the canyon. The falls may be viewed from a pretty trail that follows the right rim upstream from the Skanee Road bridge. Another 15 minutes of swift water after the falls takes you to the bridge.

WEST BRANCH OF THE HURON

This small river is rarely paddled because its size implies frequent portages around deadfalls and a short boating season.

It can provide an interesting run if you happen to be in the L'Anse area when the rivers are high, making a run on the Silver dangerous.

The river is best accessed off of Black Creek Road, a good dirt road that branches off Skanee Road about a mile west of Big Erik's Bridge. About a mile and a half after leaving the Skanee Road, you'll notice a well defined logging road branching east off of Black Creek Road. To identify this road, look for a yellow arrow painted on a tree here. If you walk in on this road you'll encounter the West Branch in less than a quarter-mile and the road will continue on the far side of the river. This is the takeout, eliminating two miles of swiftwater between this point and Big Erik's Bridge.

Where you put in depends on the time available and your mood. If time is limited or you want only the best whitewater the West Branch offers, carry your boat upstream along the river—which is easy since the woods are open and beautiful.

A carry of less than a mile will put you at the top of the West Branch canyon—if you carry up on the right, you'll be able to scout the canyon on your way. If you don't wish to carry, you can easily put in about two miles above the canyon where Black Creek Road crosses the West Branch.

The West Branch is tiny here, and will remain small for a mile until Robarge Creek, a major tributary, enters, almost doubling the flow. If you don't mind the small size of the West Branch and consequent sweeper hazard that you see at the Black Creek Road crossing maybe you'll continue upstream another half-mile on the small road paralleling the West Branch as I did.

If the water's high this additional half-mile includes a number of down trees but also a number of nice small and medium ledges. This creates class II-II+ rapids on a beautiful tree-shaded avenue of water. These small ledges continue for another half-mile below the Black Creek Road bridge, including a fun little drop near a backwoods cabin and an old railroad bridge. Then the West Branch meanders til Robarge Creek comes in, and you may have some down trees to portage.

Below Robarge Creek the riverbed is considerably bigger and less prone to sweepers. You'll encounter a couple of short pitches of class II as the West Branch runs into outcrops of slate. When you encounter continuous small ledges and the banks rise above you, you'll know that you're entering the West Branch Canyon. A couple hundred yards of slam bang III-IV ledges and you should take out on the right just above West Branch Falls, a solid twenty footer with a log strewn history.

It's around a right hand turn that was last noted to be fairly wood free. There have been reports of boaters not recognizing the drop until very late, almost dropping over accidentally.

The best portage is on the right, and you'll probably have to carry a couple hundred yards to get around the right side talus banks. Putting in again you'll have a hundred and fifty yard straightaway that suddenly drops off and is pinched left.

Here the West Branch plunges steeply into a quiet pool, creating Silent Falls, a class IV-V drop. It's easy to portage Silent Falls if you like. Another hundred and fifty yards swings you around a sharp bend and points you at Undercut Falls, another portage. It's not a bad idea to scout the approach to the right side takeout before running down.

Following Undercut Falls is a solid quartermile of class III consisting of a jumble of big boulders, ledges and, unfortunately, logs. I was able to run this section with high water channels and found it technical and enjoyable. At this point the action diminishes to class I-II until you reach the "yellow arrow" ford a third-mile away. Not of the high quality of the Silver, the West Branch canyon is a good little piece of whitewater in a pretty but accessible canyon. This run might be a good warmup for the other more difficult runs nearby.

MAP ON NEXT PAGE.

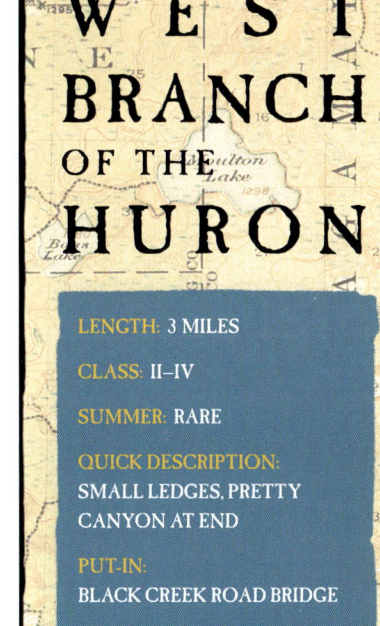

LENGTH: 3 MILES

CLASS: II–IV

SUMMER: RARE

QUICK DESCRIPTION: SMALL LEDGES, PRETTY CANYON AT END

PUT-IN: BLACK CREEK ROAD BRIDGE

TAKE-OUT: FORD CROSSING, QUARTER MILE EAST OF BLACK CREEK ROAD

tim hebrink
manabezho falls
presque isle river
michigan

©2006 dan monskey

HURON RIVER

EAST BRANCH OF THE HURON

LENGTH: 5 MILES

CLASS: II–IV+

SUMMER: RARE

QUICK DESCRIPTION:
RUNNABLE FALLS, 1 MILE CANYON

PUT-IN:
OLD RAILROAD GRADE, 1 MILE WEST OFF TRIPLE A ROAD

TAKE-OUT:
BIG ERIK'S BRIDGE

Helge Klockow runs You Turn ©2006 Steve Corsi

My first view of the Huron was on a ski trip with Greg Breining and Henry Kinnucan to check some South Shore rivers that looked promising on topo maps. We skied up from the takeout, Big Erik's Bridge, and encountered a narrow picturesque river sliding between high, pine-clothed bluffs all draped with lots of U.P. powder.

While we didn't have time to thoroughly explore the river, what we saw was tantalizing: fine ledges in a superb canyon. It has proved to be a beautiful and enjoyable run containing fun class III and IV water in an intimate wilderness setting.

The Huron remains a little-known run because of two impediments: (1) It usually has a reliable spring runoff that lasts only a week or two, and (2) When it's runnable in spring the roads are often four wheel drive country.

On the first point, the Huron doubtless is brought to runnable levels by rain at times, but the lack of boating contacts in the L'Anse area makes it unlikely that we'll hear of these cloudbursts, so plan on spring. On the second point, if you're willing to use some ingenuity you can get by without four wheel drive.

The total distance from takeout to put-in is about 5 miles on roads, 4 miles on the Triple A Road and another mile on unplowed logging roads that lead to the Huron. Sometimes you can drive up the Triple A Road early when it's still frozen and hard, unload boats for the mile long carry in on the logging road, then drive your vehicle back to Big Erik's Bridge, returning to your boats by hiking.

This way you walk the shuttle, but don't need four wheel drive. Sometimes you can get help from all the trout fishermen hanging out at Big Erik's Bridge. There aren't any "girly man" vehicles in this fishing crowd! A last option is to carry your boat up to the top! There's a cabin on river left about a half mile above Big Erik's Bridge—if you ferry across to it, you'll find a trail that goes upstream 1.5-2 miles to Big Falls (and beyond if you want to keep carrying!).

Picture a run worth carrying or dragging your boat a mile or two through snow! In the best of all possible worlds you'll have solid roads and four wheel drive. Access isn't generally a cakewalk, though. Get to the put-in by driving east over Big Erik's Bridge, swinging upstream on the road, climbing a big hill as the road veers away from the river, following a creek (usually the troublespot on the shuttle).

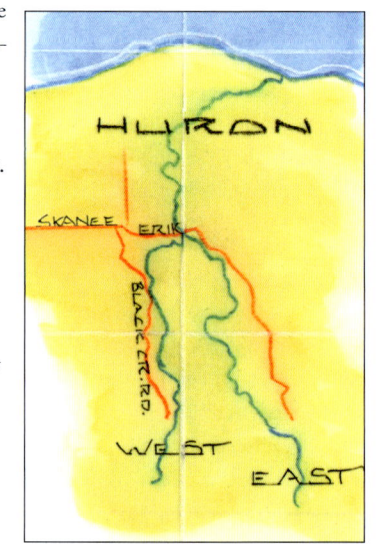

If you make it up to the top of the hill, great! Easier now, the road heads due south, then curves to run due east. Just after this curve look for a Y-junction on your right; here's where you leave the Triple A Road, about 4 miles from Big Erik's Bridge.

Go south on this logging road about a quarter-mile to an old logging camp site. From here a road should go due west—it's quite flat—I think it's an old railroad grade. Follow this to the Huron.

Now you're ready for fun. As I look back at the shuttle description I'll bet you feel woofed. The Huron is worth it! Below the put-in the Huron delights the paddler by sliding over little redrock slides (class II) amid pretty scenery.

This serene warmup lasts about a mile. Then you come to a sharp right turn which kicks off with a sloping medium height ledge and is followed in twenty yards by another ledge. The reddish rock here reminds me of Minnesota's Devil's Track.

This class III-IV drop is followed by another half-mile of easy water before Big Falls, a IV+, breaks the flow. Best scouted right, it can be portaged, but is really very benign, a fun drop. It loses 15-20 feet of vertical, starting with a steep slide and finishing with a dropoff.

On one occasion the Anokas frittered away a whole day being lost, with just enough time in the end to hike in, make several runs of Big Falls and then hike out!

Below Big Falls the river eases and swings east through a half-mile where the banks open up—usually a few logs cross the river here. When the Huron swings back north, it begins to enter the Huron Canyon. This roughly mile-long canyon is sweet and far too short . . . I wish it went for miles. Here the river zig-zags over at least a half dozen distinct IV- to IV ledges with a portage thrown in to keep you on your toes.

The high banks add to a feeling of intimacy. The portage comes after you've run four or five ledges. You'll recognize it by the river turning sharp left and running 150 feet before twisting back right in a steep drop which I call "You Turn." It has been run, but you have to negotiate a sharp turn while going downhill in a hurry, possible but gnarly.

It's easiest, but not easy, to portage on the left taking out rather close to the steep part. To aid in identification, the right bank becomes more cliff-like just above You Turn. Below You Turn are one or two more good ledges, including one that funnels into a horseshoe shaped hole that's surprisingly powerful. It can stop or backender boats. Now the banks drop away, the river becomes easy for the next mile to Big Erik's Bridge and you wish there was more. The Huron Canyon demands good boat control and is great fun for skilled paddlers.

Ordinarily, you're lucky to find enough water in it to boat the run and at these levels advanced boaters will be happy with the Huron. If it's high it becomes eye-popping expert water. You can satisfy your urge for more by running Lower Falls, the hundred yard long class III-IV that lies just below Big Erik's Bridge.

Lower Falls is a fine rapid with some nice spots, both for play and for trout, and you may have to bear the scowls of the fisherfolk on the shore. The West Fork of the Huron has joined forces with the East Fork just above the bridge, so Lower Falls has quite a bit more water and a different character than the Huron Canyon upstream.

The West Fork and nearby Slate also offer some exciting paddling, but these streams are even smaller than the Huron and so adequate flow and sweepers become more of a problem. Camping can be enjoyed at Big Erik's or at the mouth of the Huron, a few miles away.

Mark Mastalski and Brian Day below You Turn. ©2006 Steve Corsi

tim hebrink
manabezho falls
presque isle river
michigan

©2006 dan monskey

YELLOW DOG RIVER

LENGTH: 3.5 MILES

CLASS: IV-V

SUMMER: RARE

QUICK DESCRIPTION: LOTS OF BIG DROPS TO RUN/PORTAGE

PUT-IN: MARQUETTE COUNTY 510 BRIDGE OR FURTHER UPSTREAM

TAKE-OUT: MARQUETTE COUNTY 550 BRIDGE, 15 MILES NORTHWEST OF MARQUETTE

"The good folks who run the Yellow Dog have agreed to give up these photos of their fine river with some stubbornness. At my suggestion, the local paddlers should, without regret, erect a kiosk halfway down the run to sell paddles back to any newcomers as they emerge from the woods."

The Editor.

Helge Klockow runs Hills Falls, aka Barking Bitch Falls. ©2006 Steve Corsi

"Yeah, I ran the Yellow Dog – it was a bitch!" That description conveyed to me the frustration of a Hoofer boater who'd paddled the Yellow Dog, a river 15 miles northwest of Marquette that bounces down to Lake Superior with a vengeance.

If you don't like portaging or running big ledges, some in close proximity to undercuts, you'd best stay away. This is one dog whose bite is worse than its bark. A small river, the Yellow Dog makes the most of its water and gradient.

To reach the takeout, drive about 15-20 miles northwest out of Marquette on Marquette County Highway 550. The 550 bridge over the Yellow Dog is the takeout. To reach the put-in, continue northwest on 550 for about four miles, then turn left on Marquette County 510. This dirt road can be muddy, but seems solid. Now backtrack by following 510 about five miles, working mostly south til you reach the Yellow Dog.

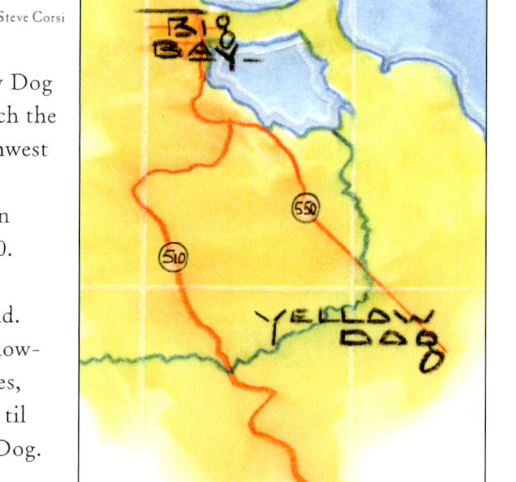

Mark Mastalski hugs river left through Obedience School. ©2006 Steve Corsi

Lenny Sheps atop Junkyard Dog Rapid. ©2006 Steve Corsi

Putting in at the 510 bridge gives about a four mile run to the 550 bridge, of which the last mile is uninteresting swiftwater. The upper three miles contains 7 big ledges, some of which we ran, some of which we portaged. Pete Cary thought they were pretty outrageous. Actually, this is only the lower half of the Yellow Dog run.

I haven't paddled the upper section which begins near Pinnacle Falls, but local paddlers have and say it's mostly class I–II boulderbed, a class III drop, lots of deadfall and a BIG drop that is best portaged. It was a source of disappointment, apparently.

If you are still intent on adding these 3–4 more miles you can reach this upper put-in by proceeding along 510 for just under three miles from 550. Then you'll see a road to the right going due west. This is the Triple A Road, and if you followed it without missing a turn, you'd come out at Big Erik's Bridge over the Huron many miles away. In spring this road can almost be a river itself as water runs downhill between banks of snow.

We couldn't make it up the Triple A, but if you can, follow it for about 6.5 winding miles and you'll see a road branch left, bringing you to the Yellow Dog in a mile and a half.

tim hebrink
manabezho falls
presque isle river
michigan

©2006 dan monskey

BALTIMORE RIVER

LENGTH: 7 MILES

CLASS: IV

SUMMER: RARE

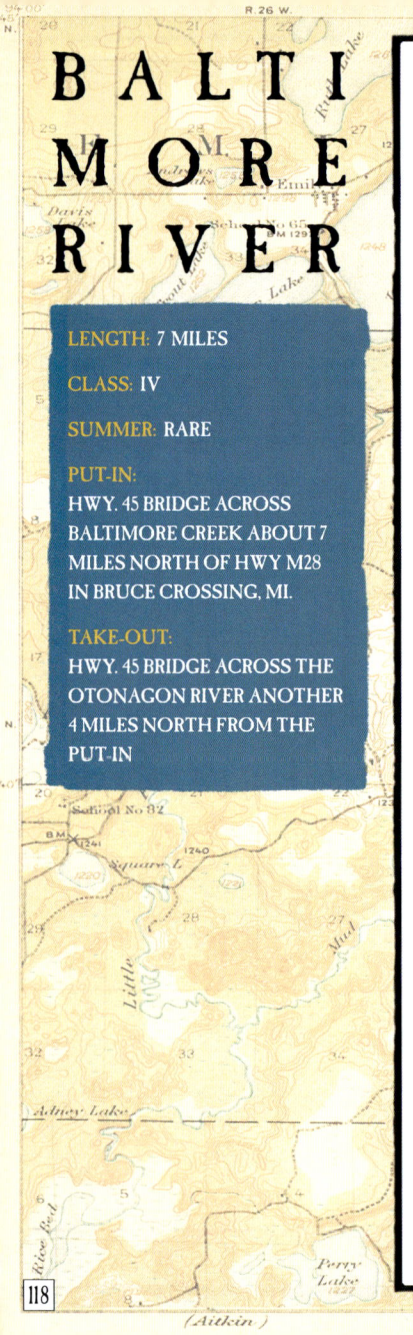

PUT-IN:
HWY. 45 BRIDGE ACROSS BALTIMORE CREEK ABOUT 7 MILES NORTH OF HWY M28 IN BRUCE CROSSING, MI.

TAKE-OUT:
HWY. 45 BRIDGE ACROSS THE OTONAGON RIVER ANOTHER 4 MILES NORTH FROM THE PUT-IN

By Thomas O'Keefe and Steve Corsi

This creek has a narrow window in the spring. We have observed it drop 8' in one week from an unrunnable torrent to a scrappy marginal run. This is a great run if you catch it at good levels.

GAUGE: Tape measurement from the bottom of the bridge support on the downstream river left side of the bridge. At 4' down the river is too high and at 12' down it is too low. 10'4" down is quite nice. The maximum is somewhere between these levels, but since this river has not been attempted many times, it is not certain exactly how high this can be run.

The run starts out and ends with a long stretch of flatwater. The meat of this run is in the middle. Creamy Peanut Butter Falls, a river-wide ledge, is the first drop on the river. Several different routes are available depending on the water level. Scout on river left. Just downstream is Okundekun Falls, a steep drop of approximately 25' falling onto several sections of very shallow bedrock. This one is portaged on river left. The footbridge below the falls will give you a good look at what the next rapid "Let Us Pray" is like. This rapid is a continuous set of 3-5' ledges that scrape the plastic off your boat at low levels, but be on your guard as a couple of them drop into keeper holes at moderate water levels and become monsters at high water.

On the first attempt at paddling this river, the group decided to turn back at this point due to a series of four river-wide holes. The trail from Okundekun Falls back to Hwy 45 is part of the scenic North Country Hiking Trail that stretches across the entire Upper Peninsula.

Harry House runs Creamy Peanut Butter Falls. ©2006 Thomas O'Keefe

The next mile or so is swift water until a fun class III rapid. The river then picks up into continuous class II-III until the river drops over Cyclops. An island in the middle of the river forms the eye and makes a good landing place to scout this drop as long as the water is low enough to leave it exposed. This drop consists of a pair of slides that drop about 10' on either side of the island.

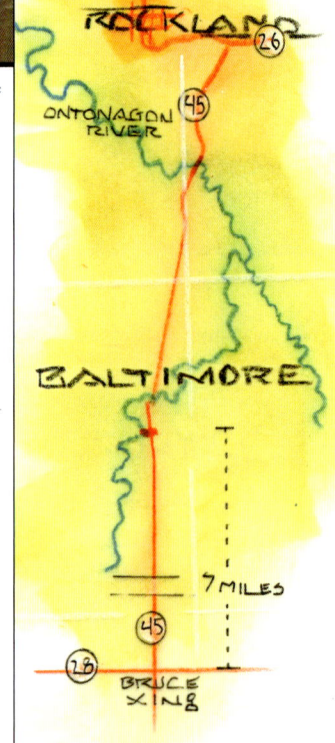

After a short distance, the river makes a turn to the left and passes under an old unsafe footbridge. Beyond this point, the river enters the canyon section. You can go beyond the point of no return if you are not paying attention. The bridge signals the best spot to take out for scouting the canyon, which is done from the river right bank, but the bridge will not last forever so stay heads up. From the bank high above the river on river right you can get a good look at "The Mass Has Ended," a long slide which funnels between several large boulders after the drop. The right side of this constriction is undercut and often holds logs and other debris underneath the water as well as careless boaters. Many solid boaters have been known to portage this first drop into the canyon and lower their boats down past the undercut boulder. If you continue along the bank on river right you can find a couple of spots to lower your boats, but it is not a trivial portage. Long, steep river banks with snow and wet mossy slopes warrant caution.

At the bottom of The Mass Has Ended begins the action packed ride through "Go In Peace," a several hundred yard class IV+ rapid formed by beautifully sculpted sandstone bedrock that is characteristic of this unique river. This area makes a great lunch spot and an easy natural pathway to scout the entire set of rapids. There are several areas where the majority of flow crashes directly into a few daunting boulders that seem to defy the laws of physics by remaining in the middle of the channel. Numerous holes and side curlers with several undercut rocks make for a challenging journey to the final slide ending in a fairly sticky hole on river left and a bumpy ride on river right. This canyon is great fun with good water, but nearly every boulder is undercut so use caution. When you hit the quiet water below, turn around and gaze at the spectacular canyon section all the way to the top, then go in peace to the Ontonagon River which takes you for a mellow 2-mile float to the takeout.

SANDSTONE CREEK

By Tom O'Keefe and Steve Corsi

After a run on the Baltimore River, don't put your gear away too quickly. A nice 30 minute diversion lies just to the south. Go about a ½ mile south of the Hwy 45 Bridge over the Ontonagon River and look just to the west side of the road. This creek is a dry roadside ditch in the summer that roars to life during the spring melt. Drag your boat another 200 yards upstream as this small gem travels into the woods away from the road, and put in just above a few gratifying ledges. The creek then floats you down a sinuous quarter-mile of narrow channel until "The Alarm Clock" wakes you up with a series of quick-hitting sandstone ledges that all form boiling, heaving holes at higher water. Take out at the bottom of the last ledge and carry your boat up the hill back to Hwy 45.

EAGLE RIVER

This one's supposed to be really nice, and I'm not surprised. It's up on the Keeweenaw, home of the biggest snowpacks in the Northwoods so even though it has a small drainage area, it's a run. Dave Bullock of Houghton and others in 1996 told me it was a hoot. Dave called it the "Silver of the Keeweenaw," high praise! The run consists of the last two miles from near Phoenix to Eagle River on Lake Superior. Apparently, even Eagle Falls has been run and one of the drops sounds like it just goes . . . and goes . . . and goes!

PORCUPINE MOUNTAIN RUNS

According to Steve Corsi and Co., there are three nice runs in the Porkies that have been run when conditions were right; the Union River, the Little Carp River, and the Big Carp River.

• The Union has a spectacular section of slides and ledges for about a mile beginning at Union Cabin, passing South Boundary road and ending below the bridge after the series of slides that make up Union Falls.

• The Little Carp has a couple nice sections of drops, but they are paid for with a couple miles of log choked channel in the center of the run ending at Wabeno Creek. The action picks up from there all the way to Lake Superior including several class IV drops connected by some picturesque continuous class III.

• The last mile of the Big Carp River has numerous class IV drops through the enchanted forest that constitutes the Porcupine Mountains. Get to these runs when the surrounding rivers are a bit on the high side.

OTHER CREEK RUNS ON THE SOUTH SHORE

You just can't keep up with all the explorin' goin' on. I've gotten reports from several expert paddlers scattered around the North Woods about some South Shore runs recently done. Some sounded good, others not so good. I haven't been able to check these out in detail yet, but if you're interested in a bodacious or abominable boondoggle, you might check out one of these.

tim hebrink
manabezho falls
presque isle river
michigan
©2006 dan monskey

THE BEST WATER

Opinions of a good spring range wildly from paddler to non-paddler. Most times the best water is snow melt; when the snow is gone, the paddler is too, off following the melt northward.

A deadfall pine awaits a future run down the Black River. The boater is Dave Bullock. ©2006 John Linn

Dave Bullock, Black River, U.P. ©2006 John Linn

Dean Johnson, East Huron. ©2006 Mike Cotten

River hardy Jay Erickson, Black River, U.P. ©2006 John Linn

From top left, clockwise to bottom left: Helge Klockow drops in on Obedience School on the YellowDog. Rod Thompson on an icy Black River in the U.P. Dean Johnson before impact on Conglomerate Falls on the Black. Harry House teeters off the bottom drop on Kuckuk's Plunge on the Slate River.

122 Manabezho Falls on the Presque Isle River, Michigan's Upper Peninsula. ©2006 Doug Nelson

Bill Obrien, Pike River.

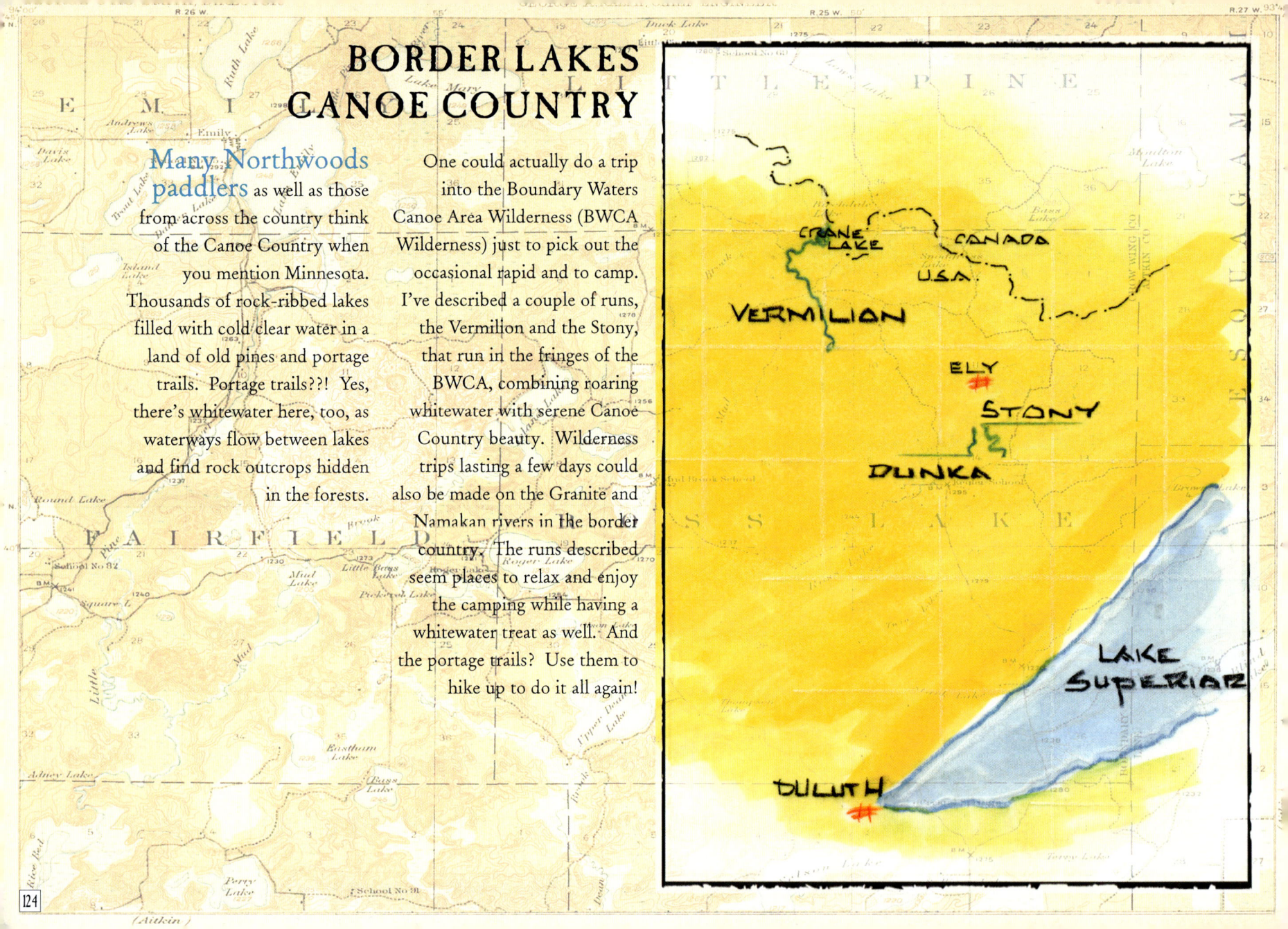

BORDER LAKES CANOE COUNTRY

Many Northwoods paddlers as well as those from across the country think of the Canoe Country when you mention Minnesota. Thousands of rock-ribbed lakes filled with cold clear water in a land of old pines and portage trails. Portage trails??! Yes, there's whitewater here, too, as waterways flow between lakes and find rock outcrops hidden in the forests.

One could actually do a trip into the Boundary Waters Canoe Area Wilderness (BWCA Wilderness) just to pick out the occasional rapid and to camp. I've described a couple of runs, the Vermilion and the Stony, that run in the fringes of the BWCA, combining roaring whitewater with serene Canoe Country beauty. Wilderness trips lasting a few days could also be made on the Granite and Namakan rivers in the border country. The runs described seem places to relax and enjoy the camping while having a whitewater treat as well. And the portage trails? Use them to hike up to do it all again!

BORDER LAKES CANOE COUNTRY

STONY RIVER
AND THE DUNKA RIVER

LENGTH: 4 MILES

CLASS: II–IV

SUMMER: EARLY

QUICK DESCRIPTION:
CONTINUOUS, FLATS, LEDGES, SCENIC

PUT-IN:
SUPERIOR NATIONAL FOREST 424 BRIDGE

TAKE-OUT:
BIRCH LAKE, EAST OF BABBITT

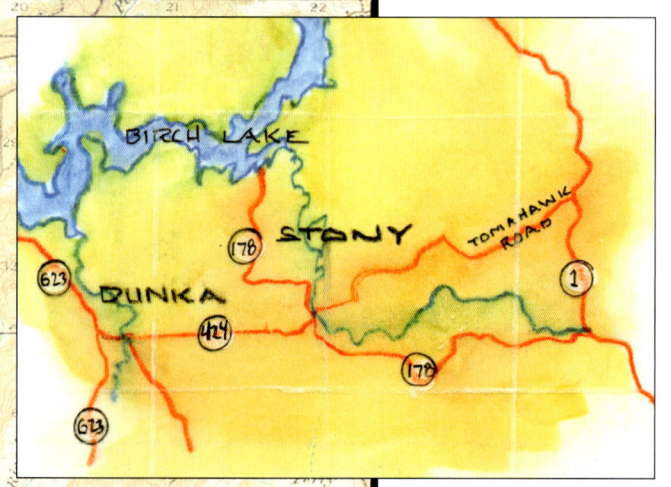

Those who started their Northwoods paddling by canoeing in the BWCA will relive memories of those days as they descend the Stony. Rock outcrops, jack pines and a finish on Birch Lake east of Babbitt give a "canoe country" feel to the run.

There's some nice whitewater, too, which starts almost immediately after putting in where Superior National Forest Road 424 crosses the Stony. The Stony displays continuous class II-III rapids for a half mile to warm you up. Oh, and I almost forgot . . .there's an eight foot sluice about two-thirds of the way through! The Anokas won't let me forget forgetting to tell them about this IV!

As the continuous rapids fade, you are immersed in beautiful flatwater. This flatwater is broken by occasional bursts of whitewater. First, a double ledge (on the left channel around an island)—class III, then comes more flatwater followed by the biggest rush on the river. Between "stone" walls the river plunges twelve feet down a slide into a foaming hydraulic.

What happens when 200 pounds of boat and paddler hits this hole? So far everything has washed out. Kayaking isn't a spectator sport, but it was a true rush to watch an open boat piloted by Dave Garren and Terry Lemke crash the Box. This drop is IV-IV+ at medium flows and is easily portaged on the left.

There's more calm, small rapids then a rapid that presents a choice at the top—go left down a narrow flume or follow most of the current right and "boof" a pleasant eight foot falls, III+.

Shortly before hitting Birch Lake the Stony shows a last flash as it slithers over a hundred yards of low ledges. This II-III rapid holds some fine sidesurfing holes. Now comes the choice—to take out at Birch Lake Resort and pay whatever the owner decides to charge for this privilege ($5 per car? $5 per person? $5 per finger?) or to paddle a quarter mile west on Birch Lake to take out where an old road comes to the water.

Taking out at this old road means you must carry your boat 150 yards to Superior Nat'l Forest Road 178. You save some money and avoid this fellow, so in my book there's no choice! After carrying your boat up the old trail you'll be able to savor the feel of a day kayaking in "canoe country."

Should you have time and should the Stony be high, you might enjoy driving six miles west of the Stony on Forest Road 424. Here you'll find the tiny Dunka—a mystery run done on a Memorial Day weekend under total secrecy. Tom Aluni made me promise not to tell Mike Cotten and Paul Douglas the location of this virgin kayaking run until we were at the put-in.

Jim Rada runs "the Box," on the Stony. ©2006 Mike Cotten

The Dunka has a few rapids, not as many as the Stony, and is quite small. It's dear to my heart, though, because it's home to "Rada's Rips," a genuine class IV–steep boulderbed fun.

Tom is a real friend, and it was very kind of him to allow me to run it first and then he named it after me. The only other whitewater feature named after me is "Rada's Rock" at Taylor's Falls... you know, the big boulder under the U.S. 8 bridge on the Wisconsin side. When I mentioned "Rada's Rock" to a woman kayakist I was trying to impress, she asked, "How come it's called that?" and I said, "Oh, no reason, I just decided it needed a name." She was not impressed. But you understand why "Rada's Rips" means a lot to me don't you??

The Vermilion
is special to me for many reasons: (1) It drains huge Lake Vermilion, which acts as a giant reservoir to keep the Vermilion boatable well into July and August. (2) It has several rapids of great character including one of the most fun sections anywhere–Table Rock Canyon. (3) It provides beautiful little Northwoods campsites where I can relax around a campfire with my low brow buddies, toasting a hot dog or a cheap steak. It's just so doggone warm and friendly from Memorial Day on into summer, for once no drysuit. It also holds rapids suitable for all. There are three principal sections starting at the Vermilion Dam: Section I (the Vermilion Dam run), Section II (the Table Rock run) and Section III (the Chute/Gorge run). I'll say a bit about each.

SECTION I
VERMILION DAM RUN

The Vermilion Dam run starts either above or below the rapids found at the Vermilion Dam at the northwest corner of Lake Vermilion. You get there by taking St. Louis County Highway 24 from either Cook or Buyck (like bike!) to St. Louis County 422. The dam is just a little slope of concrete, but the following rapid looks like a moraine of big boulders–steep, technical and filled with routes. There's a gauge on river left here which is useful in determining the level, although the Vermilion gains a lot of water before hitting Crane Lake. The Vermilion Dam rapids is a III, maybe more when high.

Now, the Vermilion alternates long flats and short rapids: Shively Falls, a twisting 150 yards of II-III water; Liftover Falls, a II+ drop of maybe four feet with a "liftover" portage; then Everett rapid, an easy class II boulderbed run; a final burst of class I, Squaw rapid. Below Squaw the Vermilion turns into a lake-like expanse. The rapids occur in about a three mile stretch and give a good warmup for beginning whitewater boaters without a lot of consequences, except in Vermilion Dam rapids. The rapids are fol-

The Gorge. ©2006 Mike Cotten

VERMILION RIVER

SECTION: I, DAM RUN

LENGTH: 5.5 MILES

CLASS: II-III

SUMMER: SOME

QUICK DESCRIPTION: VERMILION'S EASIEST SECTION

PUT-IN: VERMILION DAM AT NW CORNER OF L. VERMILION

TAKE-OUT: ST. LOUIS COUNTY 24 BRIDGE OVER TWO MILE CREEK

SECTION: II, TABLE ROCK

LENGTH: 1.5 MILES

CLASS: II-IV

SUMMER: YES

QUICK DESCRIPTION: FALLS, BEAUTIFUL III+ RAPIDS

PUT-IN: ST. LOUIS COUNTY 24 BRIDGE OVER EIGHT MILE CREEK

TAKE-OUT: CCC CAMP ONE MILE NORTH OF EIGHT MILE CREEK

Steve Stratman runs Table Rock rapid. ©2006 Chris Ringsven

lowed by a mile and a half paddle along the left shore of the "lake" until you hit Twomile Creek–then it's another twisty mile to the takeout, St. Louis 422 bridge over Twomile Creek. Want more rapids? Read on!

SECTION II

TABLE ROCK RUN

The Table Rock run starts where St. Louis County 422 crosses Eightmile Creek. Half a mile of winding later you reach the north end of the "lake" you left back in Section 1. Turn left and you'll notice a portage trail on river right. If you're new to the whitewater game, you may want to take a hike on this to check out what's ahead. Those who are bolder may paddle a couple hundred yards of class I-II water til you see a horizon line–eddy out right about twenty yards above the horizon and take a peak at Table Rock Falls. Some will portage and some will run this tiered drop.

The Vermilion dances downstream falling twenty plus feet with some fancy footwork you'll have to duplicate. Class IV-IV+ at low to moderate flows, it gets intimidating when there's actually water! On the other hand it's possible to have fun banging down this at low flows. It's smoothest in the center. I remember the Great Drought of 1977–we returned here week after week to run lower and lower water. Weekdays we'd patch our glass boats preparing for the next weekend. Ah, the world was young then . . . it was B.P., Before Plastic.

Some paddlers will come to the Vermilion looking for less radical fun, and now the Vermilion will oblige. Below Table Rock Falls comes one of the most enjoyable rapids I know: the Table Rock Canyon. The next half-mile contains a natural slalom course building from class II to III+ (IV at high flow).

The first piece is easy. Then the river narrows, a low rock cliff shows on the left and suddenly the bottom drops out as the Vermilion snakes through holes and waves, hiding its next move from view. Certainly Greg Breining didn't see what was ahead as he led our kayaks down this in an open canoe borrowed from John Wexler on our first descent. He couldn't see what was ahead, but reckoned it wasn't much worse than the Minnesota Snake (class II). A soggy camera and dented canoe proved the error of this assumption.

Eric Hobbie and others have enjoyed the slalom practice this place provides. I and others have played our way down, snagging eddies, sidesurfing holes, putting our noses into the pop up spot part way through, then carrying back up on a beautiful portage trail to do it all again and again! CANOE magazine once asked me what my favorite rapid was. I hate to choose but I think this is it. I love the action, the solitude and even the portage trail.

At high flows it's "something else," class IV+ where runs become Team Wildwater events and you just hope you blow through the holes before someone else drops in! Below the "intense" stuff, the Vermilion merrily churns along through another half-mile of class II boulderbed til you reach the flats again. On the left is a small campground and boat access, on the right is the portage trail back to the top. It's nice to camp at the takeout, and this also allows boaters to carry up from the takeout to run if they want. It's only a mile from Table Rock Falls to this camp, but what a nice mile!

SECTION III

CHUTE-GORGE RUN

Before heading downstream toward Crane Lake from Superior National Forest Road 491, take ten minutes to walk the trail up to High Falls (also called Vermilion Falls). High Falls is to my mind class VI water; it can't be run without significant risk to life, yet it is conceivable that it could be run.

I almost never use the class VI for rating rapids that are run. I think few people will intentionally run water that presents a "significant risk to life," we're out for fun, not an end to our boating days. Still, if you want to see a beautiful class VI–look at High Falls. Back to the run. The gauge used for the Vermilion River hydrograph found elsewhere in this book is located on the left, 350 feet downstream of Forest Road 491. Just beyond the gauge the current picks up–and a class I-II lead-in brings you to the Chute, a complex nine foot drop hemmed in by slabs of rock.

At low flows it's a tricky III+, as you angle down the tongue and try to avoid the left side undercuts that the river pushes toward. At medium flow, the outwash becomes wavy and boats and boaters flipped in the tongue's crosscurrents often find a way to lodge on Rebecca's Rock, a boulder along the right shore.

VERMILION RIVER

Dave Garren and Terry Lemke crash the Chute. ©2006 Mike Cotten

Rebecca's Rock sits atop other underwater giants and creates an effective sieve below water level. It has claimed and not returned at least two kayak paddles, Rebecca Aluni's being the first.

At high flow the Chute takes on a Grand Canyon feel–several huge pulsing waves throw boats around like matchsticks–big water IV+. Be warned, most boaters underestimate the Chute from shore because they don't allow for the way the Chute runs at an angle from right to left.

Below the Chute there's a lot of flatwater as you travel three and a half miles to the river's mouth on Crane Lake and then go one and a half miles east to the Crane Lake boat landing. What gets lazy whitewater boaters to do this flatwater? The Gorge and the rapids in the mile before the Gorge. After two miles of flatwater you reach the first of three separate pitches of class II-II+ water. There are some play features in these rapids that lead you through the mile preceding the Gorge: a few little surf waves and a couple of holes. Then you see the Vermilion twist sharply left between cliffs fifty feet tall. This is the Gorge.

The Gorge is a two hundred yard long cleft that is ignited by two ledges in the first fifty yards. The second ledge can generate play holes, monsters or be flooded out, depending on level. I once saw John Wexler get trashed in this hole only to roll up and then survive the 150 yards of big waves between canyon walls that remained. What was memorable about this was that John had broken off a paddle blade while underwater–but he didn't know this! He stroked and braced his way through only to look up at the end and see the other blade missing.

The Gorge can hold your attention. There are eddies in the Gorge, so it's fun to stop and admire the walls–sometimes the sun shines right down the Gorge and turns the river to liquid amber, each bubble a sparkling jewel. Times like that are the best: a bathtub warm river, beauty, fun and friends.

After the Gorge melts away a few rapids and a bend bring you to Crane Lake–now cruise to the takeout. I have spent a lot of time describing the Vermilion; it's a treasure.

Not so many rapids, but what character they have! And any river providing such warm weather paddling and camping is extra special.

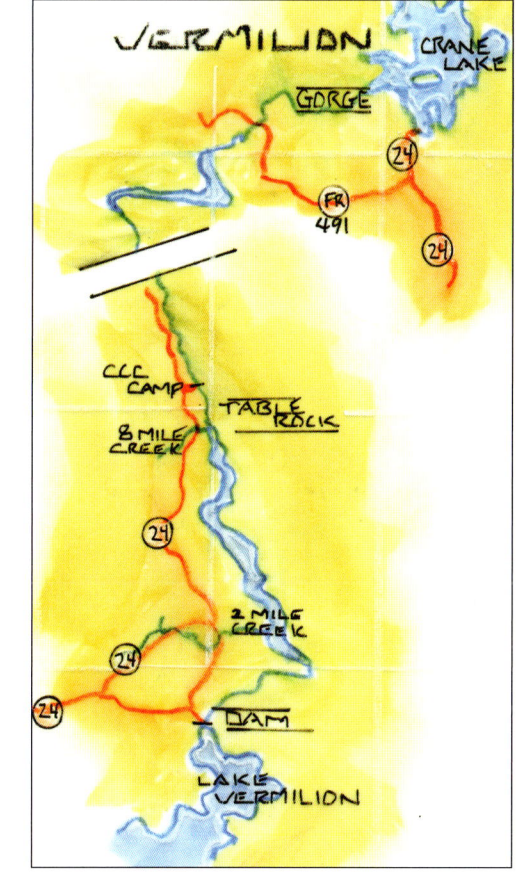

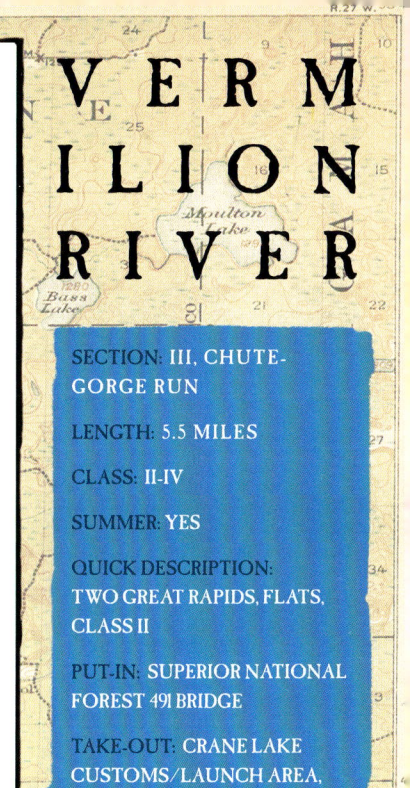

SECTION: III, CHUTE-GORGE RUN

LENGTH: 5.5 MILES

CLASS: II-IV

SUMMER: YES

QUICK DESCRIPTION: TWO GREAT RAPIDS, FLATS, CLASS II

PUT-IN: SUPERIOR NATIONAL FOREST 491 BRIDGE

TAKE-OUT: CRANE LAKE CUSTOMS/LAUNCH AREA, END OF ST. LOUIS 24

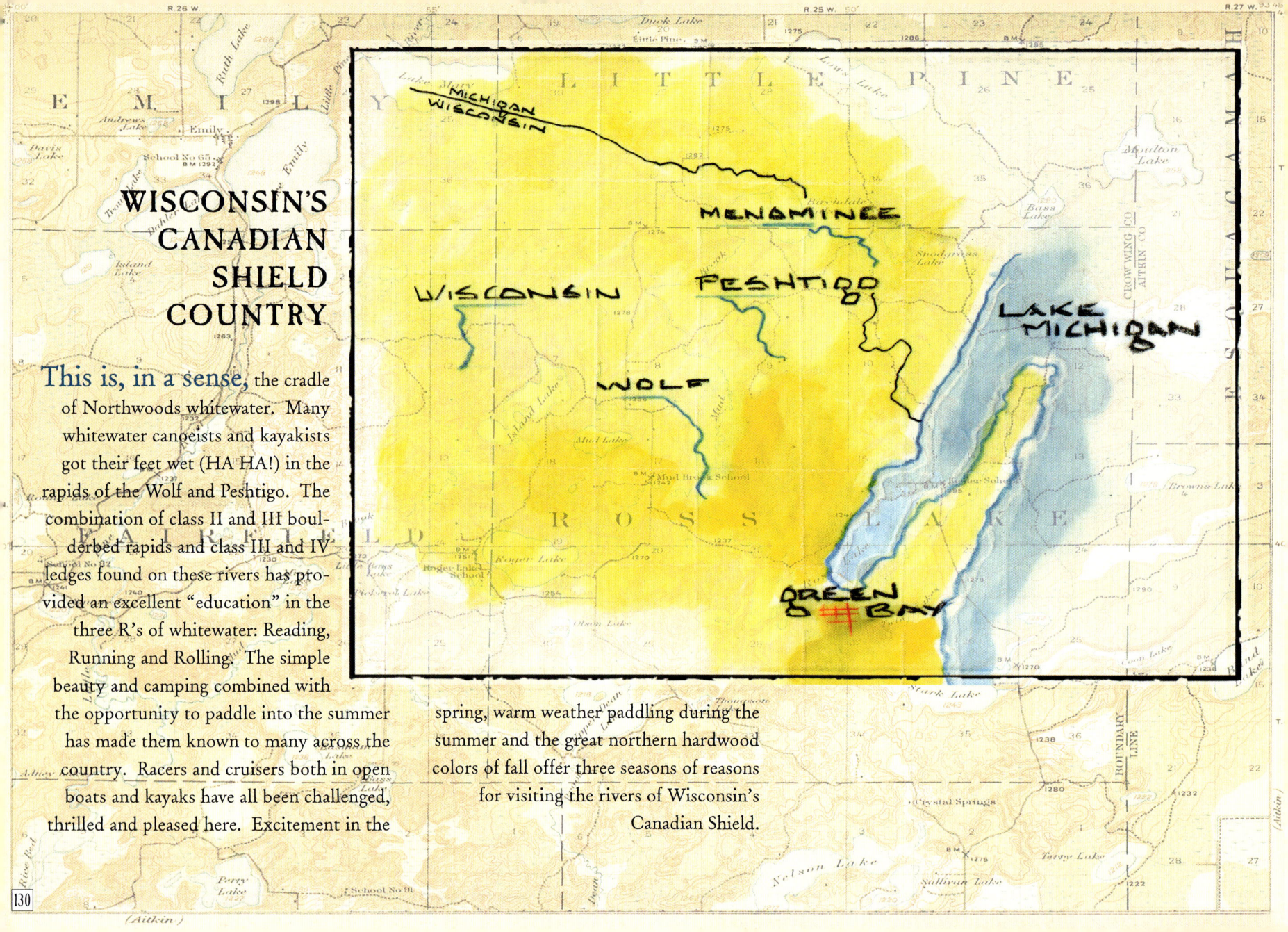

WISCONSIN'S CANADIAN SHIELD COUNTRY

This is, in a sense, the cradle of Northwoods whitewater. Many whitewater canoeists and kayakists got their feet wet (HA HA!) in the rapids of the Wolf and Peshtigo. The combination of class II and III boulderbed rapids and class III and IV ledges found on these rivers has provided an excellent "education" in the three R's of whitewater: Reading, Running and Rolling. The simple beauty and camping combined with the opportunity to paddle into the summer has made them known to many across the country. Racers and cruisers both in open boats and kayaks have all been challenged, thrilled and pleased here. Excitement in the spring, warm weather paddling during the summer and the great northern hardwood colors of fall offer three seasons of reasons for visiting the rivers of Wisconsin's Canadian Shield.

©2006 Doug Nelson

WISCONSIN'S CANADIAN SHIELD COUNTRY

WOLF RIVER

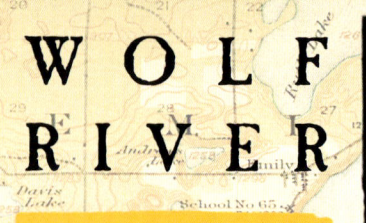

SECTION: III

LENGTH: 3.7 MILES

CLASS: II–III

SUMMER: YES, LOW

QUICK DESCRIPTION:
2 NICE, LONG BOULDERBEDS, ONE LEDGE

PUT-IN:
DNR LANDING OFF HWY M. WEST OF WILD WOLF INN

TAKE-OUT:
GILMORE'S RAPID, WILD WOLF INN, 6 MILES SE OF LANGLADE

The Wolf has probably been the "happy paddling grounds" for more whitewater boaters than any other river in the Northwoods. Canoeists, kayakists and rafters by the score have enjoyed the fine mixture of scenery, boulderbed and ledges that define the Wolf. It doesn't hurt that the Wolf, like the Peshtigo, can be paddled much of the summer albeit at low levels (see the hydrograph elsewhere in this book).

Wolf River (at Langlade) flow levels are available online on the USGS web site at http://waterdata.usgs. gov/nwis/rt and on the AW website at www.americanwhitewater.org. As on the Peshtigo gauge, the Wolf is at low, scrapey levels when around 350cfs, although the lower part, Section IV, carries the water better than Section III, the upper part. Below 600cfs is nice and above 100cfs, good.

SECTION III

Section III, as it exists today, puts in at Hwy 64 in Langlade. But a common run is to put in at the DNR landing off of County Hwy M above Boy Scout Rapids. This cuts off 6 miles of flatwater and a few rapids and makes for a 3.5 miles run of mixed flatwater and whitewater from the Gardner Boy Scout Camp, about four miles south of Langlade on Wisconsin 55 to Gilmore's Mistake. Gilmore's, a great rapid and the takeout for this section, is located near a restaurant, the Wild Wolf Inn, on Wisconsin 55 about six miles south of Langlade.

Meta Gaertnier and Mark Threlkeld run Sullivan Falls. ©2006 Roy Eneberg

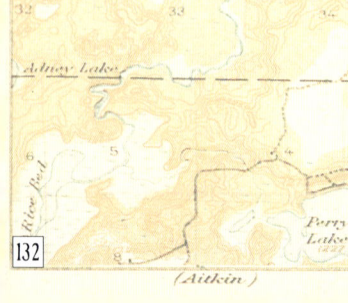

Ann Helm and Scott McKell run The Dalles. ©2006 Roy Eneberg

This section includes three principal rapids: Boy Scout, a half-mile long section of boulderbed that varies between II and III; Hanson's, another long delightful rapid with narrow boulderbed and a bit of a drop off at the top, class III; and Gilmore's Mistake, a bedrock rapid at the takeout. All three are of high quality and have been used at one time or another for putting on slalom races on the Wolf. In my paddling youth, Gilmore's was my favorite rapid anywhere because of the big waves and holes it could develop at spring flows—there are some nice playspots here, surfing and holes.

SECTION IV

Just below Gilmore's Mistake the Wolf flows into Menominee County, home of the Menominee Indian Reservation. The tribe is fiercely protective of its right to control access to the Wolf River in their reservation. They have also protected the Wolf from private development, keeping its banks free of the cabins that dot the upper Wolf.

In years past there were occasional violent confrontations between paddlers and Indians, and several years of river closure–no paddling! Now those wanting to run the 8-9 mile long Section IV from the Menominee County line to a takeout after Big Smokey Falls must obtain a permit. This can be done by calling or going to Big Smokey Falls Rafting at (715) 799-3359.

Kevin Wehrmann blasts through Big Smokey Falls. ©2006 Ann Ramirez

There are several other possible access points for Section IV including Gilmore's, the County WW bridge three miles downstream of Gilmore's, Otter Slide off Wisconsin 55 about two miles south of the WW bridge, the Dalles and Big Smokey Falls, the usual takeout.

A common approach is to purchase a permit right there at the Big Smokey Falls rafting office. Then, they will shuttle you and your boats to their put-in at Otter Slide. The takeout for this arrangement is also Big Smokey Falls. which makes for a 6-mile run.

The Dalles and Big Smokey are reached by a road that branches west off of Wisconsin 55 about five road miles from the WW bridge over the Wolf. The rapids, briefly, starting from Gilmore's are: Gilmore's, a class II-III boulder stretch (known as Burnt Shanty), then a delightful half mile long class III boulder garden called "Shotgun," followed rather quickly by the WW bridge and the short ledges of "Pismire Falls"–a III with holes when high. From Gilmore's to WW there's quite a bit of whitewater, but the three miles below Pismire are placid.

WOLF RIVER

SECTION: IV

LENGTH: 11 MILES

CLASS: II–IV

SUMMER: YES

QUICK DESCRIPTION: LONG BOULDERBED FIRST, THEN LEDGES

PUT-IN: GILMORE'S RAPID AT WILD WOLF INN, 6 MI. SE OF LANGLADE

TAKE-OUT: BIG SMOKEY FALLS, OFF WISC. 55, 13 MILES SE OF LANGLADE

the paddler resumes the flatwater mode for the next mile to the Dalles area. Along the way, you'll encounter one playspot.

On approaching the Dalles area, the Wolf will slide down and right through Tea Kettle, a hundred yards of class III with playspots. A short breather and the Wolf plunges into a small canyon, the Dalles, class III or IV depending on level. Another mile or so of flatwater and you arrive at Big Smokey Falls, the biggest rush on the trip. A steeply inclined lead-in a hundred yards long ends in a six foot hurtle off a bedrock lip with a pool at the end—class IV, and a fittingly wild ride to conclude the Wolf's Section IV.

The constricted nature of Section IV and the additional water it receives from tributaries make it a better summer run than Section III. There is easier whitewater on the Wolf, up toward Langlade and above, intermittent class II.

Since the river has reopened, I have developed new boating destinations along Lake Superior and have not returned to the Wolf in recent years. I have relied on some information provided by Whitewater Specialty, Inc. to update the political scene.

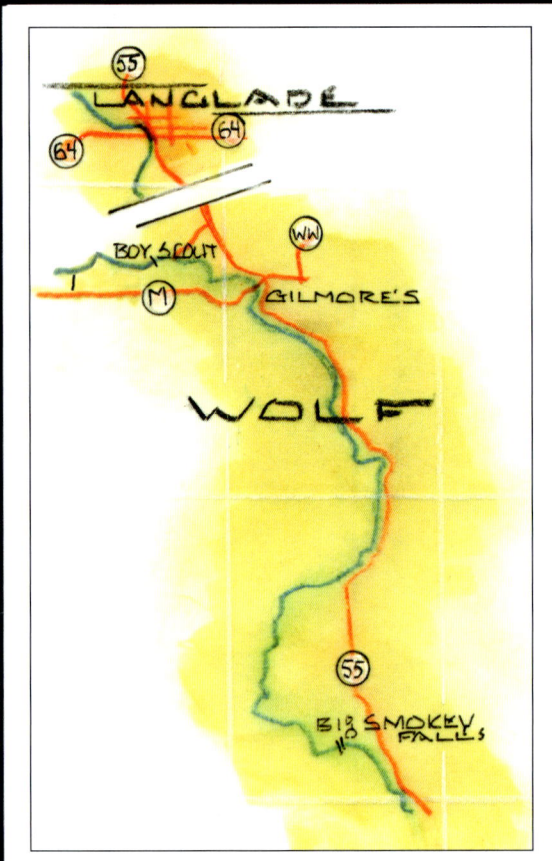

A mile below the Otter Slide access off Wisconsin 55, and three miles below Pismire, the Wolf springs over Sullivan Falls, a 6-7 foot drop; a hundred yards later the Wolf squeezes left over a sloping drop, Upper Ducknest, III+; then in another hundred yards flies into Lower Ducknest, III+ at high flow, where the water screams over a sheet of bedrock funneling into tailwaves. Calm returns and

The Wolf is a good river! There are other runs in the Wolf area with which I'm unacquainted, but which hold some whitewater: the Pike, the Pine and the Red.

The Red seems to be of the greatest interest as it is dam controlled and runnable in the summer. The section containing Monastery Falls is south of the Wolf's Section IV, towards Shawano. The Wausau slalom course is also in the area and releases are scheduled both for races and play/practice. For information on release schedules for this national caliber slalom course contact the Wausau Chamber of Commerce at (715) 845-6231.

The Peshtigo's "Roaring Rapids"

combines boulderbed, ledges and northern forest into one of the nicest runs in Wisconsin's Canadian Shield area. The takeout is just downstream of the Marinette County C bridge over the Peshtigo on river left at landing 12, a public access provided by the power company that owns the Cauldron Falls Reservoir. On the County C bridge you'll find the old paddler's gauge for the river: 0 inches (250cfs, 4' on the USGS guage) is a low but boatable level frequently found here during the summer. As of 1998, there is a new USGS gauge.

Mark Resong, a high school and college friend, accompanied me to the Peshtigo on several boat destruction outings in the mid 70's. Seven inches gave his aluminum canoe a bit of a hammering. Twelve (700cfs) is getting good, in the 20's (circa 1200 cfs) is fine boating, with holes and push and at 48 inches (circa 2500 cfs) it was wondrous big water. You get about four miles of river by driving west on County C 3.2 miles from the takeout. A mile past where County F comes in you'll see Farm Dam Lane branching right that leads quickly to the river at the mouth of Otter Creek. Putting in here gives a whitewater ride the whole way to County C.

The first mile and a half is continuous easy class I-II boulderbed and the last mile is also boulderbed, rather nice class II water. The middle mile and a half contains six distinct ledges of class III-IV nature: (1) First Drop–a sharp 6-7 foot drop with a notable hole at the base. (2) Second Drop–a sloping ledge that tends to funnel the Peshtigo into a broad hole. My first encounter with the Peshtigo at about 30 inches included seeing a raft tumbling in the Second Drop hole–it had been there overnight! (3) Third Drop–a ledge pinches the Peshtigo to the right and causes it to slide down sharply into a couple of holes. About a hundred feet below Third Drop, and a hundred feet above Five Foot Falls is a hole that is sneaky and powerful at levels above 20 inches; be wary here. (4) Five Foot Falls–as the name implies, a river wide ledge generates a five foot drop.

PESHTIGO RIVER

A channel far left is commonly run, although at high flow routes in the center develop. (5) Horserace–this is to my mind the most exhilarating of the Peshtigo's six ledges, and the longest.

Here the Peshtigo narrows and slides for 150 yards over bedrock sheets. There are eddies carved into the rock shores on both left and right and it's fun to catch these–ferrying from one to another across the jet speed wave train down the middle. Be ready for the final plunge at the end! It's probably the most difficult rapid on the run. (6) S Turn–a quick drop tight on the left side of the river.

These six drops come spaced with short sections of boulderbed between, and offer some nice holes and waves for playing. To take a look at this section, either go west on County C from the takeout a half-mile to Allison Lane and follow to its end, then walk in to Horserace, or go east on C a couple miles from the takeout to where Parkway Road heads north. After three miles on Parkway, you'll see Brandywine Lane branching left towards the Peshtigo. It will bring you close to Five Foot Falls.

The Peshtigo can be a bit crowded, as such a fine run attracts many kayakists, canoeists and commercial rafting companies. The Anokas recommend the bar at the takeout as a friendly and interesting place. The Peshtigo, while low, can be enjoyed

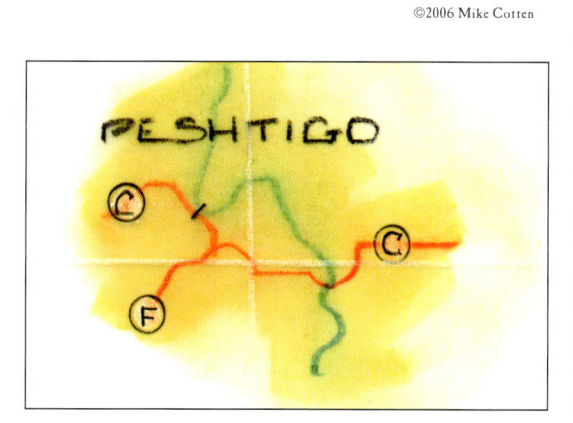

Gary DeMars puts a blade down on the Peshtigo. ©2006 Mike Cotten

LENGTH: 3.5 MILES

CLASS: II–IV

SUMMER: YES, LOW

QUICK DESCRIPTION: NICE MIXTURE OF BOULDERS, LEDGES

PUT-IN: FARM DAM LANE OFF MARINETTE CO. C, 1 MI. N. OF COUNTY F

TAKE-OUT: LANDING 12 DOWNSTREAM OF HWY C BRIDGE

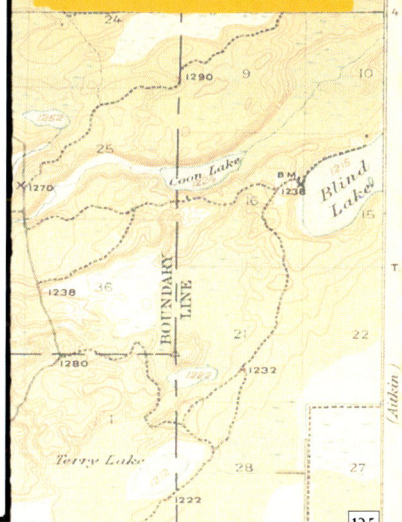

MENOMINEE RIVER

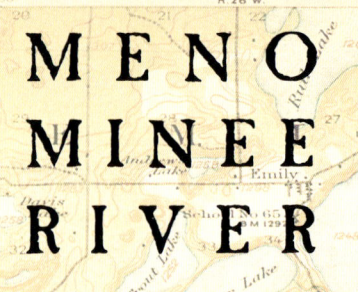

LENGTH: 3 MILES

CLASS: I-IV

SUMMER: YES

QUICK DESCRIPTION:
DAM-CONTROLLED, SHORT III-IV+ GORGE

PUT-IN:
BOAT LAUNCH IN NIAGARA

TAKE-OUT:
U.S. 8 BRIDGE OVER MENOMINEE

The Menominee has in the past been subject to industrial pollution from a paper mill near Niagara, causing some boaters to refer to it as the "Stink-on-a-me," or the "Stink" for short. In recent years, the water quality has been considerably better thanks to the Clean Water Act!

The Menominee is of interest because it is a big river that allows boating all summer. The river forms part of the border between Michigan's Upper Peninsula and Wisconsin, flowing into Lake Michigan.

Put in at the boat launch in Niagara, Wisconsin and take out 2.5 miles downstream at the U.S. 8 bridge. It's possible to avoid a bit of flatwater by utilizing the first road to the left after U.S. 8 enters Michigan. This road will bring you closer to the end of Piers Gorge where you can hike up to run just the gorge.

This run is really about doing Piers Gorge, which comes about two miles downstream of Niagara. The Gorge starts with style, crashing eight feet down Misicot Falls and roaring left at a huge boulder called Volkswagen Rock.

After this the Menominee flows through the Two Sisters and finishes off with Terminal Surfer. The whole gorge isn't that long, about a half-mile, but it does contain nice class IV water and playspots.

Steve Corsi runs Piers Gorge. ©2006 Thomas O'Keefe

Harry House and Thomas O'Keefe at Chicken Ender on the Menominee. ©2006 Elise Giddings

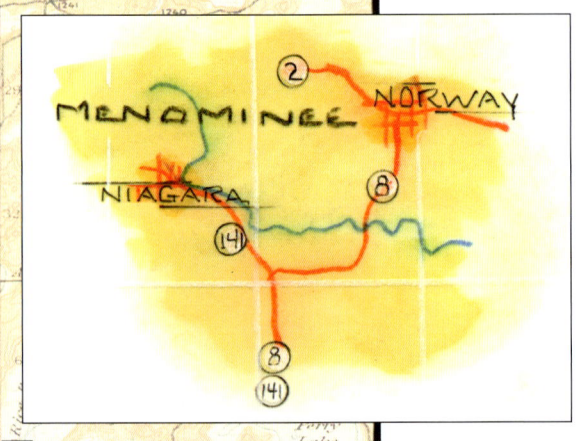

WISCONSIN RIVER

Ol' Granddad is a feisty, mean, crotchety geezer who'll give any paddler who doesn't respect him a kick in the pants.

You can meet Granddad, but only under certain conditions, as the dam-o-maniacs have funneled the Wisconsin's flow away from him, put it in a tube and bypassed the mile of river over which he presides. Let's hope this changes, as the current license expires in 2018.

To find Granddad's home, go north out of Merrill on Wisconsin Highway 107. About ten miles out of town you'll come to the Grandfather Falls powerplant (the takeout) and in another mile, the Grandfather Falls Dam (the put-in). Normally the "tubes" take all the water, but during really high water in spring, or during rarer periods of tube repair, the Grandfather Falls section receives some juice, and it does use it!

Granddad lies about two-thirds of a mile below the dam, the intervening water being good, and sometimes heavy, class III. Granddad is about eight feet tall, sloping shoulders and a red glow in his eye if you stumble into his hole. I've seen footage of a boater backendering, rolling and forward endering all in one smooth sequence—it looked planned, but I'm sure it wasn't!

The river calms down a bit after Granddad, but small ledges make for a half-mile of play water. The run is short, interesting and has easy access. I just think Gramps wouldn't be so mean if they let him have a drink more often.

How dry he is. ©2006 Thomas O'Keefe

Ol' Granddad gets a drink. ©2006 Helge Klockow

LENGTH: 1.2 MILES

CLASS: III-IV

SUMMER: MAYBE

QUICK DESCRIPTION: POWER, BIG DROP, PLAYSPOTS

PUT-IN: GRANDFATHER FALLS DAM, 10 MI. N OF MERRILL ON WISC. 107

TAKE-OUT: POWERPLANT, 9 MI. N. OF MERRILL ON WISCONSIN 107

While many boaters would love to live on the North or South Shore, jobs, families and for some, urban pleasures keep many rooted in the Twin Cities. As large metropolitan areas go, the Minneapolis-St. Paul area does pretty well. For metro residents it's nice to know that there's whitewater closer to home than Lake Superior and the runs in this section can be made as day trips. Many of the rivers in this section start running earlier than the others in this book and so give a jump on the season to paddlers looking to be out in March. Most of these runs feature only short sections of high quality water, but that develops a natural tendency to be a playboater—to learn how to surf, spin, ender . . . and roll! A couple of these runs have easier water than the usual minimum for inclusion in this book, but they provide a scenic escape close to town so I've included them–they really are too nice to ignore. I hope this section will point out a few runs that might let an evening of whitewater soothe you after a day at work or make it possible to get that kayak fix and still go out Saturday night!

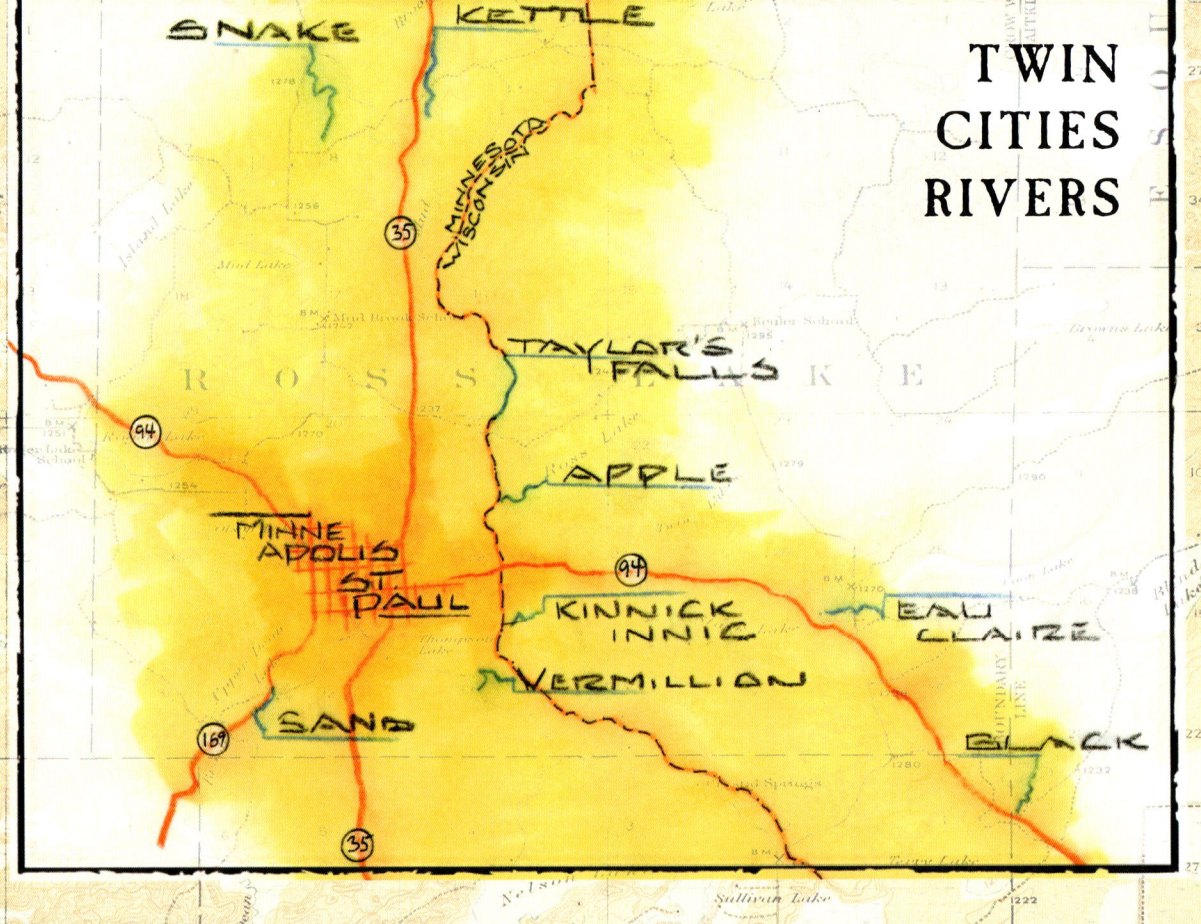

TWIN CITIES RIVERS

TWIN CITIES RIVERS

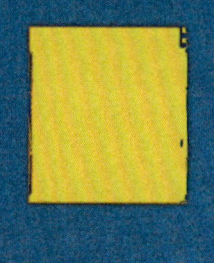

Blueberry Slide, Kettle River ©2006 Doug Nelson

VERMILLION RIVER

NEAR HASTINGS MINESOTA

LENGTH: 0.5 MILES

CLASS: II–III+

SUMMER: RARE

QUICK DESCRIPTION:
LEDGES IN LIMESTONE CANYON

PUT-IN:
JUST BELOW FALLS NEAR GRAIN ELEVATOR, PARK AT TAKEOUT

TAKE-OUT:
OLD MILL IN PARK ON MN 249, 0.5 MI. EAST OF U.S. 61

Ok you metro boatheads, here's your own best of the immediate Twin Cities area. Slap the 'yak on top of the vehicle and head on down to Hastings, an old river town on the Mississippi twenty miles southeast of St. Paul.

As you head south through town on U.S. 61, keep looking for the mill elevators. A block before you reach them on the south side of town, turn left on Minnesota State Highway 249 and go about a half-mile. Just after crossing some railroad tracks you'll see a parking lot and a park with oak trees on your right. Park here for a shuttleless run of the Vermillion's canyon.

There are two problems with the Vermillion—scanty water and poor access. To check the water, get on those railroad tracks and walk out on the trestle over the river. Do you like what you see? I hope so.

Mid-March can provide a week or two of boating here in the spring, as can summer thunderstorms. It's really flashy and we've made the trek after a cloudburst only to find matted grass—"Shudda been here this morning!"

The other problem is access. The canyon starts with a twenty-five foot falls up near the grain elevators. It's a bit hard to climb down the trails into the canyon. The best ones seem to be along the left rim

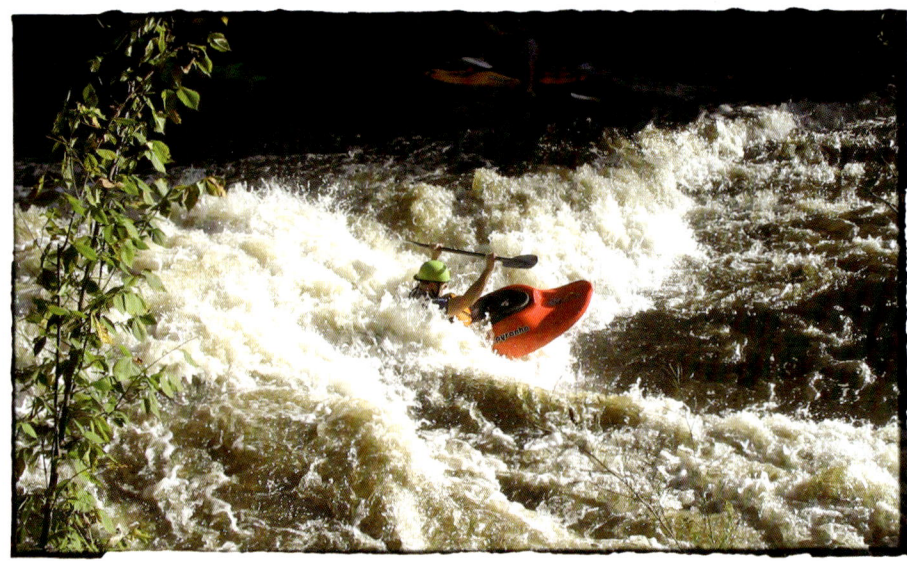

Lanny Freng surfs Donut Hole on the Vermillion River.   ©2005 Jake Vos

near the railroad tracks a quarter-mile upstream from the trestle. Carry down and enjoy!

It's a small, technical river dotted with limestone ledges in a canyon. There's lots of trash, unfortunately (I even dug a bicycle out of a silted eddy once), but there are also a few majestic white pines and lots of juniper—I like it. There are some class II play waves and ledges for a quarter mile, then the Trestle, class III at low flow, IV at high flow.

It's exciting, starting with a six foot ledge and then slamming through waves and holes for a couple hundred feet. A few eddies fly past–did you catch any? And a hole/wave at the bottom.

The fun isn't over. After a pool you encounter another hundred yards of II-II+ ledges that create some surfing opportunities when the water's up, then two medium class III ledges, each about four or five feet tall. These ledges can produce some juicy holes. At high water these holes can trash you—even Mike Vande Viver's "paddle like hell" technique proved inadequate.

A little class I warmdown and you take out river left at the ruins of an old mill—another interesting spot. So two-thirds mile of river with playspots, excitement, a little canyon, a ruined mill and no shuttle! You can spend a couple of enjoyable hours here on a cold March day and go home to warm up and eat pizza. Not such a bad way to start the season, eh?

BLACK RIVER

Guy Babbit and Mike Giddings peel out in a C2 on the Black in springtime. ©2006 Thomas O'Keefe

NEAR BLACK RIVER FALLS, WI

LENGTH: 2.5 MILES

CLASS: II–III (V)

SUMMER: SOME

QUICK DESCRIPTION: BIG RIVER, SOME PLAY, PRETTY

PUT-IN: BELOW DAM AT LAKE ARBUTUS, NEAR HATFIELD

TAKE-OUT: POWERHOUSE BOAT LANDING, 2.5 MILES DOWNSTREAM, RIGHT

During early spring 1996 I finally got to paddle this section of the Black and was pleasantly surprised by a river I'm sure I'll be back to. The Black has several traits that make it of interest to kayakists, especially those from the Twin Cities area: size, season and proximity.

By the time the Black gets to Hatfield it has drained a huge chunk of Wisconsin, making it one of our biggest whitewater rivers. I'd say it might be a little smaller than the St. Louis near Duluth. The day I paddled it there were several thousand CFS flowing down it and the nature of the rapids reminded me of those on Section I of the St. Louis.

The rapids begin with a bang immediately below the dam. The first couple of ledges exhibit a heavy class IV-V nature as the river drops furiously over bedrock. This is followed by a short pool before the river drops over a sharp class III ledge which has some playspots in its runout. Other boaters told me that at some levels a large nicely shaped surfing wave forms here.

After the bedrock ledges below the dam, the Black has a short pool before passing under the Jackson County Highway K bridge. Here the Black takes a gentler drop around a rocky island, with the better waves and water on the right. Below this rapid the riverbed broadens and the river is made up of stretches of swiftwater interspersed with broad class II rapids. In the two miles between the K bridge and the takeout, there are probably about four of these rapids. Each is about a hundred yards long and consists of boulders and/or small ledges. One of these had a small rock island near the left shore with a nice play hole between the island and the shore. With the spring flow I encountered there were also a couple of nice waves in this rapid and some of the others. Look carefully, though, the river is broad enough that it's easy to miss the good spots.

This is mainly a play run, not an adrenaline fix. I've been told that the rapids and play spots are much better when the water's high than when it's low. Apparently at some of the higher levels there are some excellent surf waves and even an ender spot. These playspots change dramatically with flow.

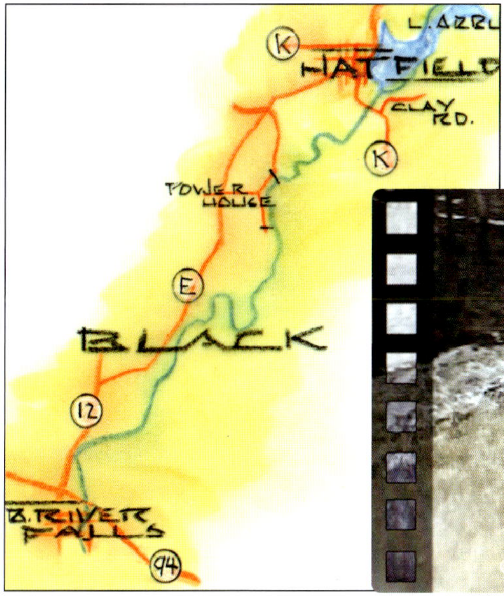

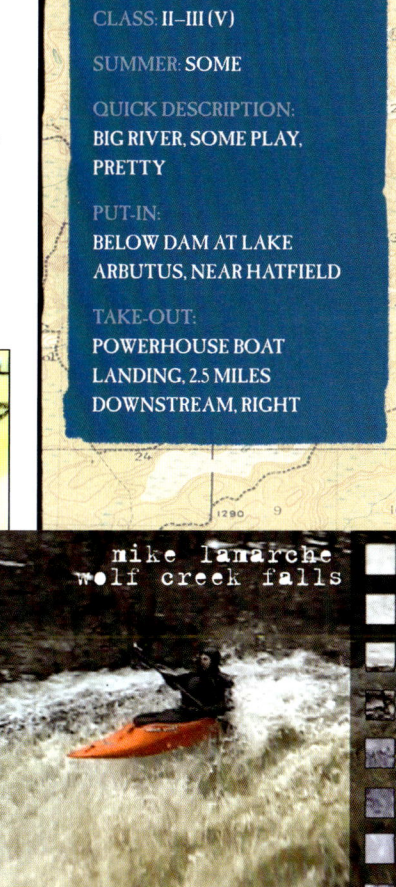

mike lamarche wolf creek falls ©2006 steve stratman

©2005 Steve Stratman

[141]

EAU CLAIRE RIVER
BIG FALLS

LENGTH: 150 YARDS

CLASS: III-IV

SUMMER: YES

QUICK DESCRIPTION: SMALL LEDGES PLUS EIGHT FOOT FALLS

PUT-IN: COUNTY PARK REACHED BY EAU CLAIRE COUNTY UN FROM THE NORTH OR FROM SOUTH BY DIRT ROAD FROM EAU CLAIRE COUNTY K BRIDGE

TAKE-OUT: SAME AS ABOVE

However, even when low the river should retain its beauty. It surprised me with fine sand beaches alternating with small rock outcrops along the bank, while the forest included both majestic pines and gnarly scrub oaks.

Though this run has a lot less whitewater than the Lake Superior jewels, it does merit a special place for whitewater paddlers. It starts running in mid to late March which allows paddlers a chance to get out and "tune up" on some easy play water. Being a big river I've heard of instances when summer rains rumbling through the southern part of the Northwoods brought it to life. The early spring paddling season was verified by Madison boaters I encountered—they had already been running it for two weeks when I came through. This was well before the Superior runs had begun to thaw! So because it runs early and can be hit by storms that miss the north, I think the Black is a good river to know about.

In recent years, thanks to American Whitewater and the National Park Service, regular releases have been scheduled on the 3rd Saturday of each month from April through August although these are cancelled occasionally subject to the water level in the reservoir behind the Hatfield dam. Refer to the AW web page for more information.

Another plus is the convenient access—it's easily reached from the Twin Cities in about two to two and a half hours by driving I-94 to Black River Falls, then going north on U.S. 12 to Jackson County E, turning east on County K. After crossing the river on K take a left and go about a quarter-mile. You can park here on the shoulder and carry to the river on a trail through the pine woods. The carry is only a couple hundred yards. To find the takeout go back to E and head south a couple miles to find Powerhouse Road, this will bring you to the powerhouse, the takeout.

As a footnote, I'll repeat Rick Klade's report that there are short class II-III runs on some of the creeks in the vicinity. Two of these are Hall's Creek near Hatfield and Robinson Creek, about six miles south of Black River Falls. I have little information on either of these, except that the Robinson Creek run apparently consists of the two miles above Wisconsin 27 and includes Polly Falls (shown on the Wisconsin DeLorme's atlas). Polly Falls was the site of a drowning in 1995. Apparently, an open canoe capsized here and one of the occupants was held in a hole at the bottom. Another boater attempted a rescue without a lifejacket and drowned while the paddler in the hole survived.

According to open boat guidebooks, there are also some rapids on both the East Fork of the Black and the Black above the Lake Arbutus reservoir. These rapids sound as if they are only class II and of lower quality than the run described here.

Eau Claire River

I love to explore, to see new places. I particularly enjoy finding new whitewater to run, so you can imagine my interest when I first heard about Big Falls on the Eau Claire. From the vague reports I had of it from non-boaters and others it was a substantial drop. Then I found photos of it in a book aimed primarily at canoeists, INDIAN HEAD RIVERS OF WEST CENTRAL WISCONSIN. The pictures and description primed me for making the drive to Eau Claire from the Twin Cities on a mid-November day in 1993 when weather forecasters predicted our last 50 degree day of the year.

I drove about nine miles east of Eau Claire on County SS and then turned north on County K two miles north of Fall Creek, Wisconsin. Within a half mile I got my first glimpse of the Eau Claire, a fairly large river, perhaps a little bigger than Minnesota's Kettle, with gleaming white sand paralleling its looping course as it wove through the pine barren country of the County Forest.

Just upstream from the County K bridge was a small rapid that obviously had enough water to run even though it had been a dry fall. Just before K dove down to cross the river I'd noticed a dirt road going west along the south side of the river with a sign for Big Falls. I followed this road for close to a mile and came to a parking lot. A broad hiking trail lead to the river and Big Falls. Later I found that there is also a parking lot on the north side river accessible by County UN off of County Q. The north side access also has a short walk to the river.

What I found was a fun piece of whitewater. A rock island and outcrops emerge from the sand, dividing the Eau Claire in two at this point. The right channel contains 150 yards of class III rapids in a curving stairstep. The right side offers a few choices of route, some tight, some broad. The main features of the right side are four small to medium ledges and several bedrock eddies to hop down. Even at the low flow I encountered it was good fun.

The left side loses the drop much more quickly: a small chute followed in fifty feet by Big Falls itself. Big Falls is a sharp drop of about eight feet with a runnable tongue at the low water level I encountered. Unfortunately, the tongue was blocked by a small, partially submerged tree, so I chose not to attempt what otherwise looked to be a solid class IV drop. After Big Falls the left channel drops another 3-4 feet in a simple rapid that ends with a play hole along the left bank.

I enjoyed my taste of whitewater and exploring that afternoon and thought about how Big Falls might appeal to Twin Cities boaters. During March it would probably be much higher which would make the right side class III juicy and Big Falls?, well I'm not sure. It's not far from I-94 so it could easily be checked out on a trip to the nearby Black (the one in the vicinity of Hatfield, WI).

In the summer it would probably run at least as high as I found it on my November run, but warm air and water could easily entice a water-starved kayakist to spend a couple of hours frolicking in the class III, blasting down class IV Big Falls, playing in the spin hole below Big Falls, working on squirt moves in the strong swirl on river left at the end of the run or picnicking on the beach. An easy 50 yard carry up on the left side allows the boater to choose his poison all over again. The pines, sand and rock outcrops make this a relaxing place.

Big Falls is certainly not a major whitewater run, but it falls into that interesting category of noteworthy isolated sections of whitewater that provide a mini-adventure. A few other such drops that I've either heard of or experienced would include Big Falls on Minnesota's Big Fork River up near the Canadian border, Big Falls on the South Fork of the Jump River about 22 miles east of Ladysmith, WI and the Dells of the Eau Claire (A different Eau Claire River!! It's located about 10 miles southwest of Antigo in northeastern Wisconsin). All of these are supposed to have "interesting" whitewater for a short distance that's easily accessible. Do some trailblazing and give them a look!

Sauk Rapids

Sauk Rapids sports several good hole/wave features. Good blunting, flatspinning and cartwheeling can be enjoyed at levels approaching 20,000 cfs (Mississippi at St. Cloud on the USGS website). At levels closer to 30,000 cfs, the "Dream Hole" appears. Remember to save enough energy for the long ferry back across the river.

Lanny Freng
©2005 Jake Vos

SAUK RAPIDS

MISSISSIPPI RIVER

LENGTH: PARK AND PLAY
CLASS: II-III
SUMMER: FREQUENT
QUICK DESCRIPTION: EXCELLENT PLAY SPOT
PUT-IN AND TAKE OUT: X PARK IN DOWNTOWN SAUK RAPIDS

mike lamarche
wolf creek falls
©2005 steve stratman

SAND CREEK

LENGTH: 3.5 MILES

CLASS: I-II

SUMMER: RARE

QUICK DESCRIPTION:
WINDING, TREES, LITTLE II, DAM

PUT-IN:
220TH ST. W, 3 MILES SE OF JORDAN

TAKE-OUT:
AT DAM IN JORDAN

APPLE RIVER

LENGTH: 0.2 MILES

CLASS: II

SUMMER: YES

QUICK DESCRIPTION:
EASY SLALOM SITE, PLAYSPOTS, TUBERS

PUT-IN:
PARK JUST DOWNSTREAM OF WISC. 64 BRIDGE IN SOMERSET

TAKE-OUT:
SAME AS PUT-IN

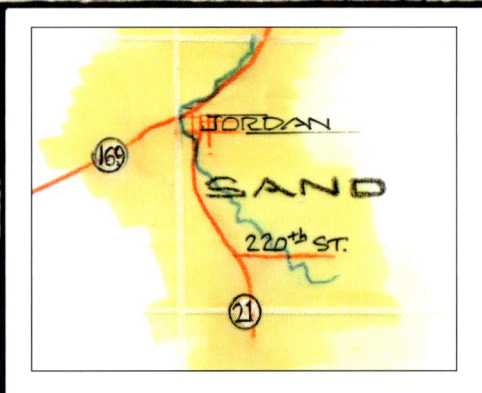

Sand Creek

The east side of the Metro area is blessed with the Apple, Kinnickinnic, Taylor's Falls and the Vermillion at Hastings. For their whitewater backyard, Minneapolis boaters can try out Sand Creek in Jordan, Minnesota, maybe twenty miles southwest of Minneapolis.

I haven't done Sand Creek lately, but my recollection is that the best whitewater is packed into the last half mile of river before it enters Jordan, including some class II-ish waves that are surfable. The other highlight is running a dam/falls of about fifteen feet in height right in Jordan.

I remember the Big Water Associates (Ralph Beer, Joerg Steinbach, Andy Westerhaus, Rick Gustafson, John Kramer, Doug Steifel and Eric Albertson) introducing me, the confident beginner, to Sand Creek's whitewater back in the early 70's.

We got to the dam and they all ran it. "How about you, Jim?" Rick asked. "Well, I don't want to smash up my boat." So Rick offered his and of course I ran it then! Are whitewater boaters clear thinkers or what??!

You can do a longer run on Sand Creek, putting in three or four miles south of town on "220th Street West." It's actually quite rural as Sand Creek winds through low bluffs and trees towards Jordan, so even with little whitewater you get some rustic slalom practice. For urban slalom practice try Minnehaha Creek!

Apple River

Many Twin City folks have their first whitewater experience on the Apple River in Somerset, Wisconsin. Not in kayaks, but in innertubes! The 150 yards of class I and II rapids near the Wisconsin Highway 64 bridge in town attract crowds of "tubers" during the warm months of summer.

These same rapids also provide a course for the Apple River slalom, often held here in early May. Somerset is roughly thirty miles east and north of St. Paul, so this can be a fun place for a few hours of practice.

You will want to avoid the hordes of tubers, which can be done by paddling early in the morning or by paddling during the cooler months, before Memorial Day and after Labor Day.

There are a couple of playspots here, a broken double ledge at the beginning and a small surfing wave at the end, downstream of the footbridge. There are dams upriver that guarantee a constant (and economically valuable!) flow during the summer. At high flow during the spring, the footbridge wave can apparently become an ender/pop-up hole. With a park on shore, it's a pleasant place for an evening paddle and barbecue.

Other sections of the Apple are paddled as well: (1) Little Falls, a class II-III ledge sequence downstream of the Polk County C bridge four miles southwest of Amery, (2) from Star Prairie four miles downstream to the St. Croix County C bridge near the little crossroads of Johannesburg–this stretch has some class I-II in the first half mile and then becomes predominantly swiftwater with occasional class I rapids and a small ledge and (3) the mile below the St. Croix County I bridge to the St. Croix where the Apple flows through a deep valley, but you must portage around the usually de-watered rapids/falls near County I and around the powerplant and canal that feeds it.

If you're just looking for whitewater, go to Somerset, but if you want a little voyage of easy exploration near town, the other sections can provide a few hours of fun.

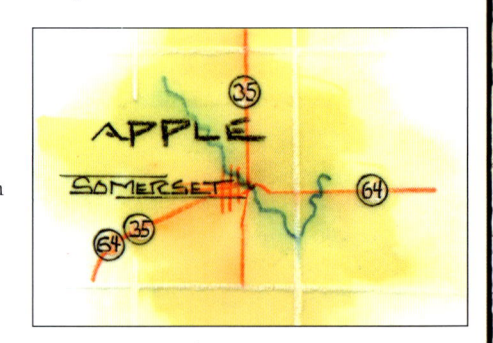

144

KINNIC KINNIC RIVER

LENGTH: 7 MILES
CLASS: I-II-
SUMMER: SOME
QUICK DESCRIPTION:
EASY, PRETTY, LITTLE, CLIFFS
PUT-IN:
OLD DAM IN GLEN PARK IN RIVER FALLS
TAKE-OUT:
PIERCE COUNTY F BRIDGE

Most of the runs in this book exhibit some fine whitewater. Some are so good that people from all over the country would enjoy seeing them. The Kinnickinnic doesn't have a lot of whitewater and I doubt that boaters will travel from the ends of the earth to paddle it. Boaters living in the Twin Cities area will enjoy the subtle pleasures of this little gem.

The Kinnickinnic offers an eight mile journey through a deep valley endowed with big white pines, gnarled oaks, occasional limestone cliffs, wildlife, and class I rapids when the water is clear, coming from springs and slow runoff, with a touch of class II when it's very high.

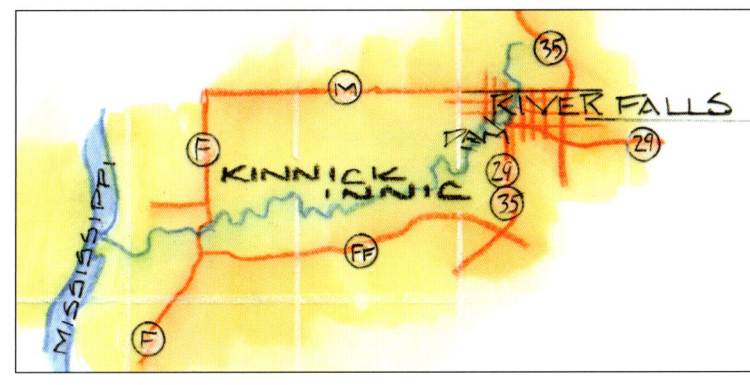

Lying about thirty miles east of St. Paul at River Falls, Wisconsin and having water early in March, it's a fairly popular early season run. The springs usually provide enough water to provide a fall color cruise on this pretty trout stream. The clean water, easy rapids, sandy bottom and nice scenery make this a good river on which to introduce nervous beginners to the addiction of whitewater.

The joy of catching little chutes and avoiding boulders quickly seduces those who thought whitewater just had to be scary. Most pools are only a few feet deep and swims lack severity. I really enjoy the run myself, and especially enjoy doing it as an "icebreaker" run to start the season and again in October near season's end.

In fall Tom Aluni and I have paddled the "Kinni" and rollerskied from the Pierce County F bridge takeout back to the put-in, Glen Park in River Falls. On another occasion I did a bike shuttle along Highway FF on Halloween as dusk settled in and jack-o-lanterns glowed at farmhouses along the way.

Ah, I digress. As benign as the Kinnickinnic is, even it has claimed a life. In March 1990 Karen Jensen and I were getting ready to carry our boats down the quarter-mile trail to the put-in below an old ten-foot dam. The river was swollen by rain that had fallen on a melting snowpack.

Suddenly a person came running up the trail yelling that two canoeists had capsized in the swirling eddy below the dam and one was missing. We hurried down to the put-in and found an amazing scene: the hundred foot diameter put-in eddy was a churning mass of foam four to five feet deep totally covering the river.

Apparently heavy agricultural runoff had created this unbelievable foampile. Two canoeists, in street clothes and without lifejackets had put in. They immediately capsized, to the horror of their friends on shore. It was an intimidating spot that day. I ran the river searching for the missing canoeist while firemen tried to push the foam aside with hoses to search the base of the dam, but it all was useless.

The paddler was found a couple of days later about a half-mile downstream, dead. This tragedy could have been avoided had they worn lifejackets, warm paddling gear and most importantly had they used good judgement. Putting in just a hundred yards downstream would've been no problem.

The Kinnickinnic really is a gentle, fun-loving spirit, which all surely will enjoy if prepared and thoughtful.

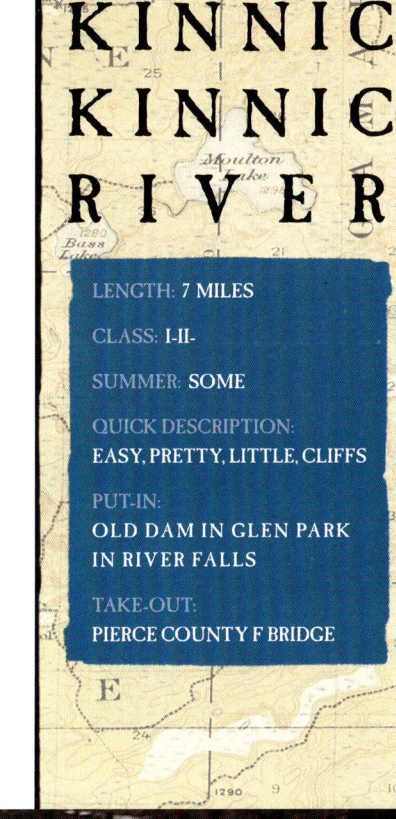

mike lamarche wolf creek falls
steve stratman

ST. CROIX RIVER TAYLOR'S FALLS

LENGTH: 0.2 MILES

CLASS: II–III

SUMMER: YES

QUICK DESCRIPTION:
BIG WATER PLAY, DAM CHANGES LEVEL

PUT-IN:
INTERSTATE PARK PARKING LOT, 0.1 MILE SOUTH OF U.S. 8 BRIDGE

TAKE-OUT:
SAME AS PUT-IN

Taylor's Falls is a godsend to whitewater-starved paddlers of the Twin Cities area. Summer has come and the fine Lake Superior runs are now good wading, so what do you do? Drive forty miles northeast of Minneapolis-St. Paul to the U.S. Highway 8 bridge spanning the St. Croix River, boundary between Minnesota and Wisconsin.

One Eastern paddler did just that. He drove to the U.S. 8 bridge looking for the site of the annual St. Croix Slalom (usually held in late August or early September). He looked upstream: riffles; he looked downstream: flatwater between scenic cliffs. Then he looked down—there it was, under the bridge!

Actually, it is short, but not that short, maybe a couple hundred yards long and adorned with cliffs, big boulders and big water. The St. Croix is a mighty river, running with thousands of CFS even in the summer.

In spring high water, big bursting, oozing waves develop downstream of the Highway 8 bridge. During summer the level can go up or down by several feet as the powerplant a half mile upstream changes the kilowatt production. Mornings can be low, with hot afternoons bringing high water.

You'll hear some paddlers referring to the level as "three wheels" or "eight wheels" depending on the number of turbines going. Eight wheels is high–squirrelly, mushy big water, with some features washed out. Three, four and five wheels is medium with a beautiful surfing wave under the bridge. A big boulder on the Wisconsin side, Rada's Rock, provides a blast-off spot for ferrying to the Wave.

Another large boulder, Joe's Rock, is in the center of the river about two hundred feet downstream of the Wave. Joe's can be exposed, submerged with a boiling eddy or washed out, depending on levels. When exposed, the Wave is good; when with boiling eddy—you can sometimes do enders just right of Joe's.

At various flows there are other ender spots and squirrelly water down near "The Neck" along the cliffs on the Minnesota side. Boating at Taylor's Falls provides excellent playing for surface boater or squirtist, and a dynamite workout as you paddle upstream using eddies to hit your favorite features again.

Joerg Steinbach, Taylor's Falls, St. Croix River. ©2006 Doug Nelson

A taste of big water boating, boatable all summer, a chance to "showboat" under the observation platform, the company of pigeons under the bridge, it all made an Iowa farmboy think he'd died and gone to heaven. If you put in on the Minnesota side, do be warned that you might be hassled about a Minnesota boat license (if your boat is over nine feet long, you're supposed to license it). This is a nice spot, and no doubt the place to learn how to play the river.

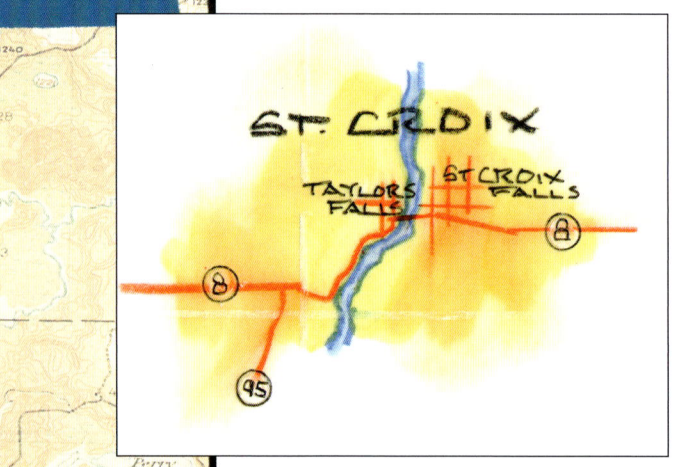

SNAKE RIVER

Minnesota's **Snake River** has two sections that are commonly run by whitewater paddlers. The "Lower Snake" from the outlet of Cross Lake near Pine City to the St. Croix holds about eight or nine miles of swiftwater dotted with rather numerous class I boulder pitches and continuous class I-II waves as you near the St. Croix. There are many runs of this nature in the St. Croix drainage such as the lower Kettle and Sunrise rivers—interesting but outside the scope of this book.

I should note here that if you're an open boater or kayakist interested in class I-II challenges in Minnesota, you should contact the DNR's Trails and Waterways Department. They offer not only excellent free maps of state parks, but also some very nice "canoe route" maps, free for the asking. The Big Fork, Little Fork, Cloquet, Vermilion, St. Louis, Kettle and St. Croix are among the many excellent canoe route maps they provide. These maps would cover many easier runs omitted in this book. Start with this web address to find the maps you need: www.dnr.state.mn.us/trails_waterways/index.html

The Upper Snake has two class II-III rapids, with the class depending on level, and some boulderbed. As it lies close to the Kettle and the Twin Cities, I'll describe it as a run that gives variety. The takeout is reached by going east three miles and then north one mile from Woodland, a crossroads about 15 miles north of Mora where Minnesota 65 and Minnesota 27 join forces to head north toward McGrath. The last piece of the dirt road to the takeout can get soft at times.

Put in at one of two spots: Silver Star Road, or a woodsy campsite reached by a narrow dirt road about a mile and a half south of Silver Star Road. The Silver Star turnoff is a bit more than five miles north of Woodland on Minnesota 65/27. From Silver Star to the campsite you'll encounter only class I boulderbed. It's about 3.5 miles from the campsite to the takeout bridge, and the first couple miles are more class I. It's quite pretty when the leaves are out as the narrow Snake ripples under a shady arch of soft maples.

Then the calm is broken by a welcome roar as you encounter Upper Falls, a class III where the Snake slithers over a series of pink bedrock ledges. Scout this short rapid from the left. After fifty yards of action the calm returns, but is soon broken as you approach Lower Falls. Lower Falls is really a misnomer, as the whitewater lasts for two thirds of a mile, with no "falls" to speak of.

When I started kayaking, information on rivers was very scarce and my "guidebook" was a set of canoe trail maps available from the Minnesota Department of Natural Resources (DNR). My "guidebook" described Lower Falls as the toughest whitewater in the state. I know now that's not true, but Lower Falls is still a delight when the water's up. It would actually make a good slalom course if high water could be predicted or guaranteed. A portage trail on river right allows easy scouting for beginners, but intermediates and others will enjoy eddy-hopping through the boulderbed, zinging in behind huge "Volkswagen Rock" and then playing the small ledges that follow. Class II with stretches of III, it's a joy . . . and I'll bet you wish it was longer.

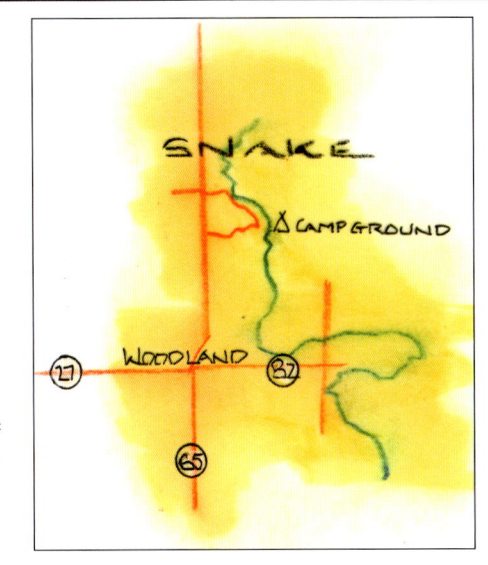

At high flow Lower Falls has claimed a number of canoes and left their wreckage strewn on shore, so it can have some power, too. The takeout bridge is only a quarter-mile below the last riffles of Lower Falls.

LENGTH: 4 MILES

CLASS: I–III

SUMMER: RARE

QUICK DESCRIPTION: EASY, WITH 2 CLASS III'S, ONE LONG

PUT-IN: CAMPGROUND EAST OFF MINN. 65, AT AITKIN/KENNEBEC CO. LINE

TAKE-OUT: KENNEBEC CO. 82 BRIDGE, 4 MILES EAST OF WOODLAND ON MN 65

mike lamarche wolf creek falls

KETTLE RIVER

LENGTH: 3 MILES

CLASS: II–IV

SUMMER: YES/SOME

QUICK DESCRIPTION: SHORT CANYON, LOTS OF PLAYSPOTS

PUT-IN: BANNING STATE PARK BOAT LANDING

TAKE-OUT: ROBINSON PARK IN SANDSTONE, JUST UPSTREAM OF MN. 123 OR AT NEW TAKEOUT AT OLD DAM SITE

The Kettle River near Sandstone, Minnesota has no doubt provided more hours of fun for Minnesota kayakists than any other river in the state. The run is short; all the whitewater occurs in about a mile and a half, but the numerous holes and waves make it possible to spend a whole afternoon or even most of a day paddling this mile and a half. Mile for mile it can be one of the best play rivers anywhere. Also, because of its large drainage area, 863 square miles, it will be runnable much of the summer, and when high can provide a big water quality hard to find in the Northwoods.

It's easily reached by interstate I-35, a hundred miles north of the Twin Cities and fifty miles south of Duluth. Being the centerpiece of Banning State Park, there are hiking trails all along the river that help boaters scout, portage back up to run again and even shuttle. Camping at Banning State Park makes for a very convenient boating trip. Another nicety is a river gauge that is read several times a week by Banning State Park personnel during the boating season. The gauge is found on both the left and right pillars of the Minnesota State Highway 23 bridge over the Kettle, about a mile and a half east of the entrance to the state park.

I've run the Kettle as low as 0.75 feet, and while very scrapey, the sandstone cliffs and pines were just as beneficial as ever and I was singing during my day on the river. During recent years of drought, I've found that it's still possible to have playboat fun at levels as low as 1.5 feet, although things become quite a lot nicer at 2 feet, when the river is class II-II+. The rapids get progressively wavier as the level goes up, and as a rough rule of thumb, I give Rada's Rule #3: The gauge reading is equal to the height of the biggest wave on the river. At 2 feet expect to see at most two foot waves, at 5 feet some five footers, etc. This actually holds up fairly well.

The rapids are formed as the Kettle cuts into layers of sandstone and this has created cliffs, potholes (the cauldrons carved into the cliffs are called "kettles"), undercuts and smooth ledges. The ledges create many fine sidesurfing holes, surfing waves, even a very nice "blasting" chute for squirt boaters. Squirt boaters will also enjoy the deep, swirling

Krista Lunde paddles the flats on the Kettle River. ©2005 Bryan Zlimen

THE MAGIC KETTLE RIVER GAUGE CONVERSION:
(From the AWA website)

Hwy 23 Bridge Level (Jim's levels) = (1.31 x Internet Sandstone Level) – 4.8.

Or call Banning State Park: 1-320-245-2668

waters that the "kettles" generate—it's a fun river for a squirtist or surface boater.

The river is prime for playing (in my view) from about 3 feet to 4.5 feet, when the river displays a basic III-III+ nature. As the Kettle rises over 5 feet, some of the play spots vanish, some holes develop quite a bit of ferocity and the river run takes on a bit of tension. At levels of 6-7 feet you see a definite big water class IV character in Blueberry Slide and Dragon's Tooth, the two principal rapids. I've run the Kettle at levels up to 11.5 feet, at which time it's a flushing big water rip—you survive Blueberry Slide and Dragon's Tooth and play in places where there are ordinarily just riffles, like at the Robinson Park takeout.

A run at high water doesn't take long, but it's packed with excitement, for while the waves get bigger at high water, the width of the river is held the same, and exploding waves and curlers can throw you around with ease—even towards the undercuts. So let's call it big water class IV+ when in flood, and remember that it could very well be ice cold, too.

The scenery is superb. I love the mixed woods of pine, oak, maple and birch that drape a pastoral friendliness on the river in summer, and provide color in fall. Icefalls and seeping icicles of spring are replaced by mossy, serene dripping and wildflowers in summer.

Let me tell you about it as it would be at moderate flow, say 3 feet.

Enter the state park, get a beautiful free map and drive to the boat landing (if you want to avoid buying a state park sticker, put in at the Highway 23 bridge). You'll have a broad river to face as you put in and only one or two hundred feet before some white starts kicking up.

The first major rapid, Blueberry Slide, is just that, a beautiful 200 foot slide followed by a couple hundred yards of curving, not-so-steep slides and ledges. At moderate and low flows, 1.5-4.5 feet, the most straightforward and exciting route down the initial slide is pretty far left, passing fairly close to the little cliff projecting from the left bank at the lip. However, a nice surfing wave occurs at these levels along far river right before the slide, so you might look for that.

The slide contains a couple of fun holes and a left side eddy so you can stop and play part way down. The outrun from the slide has surfing waves and a blasting spot (at levels of about 2 feet) just right of the main current. There are eddies along the left here, too, and you'll notice a small side channel of the Kettle rejoining the river on the left. This side channel contains a fluffy, four foot leap,

A boater finds a way out of Blueberry Slide.
©2006 Doug Nelson

"Blueberry Falls," at moderate flows. Another good hole is below the slide on river right, "Shoulder Hole," which can be pretty grabby.

The river lets up slightly after the main slide, and then begins a gradual bend to the right. The best whitewater in the last half of Blueberry Slide is along the left shore, the tamer route along the right shore. Towards the end of Blueberry Slide on the left two holes, Teacher's Hole and Teacher's Pet, provide more opportunities to

mike lamarche
wolf creek falls
©2006

149

Blueberry Slide at a beefy spring flow. ©2005 Mike Cotten

play or swim, depending on your skill and the river level. If the level is six feet or more most paddlers would find these holes "too much fun."

Many boaters will play their way through Blueberry, taking an hour or two to reach the bottom of the rapid. You can get out on river left below Teacher's Pet and carry up on the canoe portage trail to do it again!

A short calm stretch below Blueberry Slide leads you toward another rapid, Mother's Delight, class II-III at low to moderate levels. Mother's Delight is about a hundred yards long and quite straightforward. There are a couple of waves to catch at moderate levels, and a narrow hole you may wish to scrutinize at the end on the right. A projecting cliff on the bottom right and deep water encourage squirt moves.

Then another hundred yards of peace and the river drops again between low sandstone cliffs left and right: Dragon's Tooth. Dragon's Tooth is class II+ at low flows (some maneuvering), III-III+ at moderate flows (2.5-5 feet) and IV-IV+ at high flows. The name refers to a huge "Tooth" of rounded rock right of center at the narrowest part of the rapid. The "Tooth" is preceded by a similar rock outcrop and waves. At low flows both teeth can be exposed; at medium flows both teeth form healthy holes, especially the Tooth. The holes wash out into back-curling waves about 7 feet, so at 6-6.5 feet you'll encounter maximum bite. Remember Rada's Rule #3? The biggest waves on the river often occur right at the constriction next to the Tooth, that means you're flying past big holes amidst big waves at 6-7 feet. The waves become towering, shifting pyramids over 7 feet on the gauge.

The slickest run I've ever seen of the Tooth was by Grant Freiberg, a member of the old time "Big Water Associates." The Kettle was 4.5 feet or so and the Tooth was one hungry hole. Grant paddled full tilt right at the Tooth, his boat endered as his bow hit the reversal and his forward speed pole-vaulted him over and past the hydraulic! I think most Minnesota paddlers will experience the Tooth sooner or later. Swimmers, boats and paddles tend to be fed into a kettle carved into the right cliffs, so look here if you've lost something.

At moderate flows you can eddy out behind the Tooth and go after the waves in the main current. Enders, squirts, mystery moves are all possible here. For the price of a half-mile hike you can carry up on river left and do Blueberry, Mother's and Dragon's Tooth all over again, or ferry across and carry to the parking lot–a shuttleless run!

Below Dragon's Tooth the Kettle eases up and enters the Banning Rapids section. Here the river is wide open, with class II boulderbed and small ledges. The name comes from the "ghost town" of Banning on river right about a half-mile below Dragon's Tooth. A couple of stone buildings still stand from the days in the early 1900's when this was a quarry town–it's fun to investigate the buildings, easily seen from the river until the leaves come out.

There is one spot in the Banning Rapids worthy of note. About a quarter-mile downstream of the big stone building on the right, keep an eye open for a pourover/pillow rock. It's not real obvious, but when the Kettle is over 4.5-5 feet, you can get enders here–not every time–but enough to keep you here trying for "just one more."

A couple hundred yards below the ender rock, the Kettle actually becomes smooth and calm. Foam spins silently as the water slows down and big pines shade the river. You're probably tired by now, so a little drifting, quiet or chatting is just the thing–this is one piece of flatwater I really enjoy.

The tranquility lasts about a half-mile and then you enter the last major drop of the run: Hell's Gate, class III at moderate water. Hell's Gate washes out somewhat at high flows. At moderate flows there are several "goodies" tucked in here to play with–a hole at the top on the left, a nice surfing wave or two on the center-right near the beginning, more waves on the left in the middle and at the bottom a wave that becomes a "spin hole" at levels under 2 feet.

If you're on the ball and want a little thrill, pull an eddyout on the left just above the shelf of rock hanging over the river from the left cliff. You can pull into a pothole here that is open to the sky–an amazing eroded lattice. Do watch out for the undercut just downstream, though. Paddlers reluctant to quit spend their last energy playing in the waves here, or having an impromptu "rodeo" if the level is low enough for the spin hole to have formed. The squirrelies here and just downstream can pull moves squirtists don't expect. All in all, a congenial spot.

The paddle from Hell's Gate to Robinson Park is flatwater, about a mile and a half of it. You can break it up by checking out Wolf Creek Falls on the right a half mile below

Joerg Steinbach hucks an end or three in Teacher's Pet. This excellent play spot emerges around 5 feet. ©2006 Doug Nelson

Hell's Gate. Next attraction is paddling under the railroad trestle. Any kids dropping rocks? Finally, the remains of an old low dam create a few last waves–then it's time to load up at Robinson Park on the right and hit the cookies.

It's January outside now as I write this, but thinking of a fun run down the Kettle in the warm sunshine makes me glow with happiness. I've described the river at flows that are commonly found, 2-4.5 feet. The Kettle usually opens up just about the end of March and then stays above 2 feet into June. It might drop below 2 feet for a bit, but May and June rains usually boost it right up again. Summer storms will bring it up, and for some reason, it rarely fails

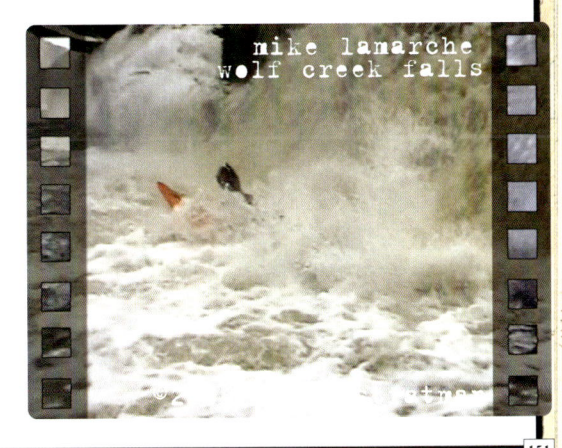

mike lamarche
wolf creek falls

151

to provide some fun in September and October. As you can see, it's bound to be well liked, probably the most popular run in the state, yet it's not crowded–just sort of a "friendly convention."

Kettle River Update

During the winter of 1994-95 an amazing thing happened to the Kettle River: a dam located about two miles downstream from the Robinson Park takeout described above was removed!! This allowed the pool backed up by the dam to drain, which was sure to reveal new rapids hidden for decades.

Speculation as to what would be found ran high among boaters. Dan Theis, who'd grown up in the area, had heard tell that there was a big drop buried beneath the reservoir waters and it turns out this was true. There was an informal race to see who'd be the first to glimpse the "hidden" rapids, and to be honest I'm not quite sure who won.

Many paddlers continued past Robinson Park in the early spring of 1995, finding over a mile of flatwater leading up to a big drop. The drop had two beautiful islands of sculpted sandstone which created three chutes, each of which dropped about ten feet. The right chute was quite small, but looked fairly easy as the gradient slid away in a straight shot. The center was where most of the water went although a good deal took the left channel as well.

Some boaters ran the center chute blind at levels of about 5 feet plus on the gauge and were shocked by a steep drop which largely funneled into a big hole. Several boaters were flattened on their decks by the impact while a couple were sent swimming. The tendency of the big hole was to blow people through, although it wasn't a gimmee. If you scout from the right island you'll discover that there is a tongue that misses the hole along the left side of the chute, and this may set your mind at ease for playing in the nice sidesurfer that beckons just above the center chute.

The left channel of the big drop is an interesting dogleg a bit reminiscent of Blueberry Slide. You go down the first pitch, eddy out and then cut back to the right. There are some fluffy looking sidesurfing holes toward the end, situated not far above a sort of pourover that finishes the left channel run. When running this side at about 3.5 feet, Karen Jensen got pinned broadside on a rock projection here that was not at all apparent from a scouting look. We should be a little wary here until we're sure all the debris has washed away.

This mighty drop rates class IV-IV+ down the center route at high flow and is a fun III-III+ down the left channel. It certainly deserves an appropriate name and I hope the boating community comes up with a good one. I understand that it had a name before it was flooded, perhaps Spring Creek Falls? I've also heard "Jailhouse Drop" and "Jailhouse Rock" suggested due to the presence of a federal prison on the river left here. I've thought it would be good to use the old name or honor the falls' reemergence

Bryan Zlimen gives Emily Tuve a push off Lunch Rock. ©2006 Krista Lunde

from under the water, perhaps "Resurrection Falls" or "Reborn Falls." In some ways a simple name honoring the mightiest drop on the river also seems appropriate, for instance "Kettle River Falls." Maybe something honoring the beautiful islands would be nice, "Sandstone Island Falls." I hope to hear suggestions from others and hopefully a good name for this great drop will arise.

There was one more nice surprise in the "new" river below Robinson Park. A quarter mile below the big drop is the location of the old dam-site and there was a rapid here, probably best rated class II-III. It's fairly long, about 150 yards, but is interesting because it has some very nice surfing waves at the top. I've been told that when the river is about 5.5-6 feet they take on "Idaho" proportions! They were still there at 3.5 feet, but not so big.

The old damsite is owned and maintained by Banning State Park as a river access point which makes a convenient takeout when doing the "long" run on the Kettle. To find the old damsite, proceed east from downtown Sandstone on Highway 123 as though going to the Robinson Park takeout. When you come to the Robinson Park turnoff, turn to the south, taking the road across from the Robinson Park road. Follow this south and it will turn into a dirt road. Continue to follow the road south and eventually you'll see it turn towards the river and go downhill. Follow it downhill and to the end of the line, where there's a small parking area.

So what has been the impact on boaters of this new piece of the Kettle? So far I've noticed that it holds its strongest appeal in the spring when the water is high and the call of the drop and surfing waves is most powerful. In general, though, most paddlers seem to arrive at Robinson Park either wasted enough or cold enough that doing two more miles doesn't sound as appealing as it did at the top. So sometimes we go on down and sometimes we quit at Robinson, but either way I think we're very happy to know that the Kettle once again roars over that reborn falls.

Dan Monskey boat scouts Dragon's Tooth. ©2006 Doug Nelson

mike lamarche
wolf creek falls

06 steve stretman

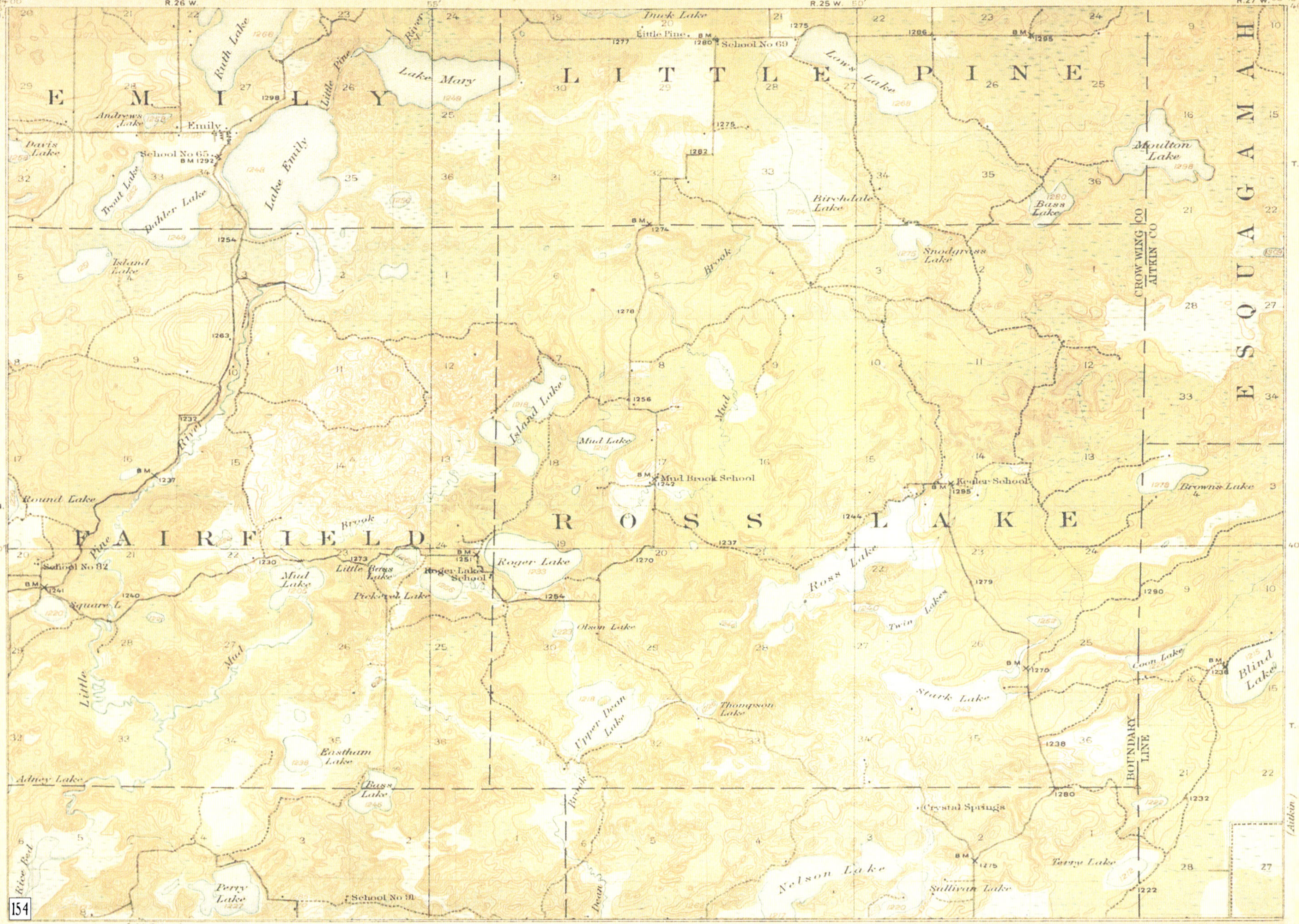

R. 26 W.
R. 25 W.
R. 27 W.
EMILY
LITTLE PINE
ROSS LAKE
FAIRFIELD
ESQUAGAMAH
Ruth Lake
Lake Mary
Duck Lake
Little Pine
School No 69
Lows Lake
Moulton Lake
Andrews Lake
Emily
Davis Lake
School No 65
Trout Lake
Bahler Lake
Lake Emily
Birchdale Lake
Bass Lake
Snodgrass Lake
Island Lake
Island Lake
Mud Lake
Mud Brook School
Keeler School
Browns Lake
Round Lake
Roger Lake
Roger Lake School
Ross Lake
Little Bass Lake
Pickerel Lake
School No 82
Square L.
Mud Lake
Olson Lake
Twin Lakes
Coon Lake
Blind Lake
Stark Lake
Thompson Lake
Upper Dean Lake
Eastham Lake
Adney Lake
Bass Lake
Crystal Springs
Perry Lake
School No 91
Nelson Lake
Sullivan Lake
Terry Lake
Rice Bed
CROW WING CO
AITKIN CO
BOUNDARY LINE
(Aitkin)

OTHER PLEASURES

OK, I'll be honest with you: it's hard to paddle whitewater year 'round in the Northwoods. Yes, Virginia, there is a Santa Claus and when he comes Northwoods rivers are frozen and buried in snow. Then there are the "dog days" of summer when you can't get excited about paddling the Kettle at 1.2 feet after seeing the big water and play levels of spring. What's a boater to do?

©2006 Doug Nelson

RIVER SKIING

In winter (late November til early March) your best option is to cross-country ski the rivers. I've heard of December paddling on the Kettle and at Taylor's Falls but even though whitewater is hard to freeze, blood isn't. Fifteen degrees Fahrenheit just doesn't seem like paddling weather!

River skiing is great fun but holds some real dangers. You should be careful on ice shelves near running water since swimming with skis on ain't easy! Fortunately, river levels tend to be low, only knee deep most places. Some rivers are safer than others, too. The smaller rivers may be frozen almost solid and those with less gradient seem to freeze better than those with falls and narrow gorges.

I'm no expert at river skiing but have enjoyed trips on these rivers: the Lester, Split Rock, Baptism, Manitou, Presque Isle, Copper Creek, Huron, Black (in Michigan), Brule (in Minnesota) as well as parts of the Cascade and Devil's Track.

It's best to go skiing after prolonged cold snaps have frozen things up good and sometimes they're safer later in the winter after the fall waters have run off under the ice. As snows drift and the rapids get smoothed out, you can easily "run" drops that would be quite difficult in a kayak. The rapids provide one of the Northwoods' best venues for those with crosscountry downhill experience, like telemarking. If you ski up from the takeout you won't need a shuttle and you'll have a fast track on the way back down. Ice formations, river noises, wildlife and tracks all give new dimension to the rivers. Skiing (or snowshoeing) also provides a way to become familiar with runs you hope to paddle. Some exploratories by kayak followed reconnaissance during the winter.

Hikers on the Black River in Michigan.

©2005 Doug Nelson

BOUNDARY WATERS CANOE AREA WILDERNESS (BWCA)

Go canoeing or kayaking in the Boundary Waters Canoe Area/Quetico. This is the traditional way of enjoying the Northwoods. Lakes, fishing, blueberries and camping are all good reasons to paddle and portage through the BWCA pines. Did I say portage? Well, yes, there are portages around RAPIDS in the BWCA! So why not paddle them?

Why not indeed! The rapids in the BWCA are largely on waterways connecting large lakes and thus are like the Vermilion in that they have a long season. The lakes act as huge "reservoirs" and the "release" of water can be pretty big. I'm aware of three BWCA/Quetico trips with some whitewater. I'm sure there must be more.

NAMAKAN RIVER

Start at Crane Lake, work east to Lac La Croix and return to Crane Lake via Canada's Namakan River. This river lies outside the Quetico and so it's unregulated. The Namakan has huge flows around Memorial Day and splits into channels around islands. Some channels have falls, others have rapids. I haven't done this trip but it has been recommended to me by several paddlers. One group towed a kayak to enjoy the playspots!

BASSWOOD RIVER

From Basswood Lake northeast of Ely to Crooked Lake the Basswood River forms part of the international boundary with Canada. The river consists of flatwater or lake-like stretches interspersed with whitewater. There are some stretches of nice class II and even some good ledges. I ran this in September with pretty low water using a plastic sea kayak and found three of the rapids to be exciting class III. I think at high water there might be some class IV water here!

GRANITE RIVER

From Gunflint Lake to Saganaga Lake the Granite connects a series of lakes along the U.S.-Canada border. Technically, part of the route is on the Pine River. In late summer I did this with a plastic sea kayak. Some of the boulderbed was low and technical but Saganaga Falls was fun. This route is part of the old Voyageur's Highway and many artifacts from fur trading times have been recovered by divers probing the rapids.

These trips combine lots of flatwater paddling and wilderness with enough whitewater to appease the kayakist. Of course there're a lot of isolated rapids in the BWCA which can be run or at least will give you a chance to theorize routes through.

KAYAK SURFING

A second summer paddling option is kayak surfing. Lake Superior really is an "inland sea" and when windy is capable of generating waves of up to 20-25 feet (this is according to a lighthouse keeper on Canada's Michipicoten Island). You certainly don't need (or maybe even want!) twenty footers for fun. I've had a good time even on three footers.

Whitewater kayaks make excellent surf boats and the sport teaches you a whole new set of hydraulic lessons. Surf waves are different from river waves! Prime surfing spots include the fine sand beaches on the South Shore (such as Little Girl Point near the Montreal), Park Point and Wisconsin Point at the mouth of the Duluth-Superior harbor and river mouths and beaches on the North Shore. Park Point is particularly well situated as storm systems over Lake Superior often bring strong northeast winds that run some big waves by the time you get to Duluth at the southwest corner.

KAYAK TOURING

Another summer suggestion is touring on Lake Superior by kayak. It's a real treat to enjoy Gitchee Gumee for a few days or a few hours. You have the pleasure of paddling, great scenery, pristine camping and watery excitement. If you don't think "sea kayaking" on Lake Superior could be exciting, you haven't paddled around Isle Royale's Blake

SUMMER OPTIONS

The summer doldrums usually strike in mid-July through August. Even during this period the real whitewater addict can still boat the St. Louis, Menominee, Wolf (Section IV), Taylor's Falls and the Vermilion near Crane Lake. Most runs, however, become low and rocky, suggesting a change of pace. Here are a few suggestions.

Point in a gale. Whitewater paddlers will enjoy this and there are many great touring destinations: the Apostle Islands, Canada's Pukaskwa National Park, the islands near Thunder Bay, Isle Royale, Michigan's Pictured Rocks National Lakeshore and others. Only time for a day trip? How about Split Rock Lighthouse, Duluth's harbor or Michigan's Porcupine Mountains State Park?

You really don't have to have a special "touring" or "sea" kayak to enjoy paddling on the Big Lake. Your whitewater kayak will be adequate, though a little slower and with not quite as much storage space as a touring boat. Still the back end of a plastic cruising boat will hold far more gear than a backpacker or cyclist can tote around, so you'll have a good time. If you'd like to try a sea kayak, it's easy to rent one at places like Trek & Trail in Bayfield and Duluth or from Cascade Kayaks just west of the Cascade River along Highway 61 up towards Grand Marais, Minnesota. Shops in the Twin Cities and elsewhere also have boats available to rent.

Still not happy? OK, go somewhere else to paddle! Many do. Quite a few Northwoods paddlers journey around the country and around the world to see rivers in those "whiter pastures" over the hill. Favorite destinations include the Appalachians or California in early March to ready for snowmelt or the Rockies in the summer or West Virginia during the "Gauley Season" releases during September. I have to admit that Rocky Mountain rivers and scenery rank right up there with our rivers, and hey?! where are those mosquitoes? But you know, those adventurous paddlers always end up back home, ready for more of our very own rivers.

That's it! This book isn't about kayak touring or surfing or running all over the world searching for the holy grail of whitewater. I just wanted you to know that life offers an unlimited supply of adventure if you just look at what's around you. There's no reason for a Northwoods paddler to whine about being "bored." I hope the "wheels are turning" in your head as you dream up that next adventure!

–Jim Rada

Lake Superior, as seen from atop Palisade Head. ©2006 Doug Nelson

©2006 Karen Jensen

Devil's Track Canyon

The water stumbles, rumbling over a notch
Golden brew falling in foaming streamers
Beneath an overturned bowl of sky blue
The waves storm against the canyon walls
as the Devil's Track races to the Lake
creating a hurried roar.

Here you can come during a certain season
A time of melting snow and naked trees
When snow and sap run in response to the
sometimes sun
You can be swept away like a log . . .
skittering over ledges . . .

Far overhead the spruce seeds spiral down
in the sunlight
With one in millions eventually rising again
to spread seed from a spire.
Sometimes nature seems to rush, as the
waters do today
Seeming so impatient, pulsing violently
And so it touches us, creatures of an hour.

Today my kayak flies on watery wings
Blasting through boils,
plunging down ledges
into copper hued
pools

To know the river today
requires acceptance of its dangers

In a month leaves will shade the gorge
and swirls gently wash the moss
With only a meditative bubbling . . .
Cooling the cliffs
It will become as once before a
babbling brook,
But I will know that beneath
the maple canopy
Amid the innocent white columns of the
paper birches
There is a primitive mind with
a resolve of rock
In which, during a certain season,
flow the watery lightning and thunder
Of the Devil's Track's
other thoughts.

— Jim Rada

Pitchfork Falls, Devil's Track River. ©2006 Tom Aluni

WATER FLOW IN THE RIVERS

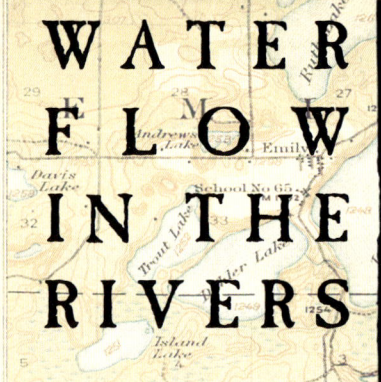

An excellent way to get water levels for the rivers in this book and rivers throughout the country is online at the USGS web site:

http://waterdata.usgs.gov/nwis/rt

American Whitewater Affiliation is also an excellent resource for water level and abounds with river running information. Their website is:

www.americanwhitewater.org

In this section I've gathered together hydrographs for some of the rivers mentioned in this book and other flow data that may be of interest to paddlers. I chose to put the hydrographs in a separate section because I think it's fun and informative to compare them. The data used in constructing the hydrographs comes from the USGS, which publishes annual records for stream flow gauges by state. These volumes can often be found in geology libraries and offer boaters with an academic bent hours of enjoyment. I picked about a dozen rivers to represent the various regions of the Northwoods and then used the monthly averages for several years (usually ten) to create a graph that would be relatively unaffected by peculiarities such as droughts or freak storms.

I've listed drainage areas in square miles so that the rivers can be compared to others in this book and elsewhere. Average peaks are given as well, this being the peak annual flow for a 24 hour period, again averaged over ten years of records. So that paddlers might estimate the flow in rivers with no hydrograph, I've included a listing of the drainage areas of several rivers for which there are only incomplete records. In a couple of cases I've listed correlations between flows in Cubic Feet per Second (CFS) and the height on a gauge commonly used by boaters. I've often heard people ask, "So how many CFS do you think this is?" I must hang out with some warped people! Part of my reason for including this section is for the benefit of those already familiar with many of the rivers—maybe they'll find something new and interesting here.

A FEW GENERAL COMMENTS CAN BE MADE FROM A BRIEF EXAMINATION OF THE GRAPHS:

- The prime whitewater period in the Northwoods begins in March and extends into June.

- Every river show a resurgence in the fall, showing a second crest in September, October or November.

- Winter is a good time to go skiing! August is a good time to go boating elsewhere or to go sea kayaking or canoe-camping.

- Those rivers farther north peak later than the southern runs.

- Big drainage areas mean larger flows.

- Rivers with lakes or swamps in their drainages rise more slowly and fall more slowly; they are moderated by the land.

With these general statements made, let me comment on the individual graphs.

ST. LOUIS RIVER

The St. Louis is one of the largest whitewater rivers in the Northwoods and this is apparent in the flow through Section I (the flow through Section II is roughly 1700 CFS less than the flow through Section I). In an average year the flow should rarely drop below 1000 CFS, but the past few years of drought have brought summer flows to levels considerably below this. In general boating is usually enjoyable when not iced over and can be very big water with peak flows of over 16,000 CFS producing some nice waves.

KNIFE RIVER

The Knife is a great example of the flashy runs of the southern half of the North Shore such as the Lester, Sucker and Split Rock. These small drainages contain few lakes and the consequence is a large amount of runoff during a short period of time—a spike of runoff in April and smaller spikes lasting a few days after summer storms. A stream's "flashiness" can be estimated by dividing the peak flow by the drainage area. For the Knife, this gives 1733 CFS/86 sq. mi., or a ratio of about 20. This is higher than the other rivers plotted. So expect small rivers with drainages devoid of lakes to rise quickly to a sharp peak and then fall quickly.

BAPTISM RIVER

The principal months for catching the Baptism with water are April, May and June, with a lesser chance in September and October. The flow in March is almost the same as during the winter because the North Shore rivers tend to break up in April. South Shore runs show more strength in March because they break up earlier, frequently opening up before March is over. As with the Knife, a river that "spikes" strongly in spring should also spike strongly with rain, responding to rain with a relatively large increase in flow that lasts only a few days. This theory proves true with the Baptism, which is usually brought up by rain a few times each year—but the magic doesn't last long!

PIGEON RIVER

The Pigeon, being on the Canadian border, is a good approximation of the flow of the rivers in the Thunder Bay area. You'll note that the peak month for runoff is May, unlike most of the other rivers here which peak in April. Its large drainage area is also much like the watersheds of Canada's Shebandowan and Kaministiquia. The presence of lakes and wetlands in the drainage moderates the peak flow and spreads the runoff more evenly throughout the year.

BOIS BRULE RIVER

Here is a river with a boggy drainage. This produces a moderated flow. The flow during April, the peak month, isn't even twice the summer flow. This amazing lack of variation was also evident in comparing one year's flow with that of other years. The flow was almost identical to the exact same CFS from one year to the next, come drought or rain. This makes the river very predictable and also allows summer paddling.

MONTREAL RIVER

Even though influenced slightly by dam control on the West Fork, the Montreal displays a hydrograph typical of the South Shore rivers, beginning its spring flooding in March. The peak occurs in April with the water falling rapidly in May, so come early!

BLACK RIVER

(Michigan's Upper Peninsula)

The Black has a hydrograph and peak flow quite comparable to the nearby Montreal. This gives us reason to believe the hydrographs are trustworthy. I say this because here we have two different "experiments," the Montreal and the Black, which give similar flows because they're subjected to similar climate and topography as they lie close to one another.

The Black actually lies more in the Lake Superior snowbelt than the Montreal and this may account for it having a slightly higher peak flow than the Montreal while having a drainage area only three-quarters that of the Montreal at the gauge location. It should be mentioned that Bessemer, the gauge site, is quite a ways from the Lake and the runs described in this book. The Black's area by the time it reaches Rainbow Falls, less than a mile from its mouth, has grown from 200 to 257 square miles. This means that the peak flow through the Lower Black run should be about a third larger than the 3000 CFS Bessemer sees at the annual peak. 4000 CFS on the Lower Black—now that is awesome.

PRESQUE ISLE RIVER

Even with only three years data, I decided to include a hydrograph of the Presque Isle at its Michigan 28 put-in because the river is of so much interest to boaters. It grows in drainage area from 261 square miles at the put-in to 358 square miles at the South Boundary Road takeout. This shows the impact of the many creeks, Copper Creek chief among them, that add to the Presque Isle's fury during the run. You'd expect about 37% more flow at the takeout based on comparison of drainage area at the put-in and takeout.

Though flow data for South Boundary Road is scarce I came on two dates when I had the flow both at the put-in and takeout. On April 25, 1975 the flow at the put-in was 2800 CFS and at South Boundary Road 4750 CFS, an increase of 70%. On August 17, 1972 the flow at the put-in was 3750 CFS and at the takeout 6750 CFS, an increase of 80%. This suggests that the area near Lake Superior contributes more water per square mile than the inland areas. Tom Schellberg would certainly recognize this as an example of the "lake effect," more precipitation on the borders of mighty Lake Superior. It is worth recognizing that Lake Superior does indeed modify the weather and climate near its shores. I'm not sure that everyone will care about these facts, but diehard "numbers" fans will appreciate these thoughts and also enjoy knowing the three CFS-Gauge correlations I uncovered for the South Boundary Road gauge on the Presque Isle:

8.41 feet = 3590 CFS,
9.07 feet = 4750 CFS and
9.62 feet = 6750 CFS.

If you've run Nokomis at 9.62 feet— you're either nuts or don't know how to read the gauge!

Editor's note: Add 1/2 foot to South Boundary Road's Boat Buster Guage. This equals the levels Jim mentions in his description. Also, Check the AW or USGS site for the U.P. Black's level; it's just next door to the Presque Isle.

STURGEON RIVER

The Sturgeon is my best hope of approximating the flows of the runs in the L'Anse area of the U.P. I think you really need a local connection for these fickle little streams, though. The Sturgeon shows the April spike and May fade typical of the South Shore. I was surprised by the strength of the October sub-peak, almost up to May flows. The gauge is downstream of the steep Sturgeon Canyon run and upstream of the mighty Sturgeon Gorge, so expect less water in the Canyon and more in the Gorge.

KETTLE RIVER

The beloved Kettle shows why it's so popular: a big drainage finds big water in spring and boatable flows during the summer. It's interesting to me that the fall peak is in October and November. Could it be because the leaves stay on the trees longer there than up north near Lake Superior? The absence of dams and lakes to moderate its flow is evident in the thin spike of its spring peak—considerably different from the nearby St. Louis' broad peaks. Gauge fiends will like the following conversion table for the Highway 23 gauge:

Highway 23 Gauge in Feet	Flow in CFS
1	275
2	700
3	1500
4	2400
5	3600
6	4900
7	6300

VERMILION RIVER
(near Crane Lake)

Here I've plotted the flow recorded at two stations: at the Vermilion Dam as the river leaves Lake Vermilion and just above the Chute, only a few miles above the river's end at Crane Lake. Lake Vermilion is a huge reservoir that spreads the spring runoff over much of the summer.

This steady flow and the narrow nature of the Table Rock rapids makes for summer fun even into early August in a normal year. As you can see, the flow through the lower section with the Chute and Gorge should be at least paddlable all of the warmer months. The difference between the upper and lower gauges is large during peak of runoff, but only a couple hundred CFS most of the summer. Tom Aluni gave me the following gauge correlation for the gauge on river left just downstream of the Vermilion Dam at Lake Vermilion:

Vermilion Dam Gauge in Feet	Flow in CFS
2	2.5
3	36
4	176
5	534
5.59	838
6	1095
7.7	2730

You could plot this data and extrapolate other levels. Another point of interest is that the Vermilion, like the Pigeon and other rivers near the Canadian border, shows a May peak—the result of later break-up farther north.

WOLF RIVER

The summer reliability of the Wolf is evident in its hydrograph. By the time it reaches Section IV the Wolf has enough water to keep its ledges runnable during the summer. While the spring peak is low for a river of its drainage area, the payback is in the broad peak in spring, with good water lasting from the end of March well into June.

DRAINAGE AREAS OF VARIOUS RIVERS

North Shore River	Drainage (sq. mi.)
St. Louis-Section I	3430
Pigeon-Middle Falls	600
Pigeon-Above Arrow R.	256
Brule-At mouth	248
Baptism-Near mouth	140
Beaver-Near mouth	126
Poplar-Near mouth	114
Cross-Near mouth	91
Knife-Near mouth	86
Devil's Track-At mouth	77

South Shore River	Drainage (sq. mi.)
Presque Isle-Near mouth	358
Montreal-Near mouth	262
Black (U.P.)-Near mouth	257
Sturgeon-Near Sidnaw	171
Bois Brule-Near Brule	120
Huron-Near Big Erik's	74
Yellow Dog-Near mouth	68
Silver-Near mouth	64
Falls-Near mouth	48

CANADIAN RIVERS

Water flows for some of the Canadian rivers mentioned in this book and others can be found on these web pages:

http://www.opg.com/envComm/wateruse/Kaministiquia/KaministiquiaRiverMap.asp

http://www.lwcb.ca/waterflowdata.html

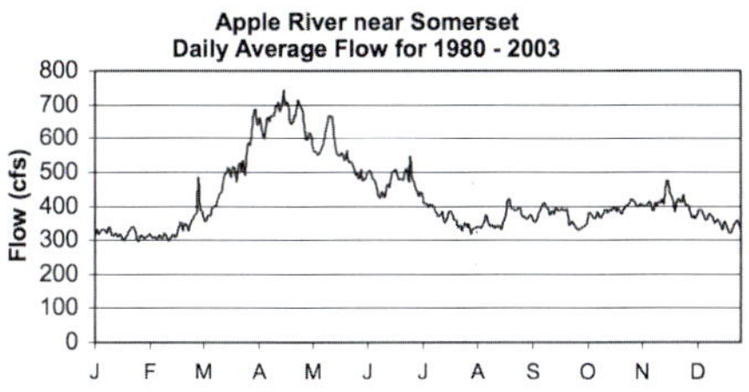
Apple River near Somerset
Daily Average Flow for 1980 - 2003
Flow (cfs)
J F M A M J J A S O N D

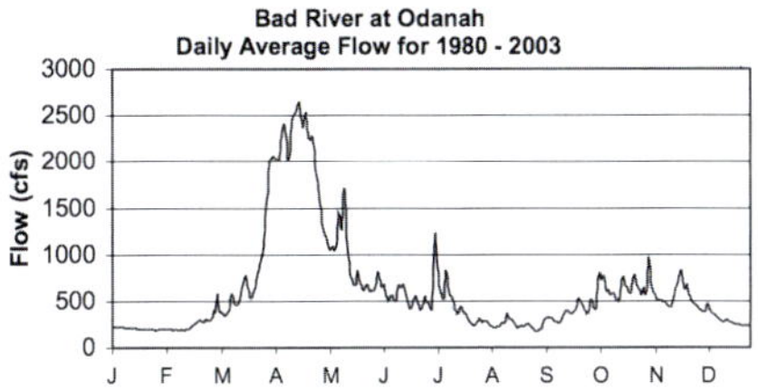
Bad River at Odanah
Daily Average Flow for 1980 - 2003
Flow (cfs)
J F M A M J J A S O N D

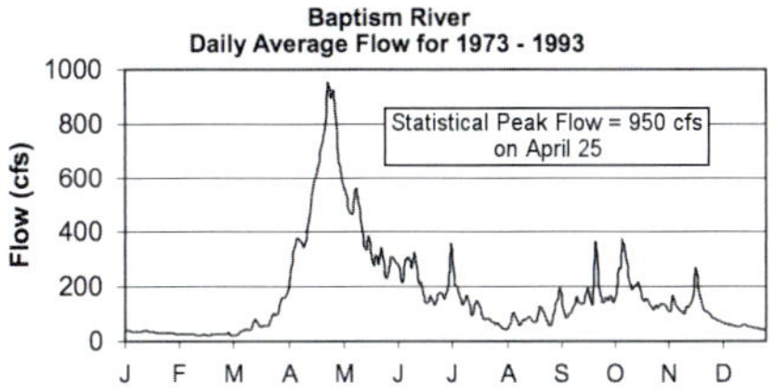
Baptism River
Daily Average Flow for 1973 - 1993
Statistical Peak Flow = 950 cfs on April 25
Flow (cfs)
J F M A M J J A S O N D

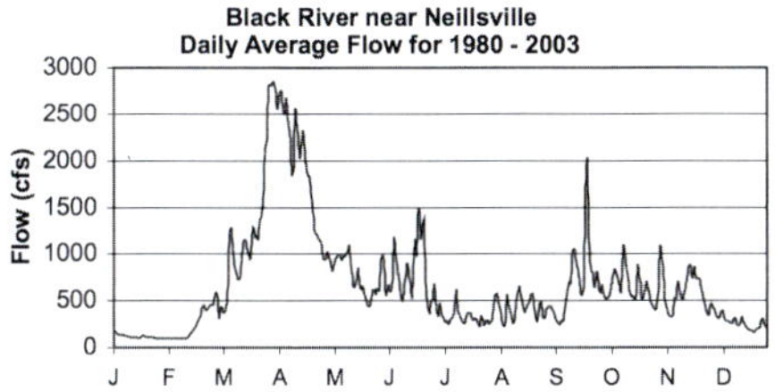
Black River near Neillsville
Daily Average Flow for 1980 - 2003
Flow (cfs)
J F M A M J J A S O N D

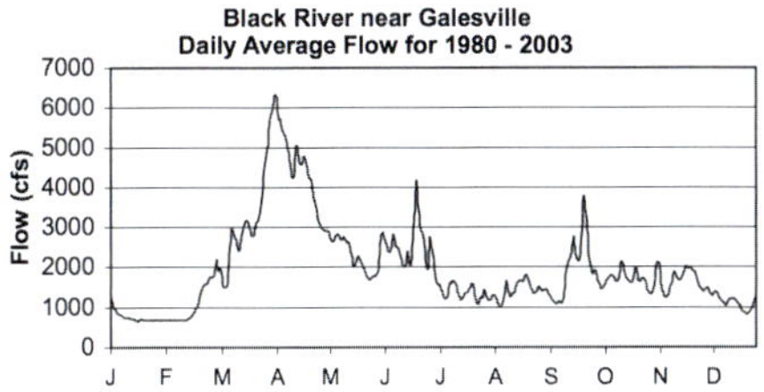
Black River near Galesville
Daily Average Flow for 1980 - 2003
Flow (cfs)
J F M A M J J A S O N D

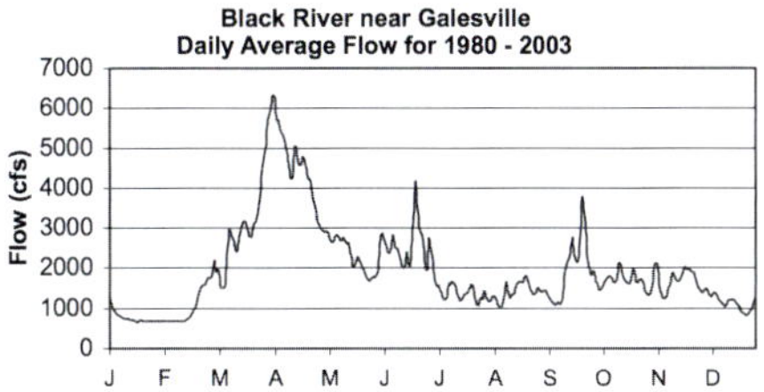
Black River near Galesville
Daily Average Flow for 1980 - 2003
Flow (cfs)
J F M A M J J A S O N D

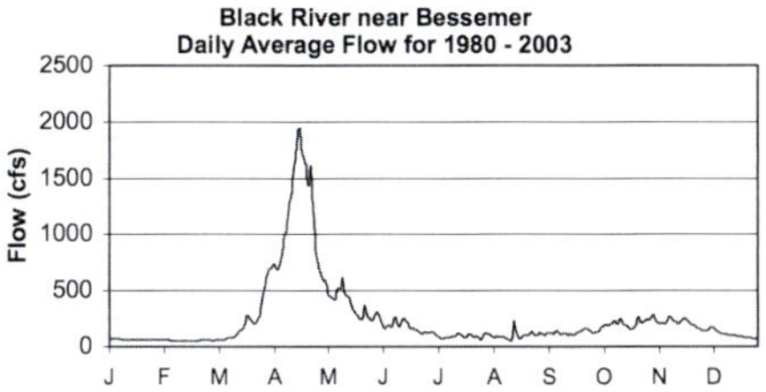
Black River near Bessemer
Daily Average Flow for 1980 - 2003
Flow (cfs)
J F M A M J J A S O N D

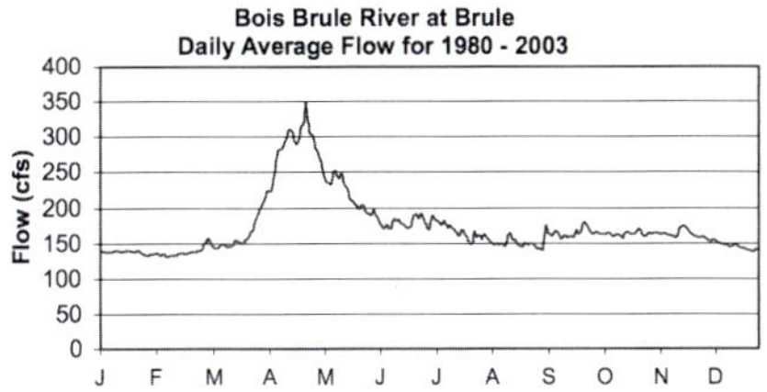
Bois Brule River at Brule
Daily Average Flow for 1980 - 2003
Flow (cfs)
J F M A M J J A S O N D

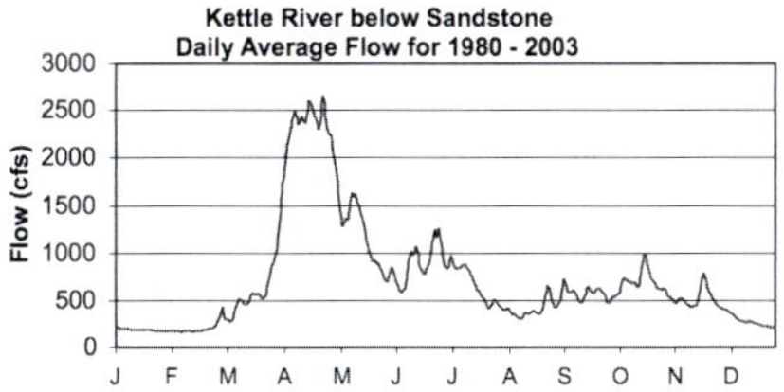
Kettle River below Sandstone
Daily Average Flow for 1980 - 2003
Flow (cfs)
J F M A M J J A S O N D

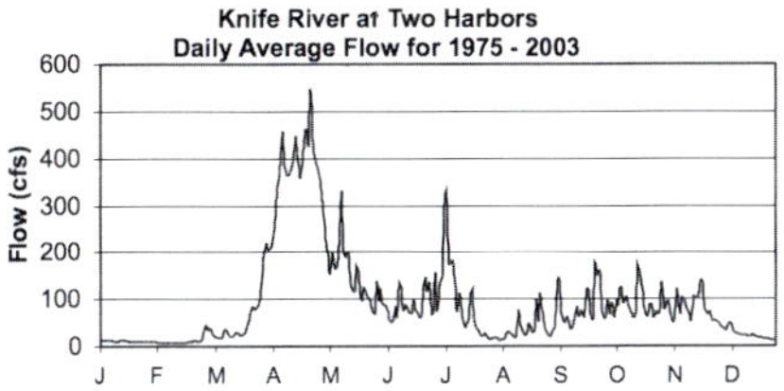
Knife River at Two Harbors
Daily Average Flow for 1975 - 2003
Flow (cfs)
J F M A M J J A S O N D

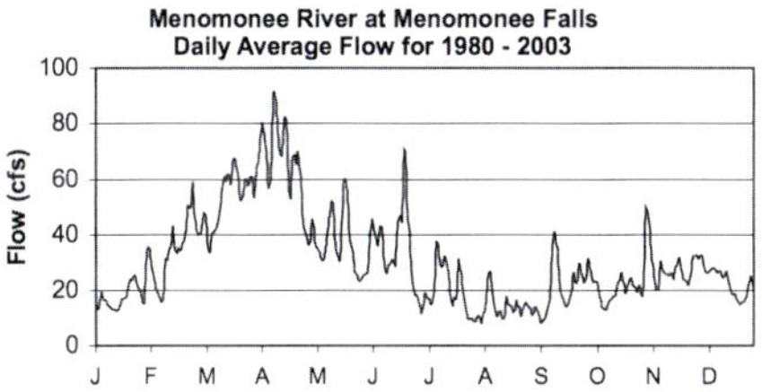
Menomonee River at Menomonee Falls
Daily Average Flow for 1980 - 2003
Flow (cfs)
J F M A M J J A S O N D

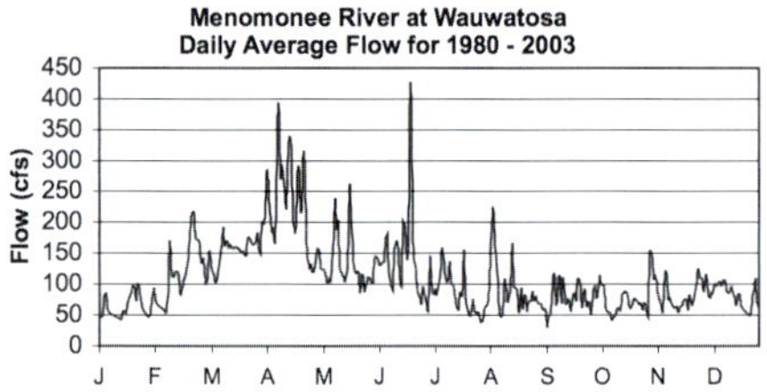
Menomonee River at Wauwatosa
Daily Average Flow for 1980 - 2003
Flow (cfs)
450 400 350 300 250 200 150 100 50 0
J F M A M J J A S O N D

Montreal River at Saxon Falls
Daily Average Flow for 1980 - 2003
Flow (cfs)
1600 1400 1200 1000 800 600 400 200 0
J F M A M J J A S O N D

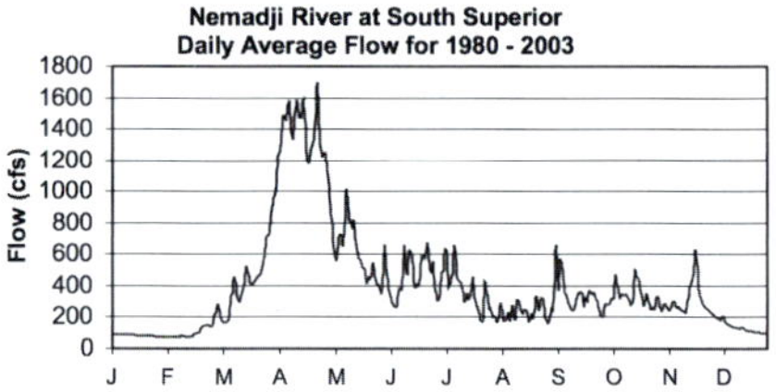
Nemadji River at South Superior
Daily Average Flow for 1980 - 2003
Flow (cfs)
1800 1600 1400 1200 1000 800 600 400 200 0
J F M A M J J A S O N D

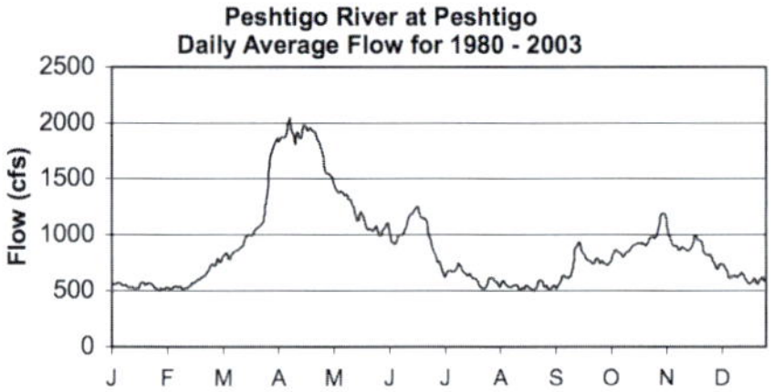
Peshtigo River at Peshtigo
Daily Average Flow for 1980 - 2003
Flow (cfs)
2500 2000 1500 1000 500 0
J F M A M J J A S O N D

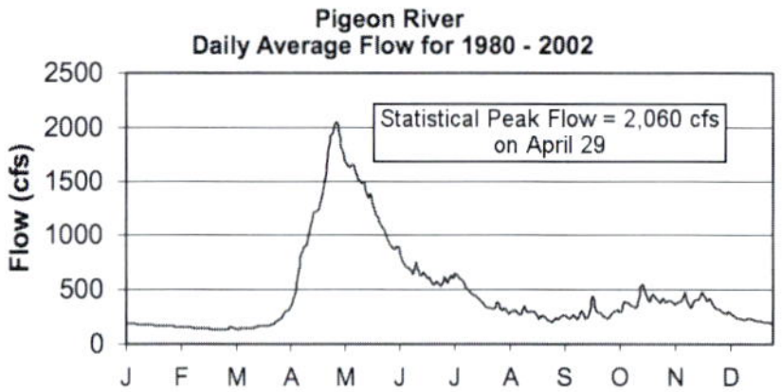
Pigeon River
Daily Average Flow for 1980 - 2002
Statistical Peak Flow = 2,060 cfs
on April 29
Flow (cfs)
2500 2000 1500 1000 500 0
J F M A M J J A S O N D

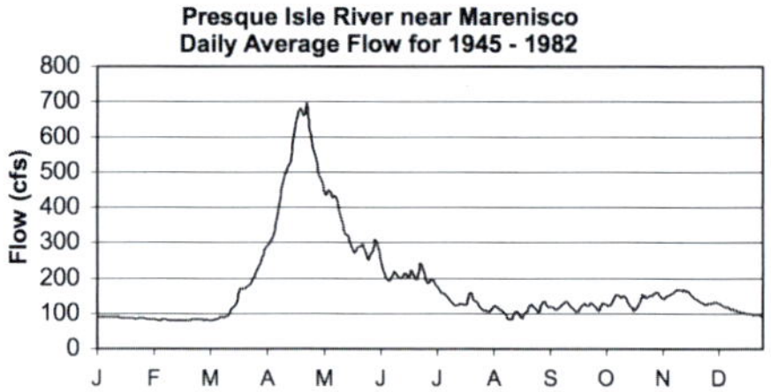
Presque Isle River near Marenisco
Daily Average Flow for 1945 - 1982
Flow (cfs)
800 700 600 500 400 300 200 100 0
J F M A M J J A S O N D

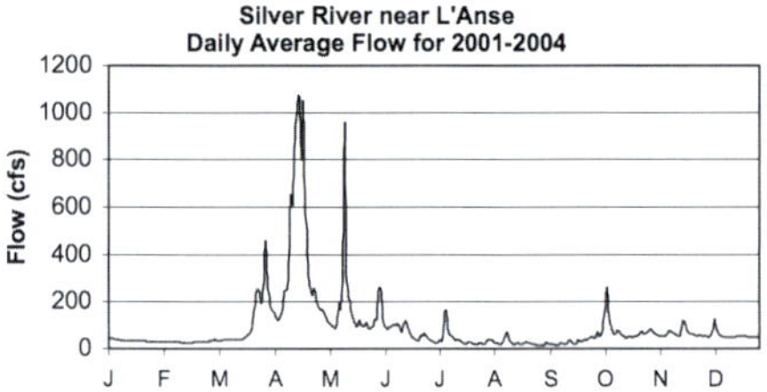
Silver River near L'Anse
Daily Average Flow for 2001-2004
Flow (cfs)
1200 1000 800 600 400 200 0
J F M A M J J A S O N D

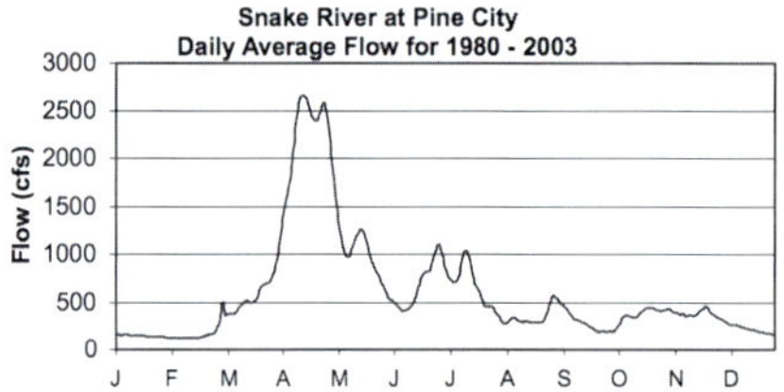
Snake River at Pine City
Daily Average Flow for 1980 - 2003
Flow (cfs)
3000 2500 2000 1500 1000 500 0
J F M A M J J A S O N D

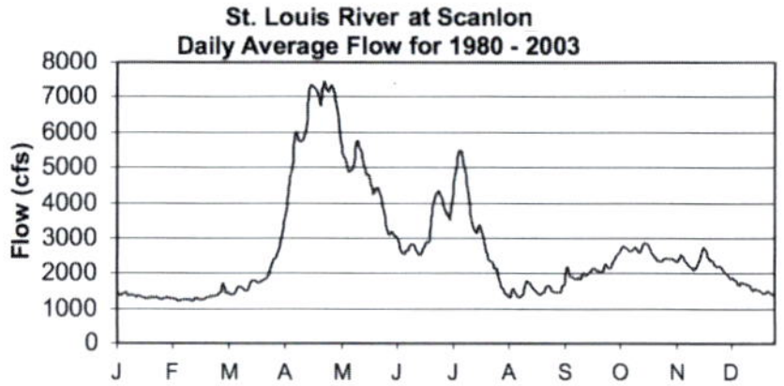
St. Louis River at Scanlon
Daily Average Flow for 1980 - 2003
Flow (cfs)
8000 7000 6000 5000 4000 3000 2000 1000 0
J F M A M J J A S O N D

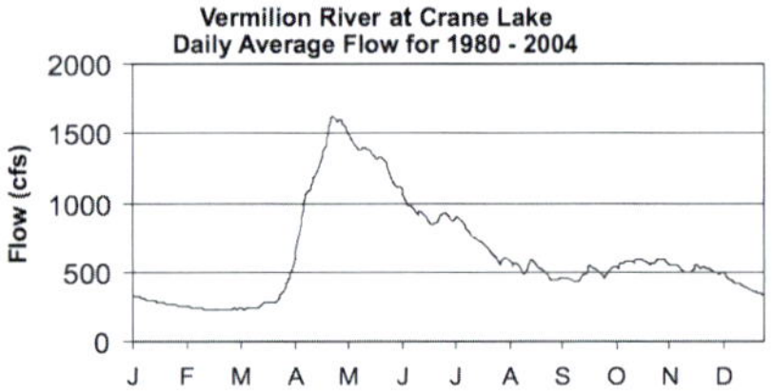
Vermilion River at Crane Lake
Daily Average Flow for 1980 - 2004
Flow (cfs)
2000 1500 1000 500 0
J F M A M J J A S O N D

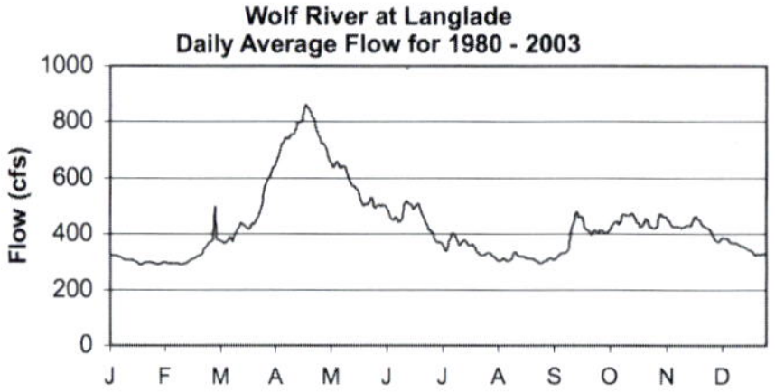
Wolf River at Langlade
Daily Average Flow for 1980 - 2003
Flow (cfs)
1000 800 600 400 200 0
J F M A M J J A S O N D

PADDLERS' RESOURCES

Kayak Clubs

AMERICAN WHITEWATER
PO Box 1540
Cullowhee, NC 28723
- Phone: 1-866-BOAT-4-AW
- Website: www.americanwhitewater.org
- Email: info@amwhitewater.org

Please join American Whitewater Affiliation, as Jim says:

"Let me say that the American Whitewater Affiliation, which publishes the Journal, is the best whitewater organization in the U.S. by far, concerned with conservation of our whitewater resources and exploring them."

HOOFERS OUTING CLUB
Whitewater Section
800 Langdon Street
Madison, WI 53706
- Phone (Outdoor Program Office): 608-262-1630
- Fax (Outdoor Program Office): 608-262-0156
- Website: http://www.hooferouting.org
- Email: whitewaterkayaking@hooferouting.org

RAPIDS RIDERS:
Whitewater Section of the Minnesota Canoe Association
Minnesota Canoe Association
P.O. Box 13567
Dinkytown Station,
Minneapolis, MN 55414
- Website: http://www.rapidsriders.net/
- Email: rapidsriders@rapidsriders.net

BOAT BUSTERS ANONYMOUS:
American Whitewater Affiliate
1019 5th Avenue South
Stillwater, MN 55082
- Email: ole.lena@visi.com

LUCK: LAKEHEAD UNIVERSITY: CLUB OF KAYAKERS
Lakehead University
955 Oliver Road, Thunder Bay,
Ontario, Canada P7B 5E1
- Website: http://flash.lakeheadu.ca/~luck/LUCK_Main.html
- Email: luck@lakeheadu.ca

Paddle/Gear Shops

MIDWEST MOUNTAINEERING
309 Cedar Ave. S.
Minneapolis, MN 55454
- Local: 612-339-3433
- Toll-free: 888-999-1077
- Fax: 612-339-7249
- Website: www.midwestmtn.com
- Email: info@midwestmtn.com

REI – RECREATIONAL EQUIPMENT INC.
Bloomington
750 W American Blvd
Bloomington, MN 55420
- Phone: (952) 884-4315
- Website: www.rei.com

Roseville
Schneiderman's Plaza
1955 County Rd B2 W
Roseville, MN 55113
- Phone: (651) 635-0211
- Website: www.rei.com

SUPERIOR COASTAL SPORTS
PO Box 215
Grand Marais, MN 55604
- Phone: 218-387-2360 or 800-720-2809
- Website: www.superiorcoastal.com
- Email: fun@superiorcoastal.com

SKI HUT EAST
1032 East 4th Street, Duluth, MN
- Phone: 218-724-8525
- Email: scott@theskihut.com

SKI HUT WEST
5607 Grand Avenue, Duluth, MN
- Phone: 218-624-5889

DULUTH PACK STORE
365 Canal Park Dr,
Duluth, MN 55802-2315
- Phone: (218) 722-1707
- Website: www.duluthpack.com

WILDERNESS SUPPLY COMPANY, LTD
244 Pearl St. S., Thunder Bay,
Ontario, P7B 1E4
- Phone: 807-684-9555
- Fax 807-344-9457
- Website: www.wildernesssupply.ca/

RUTABAGA
220 West Broadway, Monona, WI 53716
- Phone: (608) 223-9300
- Website: www.rutabaga.com

REI – RECREATIONAL EQUIPMENT INC.
7483 W Towne Way Madison, WI 53719
- Phone: (608) 833-6680
- Website: www.rei.com

LIFE TOOLS ADVENTURE OUTFITTERS
930 Waube Lane, Green Bay, WI 54304
- Phone: (920) 339 848

BEAR PAW OUTDOOR ADVENTURES
N3494 Highway 55, White Lake,
WI 54491
- Phone: 715-882-3502
- Website: www.bearpawoutdoors.com
- Email: info@bearpawoutdoors.com

Conservation Groups

AMERICAN WHITEWATER
PO Box 1540
Cullowhee, NC 28723
- Phone: 1-866-BOAT-4-AW
- Website: www.americanwhitewater.org
- Email: info@amwhitewater.org

KINNICKINNIC RIVER LAND TRUST
P.O. Box 87
River Falls, WI 54022
- Phone: (715) 425-5738

WISCONSIN LAND CONSERVANCIES GATHERING WATERS CONSERVANCY AND WISCONSIN LAND TRUSTS
211 S. Paterson St. Suite 270
Madison, WI 53703
- Phone: 608-251-9131
- Fax 608-663-5971
- Website: www.gatheringwaters.org/
- Email: info@gatheringwaters.org

IZAAK WALTON LEAGUE OF AMERICA
National Office
707 Conservation Lane
Gaithersburg, MD 20878
- Phone: (301) 548-0150
- Toll-Free: (800) IKE-LINE (453-5463)
- Fax: (301) 548-0146
- Website: www.iwla.org
- Email: general@iwla.org

Midwest Office
1619 Dayton Avenue, Suite 202
St. Paul, MN 55104
- Phone: (651) 649-1446
- Fax: (651) 649-1494
- Website: www.iwla.org
- Email: midwestoffice@iwla.org

Nature Conservancy

Minnesota, Wisconsin, and
UP Michigan Chapters
Michigan Field Office
101 E Grand River
Lansing, MI 48906-4348
- Phone: (517) 316-2277
- Fax: (517) 316-9886
- Website: www.nature.org/michigan
- E-mail: michigan@tnc.org

Minnesota Field Office
1101 West River Parkway, Suite 200
Minneapolis, MN 55415-1291
- Phone: (612) 331-0750
- Fax: (612) 331-0770
- Website: http://nature.org/wherewework/northamerica/states/minnesota/
- E-mail: minnesota@tnc.org

Madison Field Office
633 West Main Street, Madison, WI 53703
- Phone: 608/251-8140
- Fax: 608/251-8535
- E-mail: wisconsin@tnc.org
- Website: http://nature.org/wherewework/northamerica/states/wisconsin/

Michigan Land Conservancies, Central Lake Superior Land Conservancy

PO Box 7135, Marquette, MI 49855-7435
- Phone: (906) 226-2461
- Fax: (906) 227-4484
- Website: www.clslc.org
- Email: clslc@charterinternet.com

Great Lakes Bioregional Land Conservancy

1062 Morris Rd, Lapeer, MI 48446-3370
- Phone: (810) 664-5647
- Fax: (810) 664-5862
- Website: glblc.lapeer.org
- Email: ldorr@usol.com

Keweenaw Land Trust

700 Calumet St Ste 305
Lake Linden, MI 49945-1005
- Phone: (906) 296-9720
- Fax: (906) 296-9303
- Website: www.keweenawlandtrust.org
- Email: evanpmcdonald@keweenawlandtrust.org

Lake Superior Conservancy and Watershed Council

319 Lincoln Place
Petoskey, MI 49770-2593
- Phone: 231-347-9387
- Fax: (231) 347-0150
- Email: rgogawa@freeway.net

Minnesota Land Trust

2356 University Avenue West,
Suite 240, St. Paul, MN 55114
- Phone: (651) 647-9590
- Fax: (651) 647-9769 fax
- Website: www.mnland.org

Rivers Council of Minnesota

1269 Second Street N, Suite 200
Sauk Rapids, MN 56379
- Phone: 320-259-6800
- Website: www.riversmn.org

Pizza

Angelo's Pizza
210 Roosevelt Street
Ironwood, MI 49938
- Phone: 906.932.2424
- Fax: 906.932.8078
- Website: www.angelospizzaironwood.com

JIM AND KAREN THANK

My thanks to the Rada family – Charles and Della Rada, Rojean Rada and Tom Darling, Rico and Sam Rada, Leslie Cummings and Jim's darling godmother Viola Braa. Their love and good humor sustained Jim throughout his life and especially during the writing and publishing of this book. Also thanks to the many paddlers and photographers who volunteered stories, photos, and editing talents, and thanks to the many Northwoods paddlers who provided Jim and me with hours of adventures, laughs, thrills, and faithful companionship.

Special recognition is due those non-profit organizations working to protect and preserve the Northwoods rivers. I am especially grateful to the Nature Conservancy and the Minnesota Center for Environmental Advocacy.

Finally, I dedicate this book to Brownie and Whitey, whose love is as strong as an oak tree and as lasting as the rock ledges of Lake Superior's North Shore.

CONTRIBUTERS

Photographers: Karen Jenson, Paul Everson, Mike Cotten, Thomas O'Keefe, Doug Nelson Photography: www.www.agencyf.com/dougnelson/ Steve Corsi, John Alt, Tom Aluni, Henry Kinnucan, Chris Ringsven, John Linn/Adventure Creative Group: www.adventurecreativegroup.com, Roy Eneberg, Dewey James, Doug Demerest Photography: www.dougdemarest.com, Paulina Cuevas, Scott McKell, Ann Ramirez, Lanny Freng, Kevin Hill, Kay Holmgren, Kelly Fountaine, Jake Vos, Helge Klockow, Eric Strahlor, Bryan Zliman and Krista Lunde.

Video Images: Dan Monskey

Paul thanks Hal Crimmel, John Alt, Susan Cory and Joe Everson.

Extra thanks to Paul Everson, Thomas O'Keefe of the American Whitewater Affiliation: www.americanwhitewater.org and Steve Corsi who submitted photos, river descriptions and tirelessly vetted Jim's manuscript for accuracy. Steve thanks Dave Berg for his eagle eye.

Order a Print of Your Favorite Northwoods Whitewater Photograph!

Most images in the book are available as 8" x 10" color, original, photographic prints, printed on archival photo paper, suitable for framing.

VISIT OUR WEBSITE:

www.sangfroidpress.com/northwoods.htm
click "Photographic Prints," fill out the order form, and click "Buy Now."

Your print will mail to you, direct from the photographer's studio.

Check this web site out for the

NORTHWOODS WHITEWATER CALENDAR

Doug Nelson

Editor and Creative Director:
Steve Stratman

Fyi: "Helm" IS a word.

re•evolution
steve stratman
re•evolution studio
4816 clinton ave s
minneapolis
minnesota 55419
612.501.0866
sstratman@mn.rr.com

ABOUT THE AUTHOR

"We hope that Jim will journey with you in the sigh of the wind through the pines, the splash of the waves across your bow, and the sparkle of the stars in the heavens above."

– The Rada Family

Jim Rada
By Rico Rada

Jim was born in 1951, the youngest of three, but the toughest and fiercest. He spent all of his years growing up, and then some more, in Oakdale, Minnesota, in the house where our parents still live. Home was part of the anchor that he loved amidst his roaming and his adventures. He had chances to move away, even occasionally pursued a job, but only in the North Country he loved. He once said that one of the things he liked about travelling was to meet an authentic inhabitant of the region, and he hoped others felt that way upon meeting him.

As a kid, he was definitely feisty and idiosyncratic. He threatened his older siblings by clacking his teeth. He was an early opponent of sociable medicine, up to striking a boxer's pose in the corner of grandfatherly Dr. Rosenthal's office, rather than taking his shot like a boy. He once struck out, at about age 3, with a neighborhood friend, to walk along the highway to the country store over a mile away.

His Achilles heel when young was his pillow. He liked a hard pillow. So much so that he never used his, and it responded a bit like a marshmallow, gradually forgetting its given nature. If you ever wanted to pay Jim back, all you had to do was threaten to hit it.

Always a collector of beautiful things, he started with bottle caps, shiny objects in general, coins, stamps, moving up to baseball cards. Later it would be people he met in his outdoor activities and teaching, and memories of favorite places he had visited. He worked to produce beauty, too, writing poetry, haiku his favorite form. One was titled, "Jan, You Airy", in celebration of Minnesota's crispest month, and ran in the university paper. His greatest contribution was probably in the way he lived, and his acceptance of so many others.

School may never have been much of a challenge to him. He was a boy genius and National Merit Scholar, and he was never

©2006 Karen Jensen

worried about being mainstream or popular. He was always himself, interested in many things, and going hard after those which became his passions. In junior high school, he had a friend who would be president, with Jim his vice-president, and at the time they were well to the right of Goldwater.

He felt strongly that the Vietnam War was wrong and that the draft favored those from poor and minority families. He refused to take a student deferment and destroyed his draft card at age 18. Through a series of traumatic events, he was convicted of draft evasion and incarcerated in Milan, Michigan. During his four-month incarceration his quirky humor helped him cope. He taught other inmates to play chess. He won the annual footrace with its candy bar prize. He worked on the landscape crew, and at the prison entrance secretly planted tulips in the shape of a peace sign. He studied graduate-level physics and astronomy. When released, he paid extra for a homeward bus ticket that would take him through Upper Peninsula Michigan, allowing him to scout potential whitewater river runs. Jim stated that he saw the best and worst of humanity in prison, where unfortunately the greatest cruelties came from the guards. He arrived home to resume paddling and studying astronomy, rebelliously growing the long hair and beard he would wear for the rest of his life.

He loved the outdoors early on, and living in a semi-rural environment was conducive to spending many unsupervised hours outside. And his attraction to things celestial formed young, too, perhaps started initially by witnessing a great solar eclipse at age three. The great family camping trips certainly helped. He learned about whitewater boating from an old library book on Canadian paddlers and mail ordered his first kayak sight-unseen, without knowing any other paddlers. Since he didn't drive, toting the kayak was a challenge. He finally met a group of paddlers at the University of Minnesota, including Tom and Rebecca Aluni, and through them embarked on his thirty-year journey as a whitewater explorer.

He sometimes opined that he was born about 150 years too late, that he would have been suited to live in frontier times, with more wide open spaces. Hardships didn't faze him much, and he tended towards making many of the activities competitive when he was young, although he wasn't built to be one of the bicycle racers he so admired. He was a pretty healthy specimen most of his life, although he really toughened up working in the warehouse at Mom's company one summer, moving 50 pound sacks around.

Jim's slogan became "A day without fun is a wasted day." As a college professor, he was able to find slivers of time almost every day to get out for one of the activities he loved. And he also enjoyed his students, most of his colleagues, and the subjects he taught: astronomy, physics and math.

There would be no point in trying to tell the readers of this book how much Jim loved the rivers, how much time he spent around them, and the extent he and some of his friends would go to explore the unknown ones when they were just getting started. It's a happy memory for me that one of my birthday presents to him was to be his shuttle driver, taking him up to the Kettle River on a rainy May day when we were university students.

He did many things relatively late in life. Getting a driver's license. Flying on an airplane. Marrying his beautiful wife, Karen Jensen. And when he did these things, there was always some connection to the passions that became his at a much earlier age.

In thinking about Jim, anecdotes always seem the best. Many readers will probably have their own favorites. One which was retold at his funeral involved ladybugs at his cabin in northern Wisconsin. A boating friend staying over up there noticed a couple of ladybugs had gotten inside. Jim asked him to leave them alone, as he liked them. When Jim arrived in the spring, he had a ladybug infestation going if there can be such a thing.

Jim could be brutally blunt. He could be temperamental, opinionated, ornery, and crusty. His friend Tom Aluni nicknamed him "The Wolverine" (gulo gulo in Latin) after the fierce, snarling arctic mammal. But you knew where you stood with him. His joy, curiosity, honesty, sense of humor and thoughtfulness made him great company. For me it became a thing apart from time. Whether I'd last seen him the day before, or six months ago, it was the same. There was strength in being with him, and well into middle age, we were young men when we walked together. It is still a thing which bends time for me, when I remember times we had, and his strong spirit. It's fitting that one of his legacies would be a book about the rivers he loved, and along with every shimmer, gurgle, and earthy, living smell which emanates around moving water, it will remind me of him.

His life ended as he would have chosen, on a river, although his death was decades too soon. On May 17, 2003, he suffered a heart attack while paddling Triple Drop Rapid on the Presque Isle River in U.P. Michigan. It was a beautiful sunny warm day and the water was high. Doctors found that his death had been immediate, but the river carried him downstream, out of the reach of his companions, for one more ride through the currents and waves.